Lesley Stahl on U.S. sanctions against million children have died. I mean, that's more children than died in Hiroshima. And, you know, is the price worth it?"
Secretary of State Madeleine Albright: "I think this is a very hard choice, but the price--we think the price is worth it."

--60 Minutes (5/12/96)

"Saddam's goal is to achieve the lifting of U.N. sanctions while retaining and enhancing Iraq's weapons of mass destruction programs. We cannot, we must not and we will not let him succeed."
"We do not agree with the nations who argue that if Iraq complies with its obligations concerning weapons of mass destruction, sanctions should be lifted. Our view, which is unshakable, is that Iraq must prove its peaceful intentions."

—Madeleine Albright, March 26, 1997

If any child is without food or medicine or a roof over his or her head in Iraq, it's because he—Saddam—is claiming the sanctions are doing it and sticking it to his own children. ..... he is now lying to the world and claiming the mean old United States is killing his children... And if they're hungry or they're not getting medicine, it's his own fault."
"What he [Hussein] says his objective is, is to relieve the people of Iraq, and presumably the government, of the burden of the sanctions. What he has just done is to ensure that the sanctions will be there until the end of time or as long as he lasts. " (November 14, 1997)
 "Finally, I think that he felt probably that the United States would never vote to lift the sanctions on him no matter what he did. There are some people who believe that. Now I think he was dead wrong on virtually every point." (December 16, 1997)

—Bill Clinton

Amy Goodman: "... many say that, although president Bush led this invasion, that president Clinton laid the groundwork with the sanctions and with the previous bombing of Iraq. You were president Clinton's U.S. Ambassador to the United Nations.... the U.N. sanctions, for example ... led to the deaths of more than a half a million children, not to mention more than a million Iraqis.
Governor Richardson: Well, I stand behind the sanctions. I believe that they successfully contained Saddam Hussein. I believe that the sanctions were an instrument of our policy.
Amy Goodman: To ask a question that was asked of U.S. Ambassador to the U.N. Madeleine Albright, do you think the price was worth it, 500,000 children dead?
Governor Richardson: Well, I believe our policy was correct, yes

Moderator: "Did he state your position correctly, you're not calling for eliminating the sanctions, are you? "
Bush: "No, of course not, absolutely not, I want them to be tougher."

Bush/Gore on S. Hussein/Iraq/Sanctions
(2nd Presidential Debate-11 Oct 2000)

"What should we have done, just lift sanctions and hope for the best? I believed then and believe now that that was just too risky, given Saddam Hussein's past, his repeated attempts to invade his neighbors, his treatment of his own people and the weapons we knew he was developing."

"For those who cannot countenance the use of military force, sanctions will always be an option. Those who believe, as many of America's critics in the world do, that war is no longer a legitimate means in the modern world except in self-defense or with U.N. Security Council authorization will have to turn to sanctions as the ultimate method of coercion in international relations."

—James Rubin

'The concept of sanctions is not just still valid; it's necessary. What else fills in the gap between pounding your breast and indulging in empty rhetoric and going to war besides economic sanctions?"

—Richard Holbrooke:

"People say, 'You didn't recognize that it was going to have an effect on water and sewage.' Well, what were we trying to do with United Nations-approved economic sanctions—help out the Iraqi people? No. What we were doing with the attacks on the infrastructure was to accelerate the effect of sanctions.

A Planning officer interviewed
by the Washington Post reporter Barton Gellman

GENOCIDE IN IRAQ

THE CASE AGAINST THE UN SECURITY COUNCIL AND MEMBER STATES

BY

ABDUL HAQ AL-ANI
& TARIK AL-ANI

FOREWORD BY

JOSHUA CASTELLINO

CLARITY PRESS, INC.

© 2012 Abdul Haq al-Ani & Tarik al-Ani
ISBN: 0-9853353-0-0
978-0-9853353-0-4
E-book: 978-0-9853353-6-6

In-house editor: Diana G. Collier
Cover: R. Jordan P. Santos

Library of Congress Cataloging-in-Publication Data

'Ani, 'Abd al-Haqq.
  Genocide in Iraq / by Abdul Haq al-Ani & Tarik al-Ani ; foreword by Joshua
Castellino.
       pages cm
  Includes bibliographical references and index.
  ISBN 978-0-9853353-0-4 -- ISBN 0-9853353-0-0
  1. Iraq--International status. 2. Economic sanctions--Iraq. 3. Crimes against
humanity--Iraq. 4. Iraq--Foreign relations--1991- I. al-Ani, Tarik. II. Title.

  KZ4280.A55 2012
  364.15'109567--dc23

                              2012030765

                         Clarity Press, Inc.
                     Ste. 469, 3277 Roswell Rd. NE
                       Atlanta, GA. 30305 , USA
                       http://www.claritypress.com

We dedicate this book to the memory of Hashim

ACKNOWLEDGMENTS

We would like to acknowledge with gratitude the contribution of our editor Diana Collier, Joanne Baker and Richard Davoll who provided us with encouragement, editing, correction and proof reading. Any error or failure in presentation is completely ours.

TABLE OF CONTENTS

FOREWORD

When the founders of the United Nations came together after World War Two, they vowed to create a global system that would prevent the scourge of warfare from dominating international society again. To make that promise operational the United Nations Charter agreed to several founding principles. None of these principles were new as such: the refrain from the use of force, for instance, had already been debated vehemently in the inter-war period. The principle of state sovereignty, which sought to protect the state from external interference was even older in pedigree, but faced renewed emphasis as decolonisation sought to bring into being, states that were independent of hegemonic powers' interference. A third principle, the equality of states within international society, was in place to signal a brave new post-war world, where all states would have the same rights, and would merit equality in world affairs. That the vision seems unduly idealistic today, nearly seventy years later, indicates how opinion has shifted and how standards and aspirations articulated have come unstuck.

Nothing demonstrates the erosion of these values more than the fate that has befallen Iraq since the 1980s. This period includes the Iran-Iraq War, the Iraqi invasion of Kuwait, and the Halabja massacre amongst others. These events have been consistently discarded by commentators as atrocities or events perpetrated by a hegemonic ruler. To condemn them so simply however would be to misunderstand the intrinsic nature through which Iraq has been used as a puppet state in the Middle East: the manner in which Saddam Hussein was installed, the support he was initially given, the sanctions imposed notionally upon him but suffered by the Iraqi population, and the eventual invasion and destruction of the fabric of Iraqi society in the aftermath of the illegal invasion of 2003.

There are numerous questions that need to be asked before there can be full closure on Iraq. Some of these are being asked internally in the United Kingdom and the United States of America in connection with their role in the destruction of Iraq. However it is important to note that this soul-searching ought not to be merely a 'lessons learnt' history project. There is real damage done and real violations perpetrated which need to be accounted for, and real individuals who abused powerful positions for dubious motives, who ought to be punished for their roles. When discussions arise concerning reparations for past violations such as slavery and colonisation they are immediately beset by technical issues such as how to quantify the violations and who to apportion blame to. In the context of the events since 2003 in Iraq these issues do not arise. The damage perpetrated upon the body politic of Iraq needs to be assessed, addressed and remedied. The processes that engage these questions need to be free of bias and the outcomes and the workings need to be transparent.

The Al-Anis' book provides a context to Iraq that many commentators on Iraq seem unaware of. Their and our engagement with this text is crucial if we are going to begin to address the injustice that is collectively being felt in Iraq. Yet in many ways this book is not about Iraq at all. It is about the distance to which we have fallen as an international community in debasing the values contained in the United Nations Charter. Today the context for the abuse of power is Iraq, and the perpetrators who stand clearly accused in this text are, among others, two of the permanent members of the United Nations Security Council. Tomorrow's context may well be different, with different perpetrators and different victims. However unless we reiterate the fundamental principles on which international society is based, challenge those who violate them, and address real remedies where they are violated, the dream of building an international community where international peace and security reigns will remain a mirage.

JOSHUA CASTELLINO
PROFESSOR OF INTERNATIONAL LAW
MIDDLESEX UNIVERSITY

INTRODUCTION

Contextualizing Iraq within the Arab World

The events in Iraq between 1990 and 2003, which were partly precipitated by the preceding Iran-Iraq war of 1980-88, are historically significant in more than one way. Firstly, the situation in Iraq provided the first test case of the international order after the collapse of the Soviet Union and the demise of the communist movement worldwide. During that initial period, the US turned the Security Council into a rubber stamp of its policies as was attested to by Paul Conlon, a former official of the Iraq Sanctions Committee. According to Conlon, US officials drafted every Security Resolution imposing and enforcing the sanctions on Iraq for the first several years of the sanctions regime.[1] Even peremptory norms of so-called international law were breached when the Security Council put itself beyond the rule of law after the US declared that the Geneva Conventions, which were designed to lay down the rules of war, were not to be relevant anymore.[2] Secondly, Iraq has a unique position in Islam because the most significant sects in Islam look at it as the revered birthplace of their theology. Thirdly, Iraq is the only Arab state, which took part in the skirmishes of 1948, but never signed a peace treaty with Israel. It became imperative for both the US and its Middle East planners in Tel Aviv that such a state of affairs should not be allowed to continue. The opportunity to have Iraq not only sign such a treaty, but to dismantle its armed forces altogether was a golden opportunity that could not be missed. Fourthly, and consequent to the preceding facts, overrunning Iraq would open the door to the New Middle East, which the imperialists in Tel Aviv envisaged and put to their agents in Washington to implement.[3]

The destruction of Iraq during the thirteen years of siege and the following invasion and occupation achieved some of these objectives, but not all. Thus, when the plan to produce a fully compliant regime, based on a simplistic understanding of Iraq failed, new tactics were introduced. While telling people that they care so much about democracy that they will even go to war to establish it, the imperialists are fully aware that real democracy in the Arab World would mean the end to their plans. The only real allies the US imperialists have in the Middle East are those despotic regimes in Arabia and the Gulf which either have no constitutions or if they have them, they are only fig leaves with human rights light years away. [4] Realizing that it is impossible to get the civilized people of Egypt or the tolerant people of Syria to adopt such despotic regimes, and realizing the impossibility of direct rule after the failure in Iraq, the imperialists had to come up with new tactics while still maintaining the ultimate strategy of subduing the whole Arab World. As world experts in designing acronyms and composing phrases, they came up with 'Creative Chaos'.[5] What this plan means in short is that if you cannot rule the area, then leave it in chaos, which is precisely how the US left Iraq.

The new tactics under 'Creative Chaos' have taken different forms in different countries. Thus in Tunisia and Egypt they encouraged what they later called the 'Arab Spring'. This enabled them to get rid of two liabilities, Zain Al-Abedeen and Husni Mubarek, whom they had supported for decades, and thus appear to favor the will of the people. Although there was real expectation and resentment among the people in both countries, the fact remains that the political vacuum created by the departure of both leaders could not be filled by masses of protesters but by organized political parties. The only semi-organized parties were the Islamists, who despite the banning of political activities, managed to use the Mosques to their advantage and organization. It suddenly dawned on the imperialists that political Islam, as Turkey had been trying to prove, was not a threat to their interests. The 'Arab Spring' in Tunisia and Egypt was a cautioned welcome to the imperialists. It will prevent real secular democratic systems evolving in both countries and guarantees that, because of lack of vision of the Islamists, at best the expected chaos will ensue.

In Libya and Syria the conditions were different and the tune of the 'Arab Spring' could not be repeated for reasons that could not be explained in this introduction. To force regime change, a new tactic was needed. Several opposition nuclei from both countries which have been harbored and nurtured in Western states such as the US, UK and France were activated with full financial and logistic backing by the Gulf States. The plan was to imitate an armed insurrection, which could be used as an excuse for military intervention. In Libya and for many reasons, not least of which is Qaddafi's inability to understand his people correctly, the plan worked. Soon after the insurrection started in Benghazi, the West managed to pass a Security Council resolution authorizing humanitarian intervention ostensibly for the protection of civilians, which soon was used by NATO for a massive attack on Libya causing untold killing and destruction. Qaddafi was murdered and Libya was left in chaos.[6]

In Syria, the plan met different conditions simply because Syria is different. The efforts put towards regime change in Syria were massive, involving all of Syria's neighbors in the smuggling of money and weapons, and a media war by the main Arab and Western media, the like of which had never been seen before, was put in operation around the clock. However, the birthplace of Arab nationalism was not so easily amenable to plans that had worked in the Bedouin society of Libya. Equally significant was the Russian realization of their mistake in giving NATO the opportunity to destroy Libya by supporting the Security Council resolution. The Russians were not going to repeat that mistake and create an area of chaos so close to their borders. Although things are still active while we write this, we believe that Syria will survive this onslaught and come out bruised but healthier and stronger. However, should foreign interference reach a stage where the regime is forced into a corner and would feel itself threatened, then it is quite probable, in our opinion, that it may resort to a regional war to change the rules of the battle.

The Purpose of this Book

The imposition of sanctions on Iraq was one of the most heinous of crimes committed in the 20th century. Never in modern history of the world has any nation been subjected to such indiscriminate and brutal collective punishment. But that crime received very little attention in the Anglo-American world. The explanation of this failure was most eloquently summed up by Professor Thomas J. Nagy:

> Many, including the author recoil from contemplating the possibility that a Western democracy, particularly the USA, could commit genocide. However, it is precisely this painful and even taboo possibility which needs to be examined.[7]

Some books were written but only to address certain aspects of the harm caused by these sanctions. Despite the calamitous destruction resulting from the sanctions, no serious attempts were undertaken by legal professionals, academics or philosophers to address the immorality and illegality of such unprecedented mass punishment and to actually and specifically name the perpetrators against whom the charge of the international crime of genocide might be leveled and substantiated, and to provide substantiating legal and international law arguments in support of such a charge.

This book sets out to investigate the 1990-2003 war on Iraq. Iraq was attacked and put under a rigorous international blockade for over twelve years before the final invasion and occupation. We chose this specific period, rather than including the devastations resulting from the second assault on Iraq in 2003 because during this period all measures taken against Iraq were given the guise of legality under Security Council resolutions. The invasion of 2003 was without any alleged mandate and is thus an outright breach of international law which requires a separate study on its own. The objective is to show that international humanitarian law, human rights and peremptory norms of international law were breached during those twelve years. In order to achieve this, it is necessary to understand what Iraq was in 1990 and how it ended up in 2003. Iraq in 1990 was the result of decades of political and social developments in modern Iraq since the 1920s. Also modern political Iraq is inherited from the Ottomans who inherited from the Abbasids. It could be said that that a full understanding of Iraq would require going back to Sumerian times, but that would divert the purpose of the book from its real focus, that of a legal/political analysis of the last two decades.

It is accepted historically that any invader of the Middle East must conquer and occupy Mesopotamia. This is as true for Baghdad since the tenth century as it was for Babylon earlier. Chapter 2 attempts to explain the reason for the need to occupy Baghdad in modern history. It also explains the uniqueness of Iraq in being at the heart of both Sunni and Shi'a theology. This importance of Iraq, which far outweighs the significance of Arabia, at the same time sets Iraq out as a target. It is this vulnerability which the British tried to use in WWI and failed but which the US succeeded in employing in the 1990s. Imperialism thrives on occupation and usurpation. US imperialism is no different. This book argues that when contemporary imperialism realizes it cannot rule and usurp at will, then chaos and fragmentation of the nation state becomes an alternative option.

In chapter 3 we consider political Iraq between the end of the monarchy in 1958 and the occupation in 2003. The description of the Ba'ath movement and assumption of power in Iraq, which is treated in a different light to the way the Ba'ath movement have so far been treated in Anglo-American literature is inescapable in any discussion of the campaign against Iraq.

Chapter 4 describes in some detail the achievements of the Ba'ath in transforming Iraq from a semi industrialized society into a thriving society with achievements in standard of living, education, health and social welfare unknown before in Iraq or the rest of the Middle East. This was achieved in two development plans over a span of ten years. It thus puts to rest the argument made by some that other countries in the area were developed at a similar pace.[8] Such success has to be compared with the lack of any development in the eight years since the occupation of 2003.

In Chapter 5 we look at the social and political development of Iraq under the Ba'ath rule highlighting the advances made in solving the 'Kurdish' problem, political pacification, and the achievements in women's rights, education and health.

Chapter 6 demonstrates the extent of the destruction of Iraq by comparing Iraq in 2003 to what it was in 1990. The facts speak for themselves. We don't believe that any other book published in the English language has made this in-depth research and comparison of the two eras.[9]

Chapter 7 addresses the breaches of international humanitarian law and human rights law during the 1991 attack and blockade that followed, while Chapter 9 treats the much disputed contention that what happened in Iraq falls within the definition of genocide as defined in the Genocide Convention. We submit here our interpretation of the question of 'intent' and argue that it should not be viewed as some Anglo-American writers have suggested.[10]

Chapter 8 deals with the Sanctions Committee. We believe that very little has been written on this unprecedented entity which enabled one man at any time to hold the whole of Iraq to ransom by denying the export of items vital to basic survival.

We believe that this book is necessary for further understanding of what total sanctions mean. We hope that it will help in persuading people that such a regime of sanctions should never be imposed on any other nation in the future. We equally hope that it will assist those who may take legal action in the future to achieve justice and reparations for these gross crimes committed against the people of Iraq.

1

IRAQ'S MILLENNIA OF RICH HISTORY

The Unique Historical Role of Iraq

It may be a cliché to say that Iraq is different because it can easily be argued that every country is different. However we intend to argue that Iraq is unique at least among other Arab and Muslim States. This distinction will go some way, in our opinion, to explain the difficulty in understanding some of the events and happenings in Iraq over the past century.

In the recorded history of the last few millennia as we know them, Iraq stands unique in having produced more than one empire and civilization. It is the land where the world's first recorded civilizations were founded; where the wheel was invented; where writing had its first origins; where the oldest irrigation systems were implemented and where man's first laws were written. This land has had a continuum of history and its greatness is in that continuity. The fact that empires came and went in Iraq is not demeaning to its existence but a proof of its eternal existence as a state.

This unique nature of Iraq, its resilience and its capability of demonstrating its rebirth (Ba'ath) over and over again explains why it is the target of any invader of the Middle East, and the reason for the brutality and devastation of such invasions. Hulagu's forces besieged Baghdad from November 1257 until it surrendered on February 10, 1258 'leading to a week-long massacre by the Mongols, regarded as one of the most devastating events in the history of Islam'. It took Baghdad centuries to recover and the destruction of 1258 has become part of vernacular folk tales.[1]

In 2003, after having blockaded Iraq for thirteen years, denying it the necessities of life and reducing its army to a shadowy force, the Western invaders employed 'shock and awe', which in plain language meant the use of disproportionate and indiscriminate force with intent to destroy. The invasion and occupation that followed led to the total dismantling of the state; the complete collapse of the delicate social fabric that had characterized Iraq for many centuries; the death of over one million people and the uprooting of some four million others in a country of just over twenty five million, not to mention the total destruction of all utilities and public services, such as water, electricity, health and education. The whole infrastructure which had taken the Iraqis decades of labor and financing to build was completely destroyed. Baghdad has been left in ruin and will not recover for decades, if not centuries. The outcome and fate of today is no different from that of the Mongol invasion of 1258.

In both cases Baghdad posed no threat, either to the Mongols or to the Westerners. In both cases total destruction, and not just defeat, was intended and premeditated. It seems the reason why Baghdad was invaded and ransacked with such brutality is that both Imperialists realized that in order to dominate both the Middle East of the thirteenth century and the Arab World of the 21st century, Baghdad must be subjugated or ruined.

During its long history and up until the beginning of the 20th century, Iraq was either a center of an empire or part of one. How could one define the borders of what was actually the center of the Abbasid Empire? Historical Iraq was then part of the Ottoman Empire in the form of three separate *Wilaya* (An Arab word used by the Ottomans to define a sort of large Province). These *Wilayat* were: Baghdad, Mosul and Basrah. It is not a completely accidental structure. It represents what historical Iraq has always been and demonstrates its continuity. The *Wilaya* of Baghdad inherited the Babylonian and Neo-Babylonian Empires, Mosul (formerly Nineveh) inherited the Assyrian Empire while Basrah inherited Uruk and Ur - the Akkadian/ Sumerian Empire.

At no time until the beginning of the 20th century, and even after the arrival of the colonialists, had there been a political entity of any form on the western side of the Persian Gulf between Oman and Basrah. The political authority of the *Wali* (Governor) of Basrah extended, to varying degrees, down to the borders of Oman, covering most of the western side of the Gulf. Although the Ottomans did not cede any part of the Gulf, nor did the European colonialists claim any political or military authority over it, the mere fact of allowing the colonialists to establish themselves there turned out to be a very expensive blunder that has cost the people of the region dearly. As late as 1909, and after the British had established themselves in the area of the Basrah *Wilaya*, the Ottoman state described it thus in its administrative division of Iraq: [2]

> The Basrah *Wilaya*
> Located in the south of Iraq, bordered on the north by the Baghdad *Wilaya*, east by Iran, south by the Gulf and Ihsa' and west by Shammar mountain and Syria. Area estimated to be 128,800 sq. km.
> It is subdivided into four counties: Basrah - the capital of the *Wilaya*, Muntafig, Najd, and Imarah consisting of some thirteen cities, thirty two towns and 315 villages distributed as follows:
>
> Basrah: Basrah, Qurnah, Fao, Kuwait
> Muntafig: Nasseriyah, Suk as-Shiukh, Shatrah
>   Muntafig, Hay
> Najd: Hufuf, Qatif, Qatar, Riyadh
> Imarah: Imarah, Shatrah Imarah, Jahlah,
>   Majer Kabeer, Ali Gharbi

This acknowledgement of the extent of Basrah was confirmed as late as 1961 when the British Embassy in Lebanon cabled the following message to the Foreign Office: [3]

> July 8, 1961
> Sir M. Crosthwaite
> Iraqi Prime Minister, Abdel Karim Kassem [Qasim], has decided to seek the annexation of the former Basra Governorate of Iraq, usually reliable sources said here today. The Basra Governorate, which was under Ottoman rule, includes the Districts of Katif and Ahsa'a, which now form part of Saudi Arabia and are rich in oil fields.

Britain carved out most of the *Wilaya* of Basrah, according to the 1909 borders of the Ottoman Empire, and handed it over to its Bedouin clients in the Gulf and Arabia (presently Kuwait, The UAE, Bahrain, Qatar and Saudi Arabia), thus depriving Iraq of a natural outlet on the Gulf. It is a unique situation for a country like Iraq, with two major rivers terminating on its land, to be prevented from having a port on the Gulf.

Since 1990, conferences were convened and articles and books were written in order to prove that Kuwait is an ancient nation, perhaps predating Iraq, that its borders have been established and recognised from antiquity, and that all powers have acknowledged that. Some have referred to the agreement of January 23rd 1899 between Mubarak of Kuwait and Britain as recognition of Mubarak's possession of territory. In 1902, the British Foreign Secretary, the Marquess of Lansdowne, contradicted this assertion by stating that the boundaries of Mubarak's possession—the basis of Kuwait's borders—were ill-defined. He went on to state that Mubarak's territory did not extend beyond the town of Kuwait and its bay.[4]

But even more insidiously, the question of Iraq's own legitimacy as a state became part and parcel of the propaganda machine in the West, especially in the UK. Iraq isn't a proper country anyway, went the theory—it was "created" by Britain after the First World War, and before that it was part of Turkey. If Iraq wanted to emphasize its historical claims on Kuwait, it was reasoned, then Turkey could reasonably lay claim to Mosul. Iraq, they claimed, was a land called Mesopotamia, until the British came and "created" it in 1921. They do not tell us that the borders of Iraq were defined by the Ottoman and Persian Empires in the Treaty of Zohab of 1639, nine years before the Treaty of Westphalia of 1648, which defined the national borders in Europe! It is as if denying Iraq's long history would make it disappear from the memory of mankind.[5] There is nothing new in the manipulation of history for political ends. Colonialists have done it for centuries, successfully. The same pattern is repeating itself in Iraq now.

The socio-political realities in the Gulf at the end of the 19th century clearly supported the prospects of only two major countries evolving in the Gulf, namely Iraq and Iran. Both had the urban community, the tradition, the culture and history to sustain a polity. As the political authority of Iraq was expected to inherit the Basrah *Wilaya*, the whole of the western side of the Gulf would become part of the new Iraqi polity. It was obvious to British strategists that while Iran's influence on the western side of the Gulf could be neutralized, the neutralization of Iraq's power would not be so easy.

Although the Sykes-Picot Agreement was signed in 1916 between Britain and France, with the assent of Russia, for the dismemberment of the Ottoman Empire by dividing the Arab Middle East between them, British designs on Iraq, at least, started a long time before that.[6] There were two alternatives open to Britain to extend its control over the Gulf. One was to occupy Iraq at the first opportunity, and the second was to contain it while cultivating the idea of satellite statelets on the Gulf through the settling and maintaining of Bedouin tribes in return for their unconditional loyalty, as happened in the treaty of 1899 between Britain and Mubarak of Kuwait.

As the Ottoman grip started to slip, Britain found in the endless demands of the *"untrustworthy savage"*[7] of Kuwait a good means of confining Iraq. The first steps were taken by encouraging the Sheikh to lay claim to the two barren islands of Warba and Bubyan which had no value in terms of agriculture, minerals or fishing, being immersed under water most of the time. The only importance of these islands was that they controlled the access of Iraq to the sea. S. G. Knox, the Political Agent in Kuwait, wrote on 9.6.1908 to P. Z. Cox, the Resident in the Gulf, that Mubarak's claim over Bubyan could be substantiated through the testimony of the Awazim and the judgment of the *Shari'a* court whose *Qadi* (judge) was an appointee of Mubarak. However, no such luck was forthcoming regarding Warba Island, the claim to which the British at that stage thought it better not to pursue further. The India Office stated on Oct. 31, 1907 that "The Sheikh's possession right on Warba Island has never been established."[8]

As late as 1908, British official policy was that the time was not right to raise the issue of Mubarak's claim over Warba and Bubyan. Britain eventually managed to occupy Iraq, but it soon found out that direct occupation of Iraq was militarily expensive. It was in the Kurdish areas of Iraq that Winston Churchill authorised the use of poison gas showered from aircrafts against civilians for the first time in history.[9]

In 1923, Percy Cox, then High Commissioner in Mandated Iraq, defined the borders between Iraq and Kuwait. The casual way in which this was done, without their actually having been delimited on the ground, speaks volumes about the contempt of the British Government for the people of the area and its disregard for the potential for future conflict. Since Cox was an able military man and diplomat, he should have realized—and likely did—that his handling of the case of the borders with Kuwait would sow the seeds of conflict for decades to come.

Between 1930 and 1961 every government of Iraq, including those most subservient to Britain, made its position on the status of Kuwait clear. In 1938 King Ghazi of Iraq used the issue of Kuwait as a rallying point for his people, both inside Iraq major and Kuwait (then still under British rule), against British domination. He installed a radio station in his palace and played on nationalist fervour to call for the return of Kuwait. The Consultative Council on Kuwait, appointed by the Sheikh, voted twice, against British will, to unite with Iraq and called on King Ghazi to take over their land. The British response was swift: dismissal of the council, imprisonment of some of its members, and deportation of others. King Ghazi died in a mysterious car accident on April 4th, 1939. His companions in the car disappeared and his corpse was kept by Sir Henry Sinderson between the accident and his burial. Dr. Sinderson had been appointed by the British to be the monarch's physician and the first dean of the medical school in Baghdad, but in reality he was the ruler, par excellence, of Iraq.[10]

When Britain expressed its intention of ending its direct control over Kuwait in 1961, General Qasim, the leader of Iraq, welcomed the return of Kuwait to Iraq and congratulated the mayor of Kuwait, the Sheikh, on this occasion. He was wise enough not to contemplate any military action, but merely reiterated the previous Iraqi governments' stand and general public conviction: Kuwait was part of geographical and political Iraq and had to be returned one day. The British response was demonstratively swift and determined with the dispatch of military units to Kuwait. Inter-Arab rivalry played into the hands of Britain when Nasser of Egypt, the proponent of Arab unity, opposed the call for the reunion of Kuwait with Iraq. Qasim, like Ghazi before him, had to pay dearly for his conviction when a year and a half later he was toppled in the coup of February 1963.[11]

Inviolability of the Colonialists' Drawn Borders Post WWI

The underlying policy which was displayed openly in 1961 and upheld so brutally through the destruction of Iraq in 1991 and 2003 has always been the inviolability of borders drawn by the colonial powers; no correction of wrongs and no rectification of injustices are to be tolerated in any part of the colonial legacy. This is of paramount importance in the Middle East as any redress of injustice may lead to the Arabs controlling their own natural resources and possibly creating a "nightmare" (for Britain) by confronting Israel. Britain has always been opposed to any form of unity in the Arab world no matter who carries it out, even their most trusted clients, because the process of unification has its own momentum. Even the "Hashemite" union set up on 14 February 1958 between the two states of Iraq and Jordan, both of which were in the British saddle, was not welcomed in London.

British interests in Iraq and the Gulf remain fairly constant. According to the *London Times* of 19 January 1949, British Foreign Secretary Ernest Bevin was reported to have said: [12]

> British interests in the Middle East ... have changed
> little in the past 200 years and are as valid today as they
> were in the time of Napoleon. Today they are also, to
> a very large extent, the interests of the whole western
> world. The Middle East is a bridge between Asia and
> Africa and a road between the Mediterranean Sea and
> the Indian Ocean .... Oil has given the Middle East a new
> and dangerous value, but geography is still the master.[12]

Sixty years on, Bevin's statement is as valid now as it was then, almost in its entirety. There is no disputing that the US has been consolidating its influence in the Middle East while British influence has been declining. It is vital for Anglo-Saxon imperialism to control as much as possible of the oil supply to its economic rivals, Germany, China and Japan. It is also axiomatic to imperialist ideology in the Middle East that the State of Israel, which personifies Zionist imperialism, should enjoy a hegemony, which is not to be challenged or eroded in any way. All these factors were in operation when Saddam Hussein walked into the trap set for him in Kuwait while he was claiming he was reasserting Iraq's right in its coastline.

British and US interests lie in curtailing the economic might of China, Germany and Japan, and in consolidating the expansion of the State of Israel in the Middle East. The latter is for several reasons: firstly because Israel is a British creation; secondly as a deterrent for any Arab awakening and unity, thirdly because Zionism pervades business, media and politics in Britain and the US.

The hate campaign whipped up by the media with direct assistance from politicians and academics and the jingoism of the British and American public over the months leading to the destruction of Iraq in 1991 was an interesting spectacle to an outside observer. The use of depleted uranium, the burying of soldiers alive, the carnage on the Kuwait-Basrah road, the destruction of water, electricity, and sewerage systems, the devastation of all civilian factories for food, consumer goods and spare parts and the total blockade of Iraq for over 12 years, in which Britain and the USA have been prime actors, had nothing to do with recapturing Kuwait and can only be classified as the causal factors of genocide. One need not remind the reader that all these acts of destruction and the mass punishment of civilians are in violation of the same international law which the politicians in Britain and the US allegedly went to war to uphold.[13]

The imperialists demonstrated four significant principles in their campaign for the destruction of Iraq:

1. Clients who show disobedience; step out of line; develop personal ambitions on a regional or international scale; or imagine themselves partners in the imperialist designs are to be disowned and severely punished.
2. Never again should a state in the Middle East, except the State of Israel, be allowed to arm itself, develop an arms industry or acquire nuclear technology or any advanced technology for that matter.
3. The flow of oil from the world's largest reserves in the

Middle East must be controlled by the US with a minor role for the older colonial powers—Britain and France. This would ensure the control of oil supply to the other rival capitalist states of Japan, Germany and China.

4. The borders fixed by the colonial powers should remain inviolable, a principle that is to be upheld at any cost. It is not simply to protect the West's interests that these borders should be maintained, but also to entrench in the minds of the peoples of the world the Western philosophy that history can only be written by the West and by the West alone, so that when it accomplishes its mission it can advertise the end of history. Francis Fukuyama had already declared this thesis in 1989.[14]

This principle of inviolability, however, seems only to apply to nations outside the West, whereas Western nations or their forward bases like the State of Israel can change borders at will, having created them in the first place.

The reality is that history never ends. Iraq will always be there and every government in Iraq will demand the natural exit to its coastline that it had enjoyed from Babylonian times and will thus attempt to regain it. It is a matter of survival for Iraq and every nation must endeavour to survive. Military conflicts have only confirmed this reality rather than reduced its significance. Kuwait will have to be integrated into Iraq if peace and justice are to prevail in the region.

How the *Shi'a vs. Sunni* Divide in Islam Impacted Early Iraq

In order to appreciate another unique feature of Iraq, we need to shed some light on the division in Islam, which has had a much more fundamental role to play in Iraq than in other Muslim states. Islam, like other religions, has had its share of schism. However, while schism in Christianity, for example, materialized centuries later, the schism in Islam in our opinion, and contrary to conventional wisdom, started soon after its birth and long before the Prophet died.

The Quraysh, the Prophet's tribe, migrated from Iraq and settled in Mecca. Along with the tribe of Jirhem, it rebuilt the house of Ibrahim (Abraham), known as the Ka'ba and made it the centre of worship of Arab tribes, managing it and controlling all business within it. The Arab poet recorded the rebuilding of the House in the saying:

I swear by the House around which circumambulated
Men from Quraysh and Jirhem who built it.

The Quraysh became divided, like most tribes, into clans (*butoon*). Their problems arose from the battle to assume supremacy in Mecca. The most prominent clans and their members who played a role in Islam were Banu Hashim (Prophet Muhammad, his uncle Abbas and his cousin Ali), Banu Umayyah (Abu Sufyan, Uthman ibn Affan), Banu Makhzum (Khlaid ibn Al-Walid), Banu Zuhra (Sa'ad ibn Abi Waqqas), Banu Taim (Abu Bakr), Banu Adi (Umar ibn Al-Khattab). A victory for Muhammad meant the loss of Quraysh control, authority, wealth and prestige.

This political division soon developed into action against Muhammad and his small band of faithful believers of Banu Hashim and their followers.The divine command in the early stages of the mission was: 'And warn your close clan' [Qur'an 26:214]

This enmity was to be continued throughout history. In 619 AD, ten years after the start of the Prophetic mission, the year known as the Year of Sorrows, both Muhammad's wife, Khadija and his uncle Abu Talib died. The divine command to Muhammad was to immigrate to Yathrib which came to be known as Medina because his protectors in Mecca were gone. When Muhammad and his followers got to Medina, a new phase of Islam was born. Muhammad began to establish and organize his Muslim state, which went on to change the face of history. The immigration (Hijra) to Medina enabled Muhammad to contact other Arab tribes freely and call them to Islam. His power became consolidated to the anger and anguish of the leaders of the Quraysh clans of Umayyah, Makhzum and Zuhra who remained staunch enemies of the religion.

In 623 AD, one year after the Hijra to Medina, Muhammad chose to confront the Quraysh and the Umayyad Abu Sufyan in particular. Abu Sufyan had prepared a big army from all Quraysh and allied tribes and marched on Medina. The battle of Badr in 624 AD was significant not simply for its decisive victory of Islam, but because it increased the enmity between the House of Muhammad and its enemies among the clans of Quraysh. During the battle, Hamza, Muhammad's uncle and Ali bin Abi Talib, Muhammad's cousin, son-in-law, father of the Prophet's only grandsons and heir apparent killed the following chieftains of Quraysh: Utba ibn Rabi'ah, Abu Sufyan's father-in-law, his son Al Waleed ibn Utbah, and his brother Shaibe ibn Rabiah all from banu Abd Shams, cousins of Ummayds, and Al-Aswad ibn Abd Al-Asad from Banu Makhzum.

The Hashimites suffered the worst revenge when on 10th October 680 AD / 10th Muharram 61 AH of the second Umayyad Caliphate, Yazid bin Mu'awiya bin Abi Sufyan massacred Hussein bin Ali, the Prophet's only living grandson along with over seventy members of his family and comrades including children and infants. The tragedy of Kerbela on the banks of the Euphrates was probably the largest family massacre in recorded Islamic history and has marred Islam irreparably.

The martyrdom of Hussein is at the heart of *Shi'a* theology and mourning the death of Hussein is so much a part of the *Shi'a* psyche that no occasion or celebration could end without words said about the death of Hussein, if not a few tears shed. For the last thirteen centuries the *Shi'a* of the world have been keeping the first ten days of the Muslim lunar year for mourning during which the event of the massacre is retold and the *Sunnis* who killed Hussein or acquiesced in his killing are cursed. It is true, of course, that most *Sunni* Muslims do not condone the killing of Hussein but there are some, like the Wahabis of today, who justify the murder of Hussein on the grounds that he opposed the legitimate Caliphate of the day.

When Muhammad died the division surfaced clearly between the House of Muhammad and their followers from other tribes and the rest of the Quraysh. The difference centred on the succession to Muhammad. The House of Muhammad and their followers, the *Shi'a* on one side, and the *Sunni* on the other, differed politically although claiming that the difference was religious and a matter of interpretation of the will of Allah.

The Muslims differed on the meaning of the Arabic word 'Imam'. The *Shi'a* have always argued that the *Imamate* is a divine choice and not a matter for the *Umma* to select. The *Imamate* is preordained by Allah to be so and is hereditary in the House of Muhammad, starting with Ali and ending with the 12th descendent *Imam*, the Mehdi. Every *Imam* according to the *Shi'a*, like every Prophet, is infallible and must be obeyed without question as his actions are part of divine will.

The *Sunnis* have always argued that the *Imamate* is a matter for the *Umma* to decide upon and any person can become an *Imam* once the proper qualities are manifest in him.

In fairness to history, one should point out that the *Sunnis*, who have been in control of political Islam for the last fourteen centuries, did not in fact fulfill their side of the argument, namely that of free selection of the *Imam*. Abu Bakr, the first Caliph, who was chosen in somewhat disputed circumstance by popular consensus, appointed Umar ibn Al-Khattab to succeed him. Umar appointed six people, all from Quraysh, to select his successor from among them. The Umayyad, Abbasid and Ottoman dynasties all chose the Caliph on hereditary bases. It seems that what the *Sunnis* decided was that it was not the hereditary principle which they objected to but rather its connection with the House of Muhammad. The Abbasids capitalized greatly on the sympathy which ordinary people had for the *Shi'a* and the guilt felt by many at acquiescing in the persecution of the descendant of the Prophet. In 750 AD/ 132 AH they put an end to the Umayyad rule, thus signaling the beginning of the most prosperous Islamic Empire. However, no sooner had the Abbasid settled into their new acquired authority than they turned against the *Imams*, descendants of Ali, and their sympathizers. The persecution of the *Imams* and their *Shi'a* followers took many forms and passed through different periods of intensity. It suffices to say that none of the eleven *Imams* descended from Ali, save for the last *Imam,* the Mehdi who has not yet come, died a normal death. This signaled the second main division in political Islam between the Abbasids, descendants of the Prophet's uncle Abbas and their followers, and the *Alawites*, descendants of the Prophet and Ali, who have since been called the *Shi'a* of Ali or *Shi'a* for short.

It was during the Abbasid rule that the concept of *Taqiya* was developed.[15] The practice of *Taqiya* by some claiming to be *Shi'a* over centuries has been quite justifiably used by their opponents to discredit their *Shi'ism*. What the *Imams* wanted their followers to do was to forego any interest in acquiring power or being involved directly in political games. *Imam* Ja'far As-Sadiq believed that a true believer should have little interest in earthly matters because this is the kingdom of the devil, who has been given a free hand by Allah to tempt people. The Kingdom of the Lord, according to the *Imams*, will only materialize with the coming of the Saviour—the Mehdi for *all* Muslims, the second coming of Christ for the Christians, and the first coming of the Messiah for the religious Jews of today. All Muslims believe in the Mehdi. They differ on whether he is a descendent of Muhammad or not, Shi'a vs Sunni.

Building Baghdad, Capital of an Empire

In 762 AD/ 145 AH the Abbasid Caliph Abu Ja'far Al-Mansoor chose a small village on the banks of the Tigris to build his round city, Dar As-Salaam (House of Peace), and called it 'Baghdad' after the village it replaced. Between its completion in 766 AD/149 AH and its destruction in 1258, Baghdad was the capital of a very powerful and prosperous Empire. During its days of glory, Baghdad was the centre of knowledge and learning for the whole world. People from all over the world flocked there to study, develop and contribute. It became a melting pot of different races, ethnicities, and cultures. There were no barriers of any sort regarding who was allowed to reside there.

There is no element in Islamic or Arabic heritage today which does not have some root in the Empire of Baghdad. As this is not a book on the history of Baghdad, we shall only refer to its role in language and *Fiqh*. The need for writing Arabic grammar was twofold. Firstly it became necessary as the flood of non Arabs into Islam led to the weakening of Arabic which had hitherto been spoken only by native Arab speakers. Secondly, the need to study Qur'an and *Hadith* in order to develop Islamic jurisprudence created a new demand for a clear understanding of the rules of syntax and of semantics. This gave birth in c. 785 AD/ 170 AH to al-Ain, the first dictionary reported in any language. It was compiled by the genius of Arab grammatician, Al-Khaleel, and was followed immediately by *al-Kitab*, probably the first comprehensive book on grammar in any language, written by his disciple, Sibawayh. Concurrently with the consolidation of grammar and a lexicon, there arose the task of compiling the sayings of the Prophet (*Hadith*) and the story of his life and practice (*Seerah*). The needs of the state and daily life required the development of Islamic jurisprudence (*Fiqh*). Needless to say all this took place in Baghdad or its close vicinity. All *Shi'a Fiqh* developed in Iraq. Although some *Sunni Fiqh* originated elsewhere, it too was, nevertheless, developed in Iraq. The *Ibadhis*, the other smaller sect of Islam, which lives mainly in Oman today, can proudly point to Iraq as the birthplace of their *Fiqh*. Schools of thought such as Sufism and *Mu'tazilah* also developed here alongside mainstream religion. With philosophers like Ibn Sina, Alfarabi, Al-Kindi and scientists like Al-Khwarizmi and Ibn Al-Haytham (the physicist who described photons 1000 years before any European scientist), Iraq became the cradle of all Arab heritage of today.

This unique feature of Iraq as the fountain of Islamic *Fiqh*, *Sunni*, *Shi'a* and *Ibadhi* is equally its main problem. Iraq will belong to the *Sunnis* just as much as it belongs to the *Shi'a*, simply because both sides have their roots there, irrespective of the population percentage. Thus thirteen centuries of almost exclusive political control by *Sunni* has led to two facts emerging—a sense of injustice among the *Shi'a* and an expectation among the *Sunni* to maintain the status quo. Thus the *Sunni* would like Iraq under their control and refuse to accept that autonomy for the mainly *Shi'a* south may be a solution. They fear this might cause the dismemberment of Iraq, or even worse, the annexation of Iraq to an ambitious Iran which aspires to lead the Muslim world. The *Shi'a*, on the other hand, want Baghdad but without its political history which reminds them of the persecution of the *Imams*. How could the *Shi'a* want to inherit Baghdad while celebrating the blowing up on 18 October 2005 of the statute of its founder, Abu Ja'far Al-Mansoor?[16]

This sense of injustice among the majority of *Shi'a* of Iraq has become so ingrained in the culture and psyche that, when it comes to issues of principles, it seems to subconsciously affect even educated *Shi'a* and obscure their vision. This has slowly become a sense of victimization which cuts through all strata of the *Shi'a* in Iraq and has been heightened and emphasized by another feature of *Shi'a* Islam, that of *Marji'ya*. The *Marji'ya*, is the center of reference to which the populace resort when they need guidance and advice on religious matters. Technically, every *Shi'a* must follow one religious authority in his spiritual and even mundane affairs. The *Marji'ya*, which has its centre in Najaf, carries more weight and wields more power than any political party in Iraq. If this same *Marji'ya* disseminates information about the injustices to which the *Shi'a* have been subjected, it will be able to move the masses.

The Americans and to a lesser extent the British, relying on an army of Orientalists, hundreds of think tanks, numerous Iraqi so-called experts and a plethora of intelligence reports, concluded that by appealing to the sense of injustice among the *Shi'a* of Iraq, they would be able to invade, occupy it and pacify Iraq by installing a puppet, mainly *Shi'a*, government operating under their control. Even years later, they are struggling to find out why it has failed despite having first armed the *Shi'a* militia against the *Sunni* and then moved on to arm the *Sunni* so-called Awakening (when in fact it was more like a slumbering), in order to limit the excesses of the *Shi'a* militia. The reason lies in the fact that Iraq can be ruled in one way only—through a secular state. Despite bad episodes, this has worked well for Iraq over the past eighty years.

2

FROM MONARCHY TO OCCUPATION

IRAQ FROM 1916 TO 2003

Overview of Iraq's 20th Century Political History

In order to have some understanding of what happened in Iraq towards the end of the 20th century, it is necessary to see how the political system, which led to the ascendency of the Ba'ath Party, had developed.

An obvious starting point is the British invasion of Iraq during WWI. Britain was already well aware of the discontent among Arabs with Ottoman rule, especially as it became more Turkish nationalist than Islamic. The hostility between Arab nationalism and Ottoman rule was demonstrated when Jamal Pasha, the Ottoman governor and commander-in-chief in Syria (including Palestine) from 1915 to 1917, executed eleven distinguished young Arabs, both Muslims and Christians, in Damascus and Beirut on August 21, 1915 and on May 6, 1916 he executed seven men in Damascus and thirteen men in Beirut[1] on charges of sedition. Thus when it was clear that Ottoman rule was coming to an end, Britain started looking for allies inside the Arab world. It would have been unthinkable for Britain to rely on the Arab Nationalists of Greater Syria as those were clearly out to rid the Arab world of any kind of occupation or foreign domination. Britain saw a good tool in Hussein bin Ali, the Sharif of Mecca with a claim to be a descendent of the Prophet Muhammad. He had some aspiration of becoming a ruler. In the ensuing communication between Hussein and MacMahon,[2] the British promised him an independent Arab land once he sided with them against the Ottomans. Hussein mobilized people in the Arab world against the Ottoman rule and on 10 June 1916 declared a rebellion against them. Although the scale of operations conducted by Hussein's followers was not great, they had great demoralizing effect on the Ottomans. Unbeknown to Sharif Hussein, the British had no intention of honoring these commitments. Concurrent with the correspondence with Hussein, the British were drafting the Sykes-Picot Agreement with the French to divide the Arab world between them. Moreover the Zionists were nearing their ambition to have Palestine promised to them, which eventually materialized with the Balfour Declaration of 1917.[3]

By 1918 all the Arab Middle East, except Arabia, was under military occupation. Sharif Hussein was forced to flee to Cyprus. He then went to live in Amman, Transjordan, where his son Abdullah was king,[4] and died there in 1931, a poor depressed man. It was no accident that although France was given most of Greater Syria in the Sykes-Picot Agreement, Palestine was retained for Britain. The reason was that the Zionists, who have always had London as their capital, made sure that the future of Palestine was decided at their hands and not subject to a lesser or perhaps unpredictable Zionist enclave in France. The decision was, as accurately argued by some staunch Zionists of today, to grant all of Palestine to the Jews and thus a new political entity by the name of the Emirate of Trans-Jordan was created on the east bank of the river, envisaged to become the home of the Palestinians once the Jews became a majority in Palestine.

The new colonialists wanted it to appear that they were responding to Arab sentiments and rewarding their support for defeating the Muslim Ottomans. Thus they appointed Faisal ibn Hussein as King in Syria and Abdullah ibn Hussein as Emir of Trans-Jordan. These appointments achieved two objectives. Firstly, they demonstrated some gratitude for Hussein's rebellion against the Ottomans. Secondly, and more importantly, they insured that both Faisal and Abdullah, brought from Hijaz, would be reliant upon the British for their survival and rule. The Syrians soon rejected Faisal but the British immediately considered him to be a good candidate to rule Iraq. On 23 August 1921 Faisal I became King of Iraq by British dictate. However, the real ruler of Iraq was Percy Cox.[5]

It is unavoidable for a student of history or international relations to draw parallels between what happened in Iraq during the two invasions at the beginning of the 20th and the 21st centuries. Both invasions were allegedly made to liberate the Iraqis although we are not told whether or not the Iraqis asked to be liberated! The first invasion put Iraq under the dictate of the British Captain, Percy Cox, and the second invasion made Iraq a corporation run by the US ambassador, Paul Bremer. Both men ruled by decree to the exclusion of everything Islamic or Iraqi. All legislation was in English with an Arabic translation, but wherever conflict arose, the English version prevailed. Following the first invasion of 1916, the League of Nations, dominated by colonial thinking, put Iraq under British mandate, which was the sanitized word for occupation. Following the second invasion of 2003, in accordance with the covert imperialist dominance since the demise of open colonialism, the UN authorized the US and UK to occupy Iraq and rule it. Both invasions produced a new constitution for Iraq which was claimed to reflect the will of the Iraqi people. In 1920 Percy Cox appointed a Constituent Assembly and in 2003 Paul Bremer appointed a Governing Council. Both invasions utilized the sectarian divide amongst the Arabs of Iraq to further strengthen their hold over the country. Both invasions resulted in treaties which left Iraq with reduced sovereignty and the indefinite positioning of foreign forces on its land. Both invasions resulted in imposed agreements in which Iraq's oil was usurped by the invader. Even the alliances and allegiances have changed very little. Thus the descendants of Ali Suleiman, the Anbar tribal chief, who sided with the British in 1920s, sided with the invaders of 2003, while Harith Ad-Dhari, the grandson of Sheikh Dhari, who killed Colonel Gerard Leachman in 1920, led a powerful opposition movement. In short an observer could easily conclude that the events since 2003 show a remarkable similarity to the events of the early 20th century. It is as if Iraq had not gone through eighty years of political maturity. Neither the Iraqi politicians nor Anglo-Saxon invaders appear to have learnt the lessons of history.[6]

Collaboration with invaders is mostly done by political minorities or oppressed groups and even such a minority consists of smaller minorities, each collaborating for a different reason, but all lacking in principles in varying degrees. At the bottom of the ladder of collaborators are those who aspire to power, money, or social position which they otherwise would never acquire in normal circumstances. Another group of collaborators consists of those who have suffered from the regime in power and are willing to seek vengeance at any cost. There are some among the collaborators who genuinely mean well for their people but because they suffer from a sense of inferiority they believe that collaborating with the invader would lead to better times. We believe that Nuri As-Saeed,[7] who along with Yasin Al-Hashimi made up the two most prominent Iraqi political players of the first half of the 20th century, was from this last category. Nuri Pasha was Iraq's Prime Minister eight times between 1930 and 1958, when he was tragically killed some 50 meters from where we lived.[8] Even when he was not heading the cabinet, he held such power that it is safe to conclude that he was the real ruler of Iraq for nearly 30 years. It is necessary to pause here and reflect on one important fact relating to Nuri Pasha. This man who held power in Iraq for so long was born a Kurd and educated as a Turk. We have been fed a great deal of propaganda by the ill-informed or ill-intentioned Western media about the oppression of Kurds in Iraq until it has become a mantra. We shall address this campaign of falsehood later in the book, but it must be highlighted here that a country that had oppressed and persecuted the Kurds throughout their history could not have had a Kurdish ruler for thirty years. In fact Nuri was not the only non-Arab Prime Minister of Iraq for much of the time between 1921 and 1958. There were several others. Notable among them were: Jafar Pasha al-Askari, a Turkoman, (1887–1936) Naji Shawkat, Turkish-Caucasian, (1893–1980),[9] Hikmat Sulayman, Turkoman, (1889–1964),[10] Ahmad Mukhtar Baban, Kurdish, (1900–1976) [11] and other top army officers and ministers who are too many to count. In fact Iraq is very similar to Britain where the Scots, like the Kurds, have normally held higher number of positions in government than their percentage of the nation would have entitled them to hold, had there been any intention of national favoritism.

Nuri As-Saeed's Rule

Nuri graduated as an army officer in 1906 and served in the Ottoman army. Although he witnessed the birth of the Turkish national movements, he was never an Arab nationalist. If anything he opposed the movement as was clearly shown during his last years in power. Like his successor General Qasim, Nuri believed that Iraq should be isolated from the effect of Arab nationalism that was sweeping across the Middle East. Both, in our opinion, were clearly wrong. Nuri seeing the inevitable demise of the Ottoman Empire, sided with the winner in order to realize his early ambition of ruling Iraq. Although he was pro the West and needed the British to support his rule, he asserted his independence within reason. One example is an acrimonious encounter between Nuri and the British ambassador in the late 1950s over a request for new armaments.[12] The legacy of Nuri As-Saeed in Iraq may be summed up in four developments that shaped Iraq's political life during the monarchy and beyond, resurfacing again after 2003. These were the treaty with Britain, the award of Iraqi oil to the British, the setting up of Baghdad Pact and the setting up of the Hashemite Federation with Jordan.

By considering how Nuri reacted to the calamity of Palestine and the rise of Nasser, it becomes easier to understand where he stood vis-à-vis Arab nationalism and consequently, albeit partially, his own demise. Very much like many pro-Western imperialist Arabs, whether highly educated and informed like Dr. Fadhil Al-Jamali[13] or primitive and ignorant like Abdul-Aziz bin Saud, Nuri had no problem with political Zionism. However, they wished and sometimes even tried to convince their Western patrons to moderate the Zionists' ambitions, if not to prolong their own political survival then to sell the concept of coexistence to the Arab public. It was reported that in the Bludan conference called in September 1937 on Palestine, Iraq was represented by moderates like Tawfiq al-Suwaydi and Nuri As-Saeed.[14] (Moderates, when referred to by Western writers in reference to Arabs, means those who acquiesce in Zionist and/or Western hegemony.) In 1930, during his first term as PM, Nuri signed the Anglo-Iraqi Treaty, which granted Britain the unlimited right to station its armed forces in and transit military units through Iraq. It also gave the control of the country's oil to the British.

The second manifestation of Nuri's rejection of Arab Nationalism was in his opposition to Gemal Abdul-Nasser (better known as Nasser) of Egypt. Nasser epitomized the aspirations of the young post-WWII Arab generation to freedom, national independence, and some form of social justice while at the same time rejecting corruption in their midst. They were mostly anti-Communist but Western policies forced most of them to seek Soviet backing. Nasser only turned that way after the West refused to finance the vital high Aswan Dam, and declined to provide the Egyptian army with the necessary armaments. When the Russians offered assistance he accepted it while at the same time prohibiting any activity by the Communist Party of Egypt.

Nuri's aversion to Nasser and his Arab nationalism, apart from giving rise to anecdotes such as the one in which he invited Antony Eden to attack Egypt following the nationalization of the Suez Canal,[15] materialized in two actions, namely the setting up the Baghdad Pact and the Hashemite Federation. The Egyptian revolution of 23 July 1952 was a milestone in the history of the Middle East. Nasser and his cohort of young revolutionary Egyptian officers were initially determined to rid Egypt of widespread corruption and build a socially just society. Even if Nasser and his colleagues were not Arab nationalists on the eve of 23 July 1952, they soon became so. The appeal and its reverberation across the Arab world rattled many pro-Western leaders along with their patrons in the West. Nuri was determined to set up his own pact, not because he considered Israel as the main enemy,[16] but rather to oppose Arab nationalism which he considered to be the main threat to his power and to the interests of the West. After some negotiation and persuasion, he and Adnan Menderes, prime minister of Turkey, signed, on 23 February 1955, the Turco-Iraqi Treaty of Mutual Cooperation, which came later to be known formally as the Baghdad Pact following the accession of the UK, Pakistan and Iran. According to one US State Department Report, the Turco-Iraq Pact was motivated by a desire to "promote Iraqi-Syrian union by bringing Syria into the Turco-Iraqi pact".[17] However, the Baghdad Pact did not manage that because Syria and Egypt forged, on popular demand, a union in February 1958, which consigned Nuri's dreams to ashes.

Arab nationalism had its heyday between 1956-1961, i.e. the period between the Suez fiasco, when Britain and France agreed that Israel should attack Egypt so that they themselves could use this as a pretext to attack Egypt, topple Nasser and regain the Suez Canal; and the dissolution of the Union between Syria and Egypt. The failure of Western Imperialists and their protégé, Israel, was seen by the Arab public as the first victory against outside invaders since the end of the crusades. The union between Egypt and Syria was seen by the Arab masses as the realization that, after eight centuries of being subjected to division, invasions and occupations, the Arabs were capable of real union as opposed to phony organizations such as the Arab League created on British initiative to maintain division.

Nasser was everything Nuri was not but wished he was. Nasser had the charisma of a leader while Nuri looked like a Baghdadi thug with two pistols sticking out of his trousers and surrounded by a gang of hoodlums.[18] Nasser was a great orator who could mesmerize people when he talked while Nuri was such a poor speaker that he could not even read well from a prepared text. But more importantly Nuri had no cause to which the people could relate. The message that the only way forward was to have alliances with the colonialists was not going to get a good hearing. The people had had enough of foreign domination and wanted a change. Nasser, on the other hand, had a cause with which the people could identify—a move from the old regime of subjugation to a world of free will and free choice, which is completely in harmony with human nature.

While the Syrians and Egyptians were preparing for the announcement of the union between their two states, Nuri managed to convince the two second-cousin monarchs of Iraq and Jordan to enter into a loose federation by the name of the Hashemite Federation. The formation of such Federation was announced on 14 February 1958 and the protocol was signed by the two kings on 19 May 1958 with Nuri being the Federation's first prime minister.[19]

Nuri, a product of the Ottoman regime, switched sides to the British and told the Iraqis to follow him as he knew best. His position did not have much legitimacy. The Islamists rejected him for having sided with the infidels against their brethren Muslims. The non-Islamists—we hesitate to use the term secular as there were no secular Iraqis—wanted freedom from foreign domination under whatever name. He could not even form a proper political party to act as his base, yet he repressed all political opposition from the communists to the Ba'athists. Not even the mildly pro-Western National Democratic Party seemed to have been to his liking.

The only good in Western political order is its ability to ensure the peaceful exchange of power between different parties and different leaderships. It seems that power with its success brings a sense of grandeur that with time blinds the ruler's vision and fogs his perception and understanding. In his last speech made towards the end of spring of 1958, only a few weeks before his downfall, Nuri told his Iraqi listeners to sleep soundly because as he put it: *"Dar Es Sayyid Ma'mounah",* The House of the Sayyid (Master) was safe. Only a few weeks later his body was dragged through the street of Baghdad.

General Qasim's Rule

While Nuri was promising Iraqis that his house was safe, young Iraqi officers had come together and decided to work towards ridding the country of its rulers and set up a revolutionary Iraq. This small nuclei of Free Officers was made up of men from varying backgrounds. The two main officers among them were Brigadier Abdul-Kareem Qasim (1914-1963) [20] and Colonel Abdul-Salam Arif (1921-1966). [21] Both came from humble backgrounds, with Qasim being the bright Iraqi achiever, distinguishing himself at every level of education and training from primary school to military staff college. Qasim was chosen by the Free Officers to head their meeting as he was of the highest rank among them.

On the morning of 14 July 1958, and only a few hours before King Faisal II and his aides were due to fly to Turkey for an official visit, the movement of the Free Officers led by Qasim launched a coup which ousted the monarchy and killed members of the Royal family, the Prime Minister, his son and a few others. [22]

Iraq had two main powerful political blocks—the communists and the Arab nationalists. There were other political groupings such as the democrats, the Muslim Brotherhood and smaller Arab nationalist groups especially the Nasserites, but they had little influence among the public at large. The Iraqi Communist Party was the oldest and the best organized, drawing on the expertise of the international communist movement, and it managed to rally more people behind it in the few months following the July coup. As most communist parties of the world during the second half of the 20th century were appended to Moscow, they had little freedom of policy or decision. Moscow's line post WWII was that any government formed by the national bourgeoisie should be supported. Qasim's regime was such a government and the Iraqi communists were obliged to support it. Thus the communists had to support the regime which oppressed them and imprisoned their members and on the day it fell, on 8 February 1963, they had to come out to the streets fighting for it.

Moscow wanted to ensure that Iraq's new Government established strong links to the USSR. Thus the slogan of the Iraqi Communists from day one was Soviet Friendship. The Arab nationalists, led by the Ba'athists, wanted an immediate union with the United Arab Republic of Egypt and Syria (UAR). Neither the union with the UAR nor the 'very close' friendship with the Soviets suited Qasim. He wanted an independent Iraq capable of withstanding both pressures. He believed in Iraqi Nationalism and looked for it in Iraq's history. When he selected a new flag for the Republic he chose the Babylonian sun as an emblem. His vision lacking in ideology, was contrary to the established political wisdom prevailing in Iraq, and was not even understood or appreciated by the masses who genuinely supported him.

When the conflict with Arif surfaced, Qasim was supported by his faithful Qasimite officers and all the communist officers in the Iraqi army and air force, of whom there was an appreciable number. The Ba'athists and other Arab nationalist officers sided with Arif. Arif was removed from his position as deputy prime minister and later sentenced to death, which was later commuted to life imprisonment, and then he was put under house arrest. That meant a consolidation of the position of the communist officers and their sympathizers throughout the armed forces. The Arab nationalists in the armed forces, some of whom were founders of the Free Officers movement, feared that Iraq was being diverted away from its supposed Arab nationalist path. In March 1959 they staged an armed rebellion in the garrison of Mosul, which was supported by other army units in the rest of Iraq. Qasim put it down with the assistance of the communist party and its officers. Qasim had no alternative but to sign the death warrants of the rebels, if he was to establish his authority. He thus committed the most unforgivable cardinal offence of a revolutionary, the killing of his comrades. On 20 September 1959 some twenty Iraqi officers, including the founder of the first cell of Free Officers, Rif'at Haj Sirri, were executed. The executions brought back the memory of the death sentences of the four rebel officers on 6 January 1942,[23] and the further execution by the monarchy of these four officers and one civilian leader.[24] The damage to Qasim's reign from the execution of these officers, some of whom were highly respected, was irreparable.

On 19 July 1959 in a major speech inaugurating a Christian church in Baghdad, he referred to the Iraqi Communists as anarchists and followed that with a press conference on 29 July in which he called on the communists to stop spreading malicious rumors about an impending reactionary conspiracy against the regime.[25]

Qasim's greatest legacy was the promulgation of Law Number 80 of 1961.[26] The law meant that 99% of Iraq, with massive known oil reserves, was back in the hands of the Iraqis.[27] A short summary

THE STORY OF OIL

Although Iraq is one of the world's richest counties in hydrocarbons, the oil of Iraq is one, but not the most significant, reason why it was attacke, invaded and occupied twice during one century.

In June 1914, the Ottomans granted exploration concessions in the Wilayet of Mosul through a Letter of Intent, to the British owned Turkish Petroleum Company (TPC). The San Remo Oil Agreement of 1920 rearranged the shareholding in the TPC which divided the rights in Iraq's oil into 70% for Britain, 25% to France and 5% to Mr. Gulbenkian, the Armenian who brokered the concession for the TPP. In 1929 the TPC became the Iraq Petroleum Company (IPC). The rising US imperialism which started taking shape post WWI went into full action to exploit Iraq's oil. By 1928, the shares in IPC was rearranged again resulting in Britain controlling 47.5%, France 23.75%, the US 23.75% and Gulbenkian retaining his 5%. In 1931 the Iraqi Government granted the IPC a 75-year concession.

The problem of the usurpation of Iraq's wealth did not stop at the distribution of shares alone but went further into the pricing of oil. This was so because "the pattern of relationships between Iraq, as well as other oil-producing countries, and the oil companies exploiting oil resources was regulated by concession agreements. According to the provisions of the concession, the foreign-owned oil company obtained an exclusive right to develop and export Iraq's oil; it was the sole determinant of the level of oil output and export; and it alone had the prerogative to set the price of oil. In short the government had no input in the development or the pricing of what became the most important commodity of the national economy. The role of the government was a passive one; it became a recipient of a fixed sum per unit of export."

Furthermore, the IPC "was not to be operated as an independent profit-making company. It was essentially a cartel for producing and sharing crude oil among the individual oil corporations who owned it. As such, each company lifted, transported and marketed its own corporate share of the produced crude. No doubt this arrangement was quite contentious and indeed it did open the door for crude oil pricing, transporting and marketing manipulation which would result in an underpayment of royalties to the host country coffers."

The nationalization of oil by Iran in 1951, despite having failed, created an atmosphere that forced new negotiations between the oil companies and the producers for profit-sharing which culminated in the agreement of 1952. As the oil companies alone had the power to fix oil prices, they started a spree of price cuts. This movement of price cutting was a major reason the oil producing countries set up the Organization of Oil Producing Countries (OPEC), which struggled for many years to stabilize oil prices. This was in vain as the oil companies ignored its calls to restore oil prices to their 1960 levels.

Oil exploration in Iraq, following the drilling of the first well in Kirkuk in 1927, slowed down during WWII but resumed soon after its end. The IPC discovered several large oil fields between 1948 and 1954, notable among which were the super fields of West Qurna, Rumayla and Majnoon. The unfair concessionary agreement granted the oil companies permission to explore anywhere in Iraq for a period of 75 years without Iraq having any say in the matter or having the right to buyback. These facts created a sense of resentment among Iraqis in general, both government and governed. Thus General Qasim received total support, including from his political enemies, when on 11 December 1961 he promulgated Law Number 80 which dispossessed the IPC of some 99.5% of its concession, that being the Iraqi territory that had yet been explored.

In 1964 the Iraq National Oil Company (INOC) was established to develop all Iraq's oil reserves. INOC went on to enter into several service agreements with Soviet, French, Japanese, Italian and Brazilian oil companies in which these oil companies explored for oil in Iraq under INOC control. Once oil was discovered, it would be surrendered to INOC and the oil produced would be sold to these companies at an agreed discount. The success of INOC was demonstrated by its ability to raise Iraq's production capacity from 1.5 million barrels per day in 1968 to 3.5 million barrels per day in 1979. By 1979 all of Iraq's oil was being produced by Iraqis under the control of INOC.

It is not difficult to see how the imperialists concluded that they had reached a dead end with Qasim. One of the earliest signs of their giving up on Qasim was the imperialist incitement and support for the military rebellion of the Kurds in northern Iraq. On 6 October 1958 the Kurdish leader, Mustafa Al-Barazani, returned from exile on Qasim's invitation and was given an official hero's welcome. Under Qasim's rule, just as much as under Nuri's rule before him, the Kurds could not argue that they were oppressed. Yet on 21 September 1961, Mustafa Al-Barazani declared an armed insurrection against Baghdad. On and off fighting between the Kurdish rebels and the central government in Baghdad ensued and was carried through and beyond Qasim's rule.[28]

On the morning of 8 February 1963, some tanks advanced on Qasim's head office in the Ministry of Defense, next to the middle gate of old Baghdad, and a few MIG-fighters took to the air to attack the Ministry. Top commanders were assassinated in their homes in what was a cleverly hatched plan led mainly by the Ba'athists and supported by other Arab nationalists and Islamists in the Iraqi army. Qasim and his faithful soldiers fought bravely but with no help from any other unit outside the Ministry, he was doomed. On 9 February 1963, Qasim was arrested with a few of his most loyal officers in the Festival Hall next to the Ministry. He was summarily tried and executed. The events of 14 Ramadhan (8 February) were in actuality not purely a military action by army officers but rather a revolution in which the whole civilian Ba'ath Party and their allies took part. In fact had it not been for civilian action in eliminating some top figures in the Iraqi army and air force, the operation might not have succeeded.

From the first hour of the military activity, the Iraqi Communist Party issued a statement calling on the people of Iraq to resist the revolution. They were out on the streets led by no less a figure than Salam Adel, the Secretary General of the Politburo. What followed was a bloody oppression with killing, torture, and imprisonment on a scale which Iraq had not seen before. Historians have argued and undoubtedly will go on arguing as to whether or not a less bloody fate would have befallen the Communists had they not resisted the Ba'ath revolution of 1963.

The Arifs' Rule

Following the failed assassination attempt in 1959 on Qasim, the Ba'ath Party in Iraq went through a rearrangement phase in which a new leadership was installed by the Pan-Arab National Leadership of the party. The new Secretary General to replace Fouad Ar-Rikabi was Ali Salih As-Sa'di who, despite being a charismatic person, lacked Fouad's organizational skills and the ability to impose authority.[29] No sooner had the Ba'thists dealt with the Communists than they started conspiring against each other.[30]

It has since been argued, when comparing Arif to Qasim, that while Qasim reprieved Arif from the death sentence when he was convicted of an assassination attempt on the latter's life, Arif either demanded the execution of Qasim on 9 February 1963 or did nothing to stop it when as President he had the authority to do so. Although Arif declared in July 1958 that he wanted an immediate union with Nasser of Egypt, he did not seem so enthusiastic about such a union when he became the President of Iraq in 1963. It seemed that he began to have his own vision about his role in history and for once probably naively thought he could have been a challenger or successor to Nasser. His control of Iraq was due to the current political situation, rather than his own political skills. The Ba'ath had undergone a meltdown[31] and the communists were in such disarray that they could be regarded as non-existent.

Arif needed the support of the other Arab nationalists after having removed the Ba'athists from power. However, he soon faced a plot against him by a number of Nasserite officers while he was visiting Egypt. But the attempted coup was an instant failure and its leaders fled to Egypt.[32] Two main features of Arif's rule are worthy of note. Firstly, Arif emulated Nasser by introducing some form of socialism. To distance himself from the communist socialism and to avoid Islamist criticism, it was given the odd name of 'rational socialism', a term which may be attributed to the Belgian thinker, Hippolyte Colins.[33] Secondly, and perhaps more significantly Arif's rule witnessed intensified battles in the north between the Iraqi army and the Kurdish rebellion that was started by Mustafa Al-Barazani in September 1961. The intensified fighting could be attributed partly to Al-Barazani's attempt to take advantage of the chaos in the Arab nationalist camp in Baghdad, and partly to Arif's chauvinistic nationalism and his distaste for Kurds.

On 13 April 1966 Abdul-Salam Arif was killed along with a number of his ministers in a helicopter crash while on a visit to Basrah. His death remains a mystery. The sudden death of Arif created a political vacuum that many of the officers around him sought to utilize to their advantage. There were tense hours before wisdom prevailed and his brother Abdul-Rahman Arif was chosen as the next President signaling the era of the second Arif presidency. In fairness to Abdul-Rahman, he was not chosen by virtue of being the brother of Abdul-Salam. Abdul-Raham was one of the early members of the Free Officers nuclei in the Iraqi army prior to the coup of July 1958. He was a highly respected army officer and served under Qasim despite his brother's rift with the latter. He was a wiser Arab nationalist than his predecessor brother, and many Arab nationalists, including the Ba'athists, were able to deal with him. He was acceptable to the remnants of the Communist Party because he was not directly involved in their persecution. His era was one of a genuine freedom that Iraq had not witnessed for some time. Most of the communists who had lost their jobs in Government were reinstated. Many political detainees were released and people were openly discussing political issues and expressing dissent.

As this freedom started to permeate Iraqi society, political parties began to reorganize themselves. However, it seems such an atmosphere was ominous for the imperialists in Washington and London. A free Iraq would produce a genuine nationalist state which is anathema to the imperialists' design for it and its neighbors. A stable free and 'democratic'

Iraq would assert itself in every field and that would be contrary to imperial interests.

The US started to look for some solution to forestall the eventuality of a free Iraq. They managed, through their trusted and respected Iraqi academic, Dr. Nasser Al-Hani, to establish contact with some ambitious officers around Arif. As money is never a problem for the US,[34] they were able to finance the coup and reward these young officers with promise of high positions in the new government provided they toed the line.[35] Abdul-Rahman Arif told Batatu that he knew that An-Naif was bought by oil companies through Saudi Arabia and by the intermediary of Bashir Taleb, the military attaché in Beirut and Nasser Al-Hani, Iraq's Ambassador to Lebanon.[36]

The Ba'ath joined the conspiracy against Arif. Only two weeks after the coup of 17 July 1968 the Ba'ath ousted their co-conspirators and the Party formed a new government consisting only of Ba'athists. Ahmed Hasan Al-Bakr remained the President and Chairman of the Revolutionary Command Council and added the post of Prime Minister. Saddam Hussein became the Vice-Chairman of the Revolutionary Command Council. The smaller coup of 30 July 1968 signaled the Second Coming of the Ba'ath which was to last until it was removed with the US led invasion in March 2003.

The Significance of the Ba'ath Movement in the Arab Middle East

No political movement has had such a profound impact on the history of the Middle East during the 20th century as the Ba'ath. It was born in Syria where it has prevailed since 1963, it ruled Iraq between 1968 and 2003 and it has had branches in almost every Arab country and played a significant role in varying degrees in all of them. This book sets out to show how the Ba'ath did indeed build a semi-industrialized state as UN Under-Secretary-General Martti Ahtisaari said in May 1991[37] and how it was destroyed through genocidal sanctions and wars.

However, some background is necessary to appreciate the reasons for the rise and fall of the Ba'ath movement in Iraq. The birth of the Ba'ath movement in Syria and how it took root in Iraq has been covered, albeit briefly, in a previous work, *The Trial of Saddam Hussein*,[38] and we do not intend to reproduce it here. It suffices to restate the reasons why the Ba'ath succeeded in Iraq. We believe there were two main reasons—their ideals were simple and appealing, although the methods used to implement them were oppressive toward dissent. The Ba'ath believed that the Arabs make one nation which has been divided by different episodes of colonialism. In support of such belief they would cite the common language, culture, history, religion and enemy. The only salvation for the Arabs, the Ba'athists believe, is for them to unite. The second ideal of the Ba'ath called for some form of social justice which it called, in line with the mood of the 20th century, socialism. In order to see why such an ideal would appeal to the Arabs at large, one needs only to consider it from the perspective of the deprived Arab masses, who look with disgust at their wealth being squandered by corrupt regimes, installed by the same imperialists who created the division among Arabs and who endeavor to maintain it.

Learning the Lessons of the 1963 Failure of the Ba'ath

On 30 July 1968 the Ba'ath Party assumed full control over Iraq and started its second, longer and eventful era of rule over Iraq. In order to avoid the power struggle for leadership, an understanding was reached between the two most powerful men, namely Ahmed Hasan Al-Bakr and Saddam Hussein. Al-Bakr commanded a great deal of respect among officers in the Iraqi army and not just the Ba'athists among them.

Saddam Hussein was a young ambitious Ba'athist who had been denied any role in the party due to his exile, following the failed assassination of Qasim in 1959, until 1963. When the party disintegrated in November 1963, Saddam and Al-Bakr worked together to regroup old members into a new organization. They succeeded after they assumed power in July 1968. Increasing numbers of former Ba'athists started returning to the fold of the new party. This move was in line with the premise, which Saddam reiterated to his comrades, that the party would be built once it assumed power.[39] Once the Ba'ath assumed full control in Iraq on 30 July 1968, an understanding was reached between Saddam and Al-Bakr. Saddam started with building the party and setting up the nucleus of Iraq's first real intelligence service. Al-Bakr took control of the army and the running of government.

The one thing the new Ba'ath was not going to tolerate was dissent within the party. As there were only a few members who had a gift of formulating and reflecting on principles, the only dissent that could have arisen would have been based on personal allegiances and ambitions of power. This policy of ruthlessly eliminating dissent worked to the Ba'ath's advantage at some times and to its detriment at others as we shall see later.

Saddam Hussein, who had a grand vision of building a powerful Iraq, understood the importance of oil in the realization of this vision, and took control of the oil issue right from the beginning. He set up, and presided over, the Follow-Up Committee on Oil Contracts which effectively made him supreme in all matters dealing with oil, especially existing and impending negotiations with oil companies. Thus while OPEC was negotiating with the oil companies, negotiations which led to OPEC member states securing a share in the oil production by the end of 1972, Saddam Hussein was planning something even grander. In June 1972, Iraq nationalized the IPC concessions. Following the Arab Israeli war of October 1973, Iraq nationalized the American and Dutch interests in the Basrah Petroleum Company (BPC) and by 1975 all foreign oil interests in Iraq were nationalized. Iraq set up the Iraqi Company for Oil Operations (ICOO) to operate and manage the nationalized oil fields. "Thus fifty-five years after the humiliating San Remo Agreement Iraq finally achieved complete sovereignty over its oil fields." [40]

The sequence of events from the Tehran Agreement to OPEC's modest success to Iraq's nationalization led to a new era for the Ba'ath in Iraq. Some six years after assuming power and after a few austere early years, the Ba'ath was basking in the glory of success having raised Iraq's oil revenue from ID 214 million (approx. $710 million) in 1970 to ID 1.7 billion (approx. $6 billion) in 1974. Oil revenue increased from 16% of Iraq's GNP in 1970 to 57% in 1976. [41]

The Ba'ath Succeeds in Freezing the Kurdish Problem

Saddam Hussein realized even before assuming power in 1968 that the Ba'ath would not be able to set in motion its plans to build the Iraq it desired so long as the Kurdish problem was festering. The Kurdish problem arose from a sense of injustice among the Kurds of Iraq, and belatedly among the Kurds of Iran and Turkey, at not having their own national home. The history of the problem is too long and too complex to adequately argue here. It would suffice to say that Saddam Hussein and his comrades genuinely wanted to put an end to the fighting in northern Iraq between the government forces and the Kurdish rebels, which had been intermittent since September 1961.

One of the earlier indications of good intention on the part of the new leaders of Iraq came in Revolutionary Command Council decree number 677/1969, which set up a committee headed by the Vice President to coordinate the implementation of laws and decrees relating to the Kurdish region. This was followed by a general pardon of all civilians and military personnel who participated in the rebellion in the north of Iraq. Among the other decrees that indicated a real willingness to address some of the legitimate national grievances of the Kurds were: decentralization through Governorate Law; creation of the new Dihook Governorate; the building of Sulaimaniyah University; setting up the Kurdish Scientific Council; setting up the Kurdish Culture Directorate, and making Nowruz (The Kurdish/Persian Holiday) a national holiday in Iraq.[42]

Negotiations led to a Manifesto for Kurdish Autonomy. This was signed by Saddam Hussein, representing the Government, and Mustafa Al-Barazani, representing the Kurds, in what came to be known as the 11 March 1970 Manifesto. It was certainly a revolutionary Manifesto and gave Iraqi Kurds far greater rights and status than Kurds in both neighboring Iran and Turkey, where the total Kurdish population is nearly ten times that of Iraq. Amongst the Manifesto articles was the acknowledgment that Iraq consists mainly of two nations (Kurdish and Arab), and that the Constitution should incorporate this. It also decreed that the Kurdish language become the official second language in the Kurdish area and taught alongside Arabic (note that even today neither the Welsh nor the Scots in Britain enjoy such rights); that the Kurdish language should be taught as a second language in Arab schools of Iraq; that there should be no discrimination against the Kurds in official government positions or military command; that those appointed to positions of power in Kurdish areas should be Kurds or, alternatively, Arabs who had mastered the Kurdish language; that a Kurdish Vice President should be appointed, and the Kurds should have a proportional representation in the legislature body. The Manifesto set four years for the implementation of its terms.[43]

On 12 May 1971, the Revolutionary Command Council in Baghdad set up a committee headed by Saddam Hussein to implement the Manifesto whose success was in the interest of the Government in Baghdad. As part of the Ba'ath attempt to pacify the political sphere in order to get on with the ambitious development plan, it set up the National Progressive Front (NPF) as a political front of the main political parties in Iraq including the Ba'ath, the Communists and the Kurds with some other small political parties.[44] The Ba'athists went further than any had expected and, in 1972, signed a Treaty of Friendship and Cooperation with the USSR. Article 1 stated that the treaty's objective was to develop broad cooperation between Iraq and the Soviet Union in economic, trade, scientific, technical, and other fields on the basis of "respect for sovereignty, territorial integrity and non-interference in one another's internal affairs." Under the treaty, Iraq obtained extensive technical assistance and military equipment from the Soviet Union.[45]

As the deadline for the implementation of the 11 March Manifesto got closer Al-Barazani was adamant not to negotiate any further until his new demands (including the inclusion of Kirkuk within the Kurdish autonomy region, and the abolition of the Revolutionary Command Council) were accepted. Both parties in the NPF, the Ba'ath and the Communists, proceeded to legislate accordingly. On 11 March 1974, four years after the declaration of the 11 March Manifesto, The Autonomy Law was promulgated and the provisional constitution was amended accordingly. On March 12, 1974 the Government invited Al-

Barazani to join the NPF but he declined. However, as a sign of good will and in line with the 11 March Manifesto and Law, the Government appointed Abdullah, the eldest son of Mustafa Al-Barazani, as a member of the cabinet and Taha Muhiydeen Ma'rouf as Vice President.

None of these political measures, however, appeared to work and the Kurds again took to the mountains to resume their insurrection. This time the fighting was fierce because the Kurds had managed to acquire from the Shah of Iran new and heavy weaponry. It was clear to the leadership in Baghdad that the only way to stop the insurrection, which was distracting the Government in Baghdad from its development plans, was to stop the Iranian supplies and the only way this could have been achieved was by striking a deal with the Shah of Iran. Algeria brokered such a deal which was signed, during an OPEC meeting, in Algiers on 6 March 1975 by Saddam Hussein and the Shah of Iran. By this Agreement, Iraq ceded part of its waterway in Shatt Al-Arab to Iran in return for the latter closing its borders and ceasing all supplies and support to the Kurdish insurrection. No sooner had the Agreement been signed than the Kurdish rebellion evaporated, thus proving that it had been maintained by the Shah of Iran. On 18 March 1975, Mustafa Al-Barazani fled Iraq to Iran and then to the US where, on 2 March 1979, he died a broken depressed man. The meltdown which ensued within the Kurdish political structure was so severe that it took the Kurds more than fifteen years and two invasions to regroup. There is also evidence of Zionist cooperation and aid from Israel to the Kurds. Several books and articles have been written detailing such cooperation with photos of Al-Barazani and several of his aids and other Kurdish leaders with Israeli officials in the North of Iraq or in Israel itself.[46]

Although the Algiers Agreement of 1975 is regularly cited when the Kurdish problem is discussed, we believe its true significance, regarding subsequent events in Iraq, has never been acknowledged. It is true that it enabled the Ba'ath to pacify the whole country and embark on its development plan, and that it saved bloodshed and destruction on both sides. However, it is equally true that it was one of the causes of the Iran-Iraq war which include the awakening of the Shi'a after Khomeini revolution and the consequent competition within Iraq between Arab nationalism and revolutionary Islam, which had a greater grip on many among the Shi'a population and all that followed, from the attempt to recover Kuwait, to the destructive sanctions, to the calamitous invasion and occupation of 2003. It would have been inconceivable for an Arab Nationalist, like Saddam Hussein, to cede Arab land in difficult times without planning from the outset to recover it one day. The 1980 invasion of Iran was, inter alia, Saddam's attempt to reverse the humiliation of the 1975 Algiers Agreement. He may have seen himself as a proud Arab Nationalist who had been forced to kiss the hand of the archenemy

Persian Emperor now reversing the victory of Qadissiay of 637 AD when Islam overran the Sassanid Persian Empire.

The development plan, the details of which will be examined in later chapters, executed by the Ba'ath between 1975 and 1980 brought prosperity to Iraq unknown before. Most Iraqis, who lived through that period, remember it today with nostalgia. Along with full employment and solid infrastructure, the rulers of Baghdad managed to arm their military to a degree and sophistication hitherto unseen.

By the end of 1979, while Khomeini was struggling to build a new Islamic Iran with the Iranian army almost disintegrating, Saddam Hussein felt powerful and almost unstoppable. He thought the time was right to rectify the humiliation and injustice of the Algiers 1975 Agreement. Saddam Hussein believed that Iran's attempt to export the Islamic Revolution and the violation of the border including exchange of gun fire was sufficient justification for the Iraqi army to invade. He genuinely believed that Iran was very weak and that he was about to topple Khomeini and assume supremacy throughout the Gulf. We are not speculating but basing this conclusion on statements he made to that effect to a few of his closest lieutenants. [47]

The Iraqi Night of the Long Knives

One of the main elements of the rise and fall of the Ba'ath in Iraq had been Saddam Hussein's ambition, right from the beginning, to lead the Party, rule Iraq and consequently the Arab World. The most formidable party member who worried Saddam Hussein had always been Abdul-Khaliq As-Samarrai' whom he had to remove in order to have the stage for himself. Abdul-Khaliq was a highly respected Ba'athist, loved by most party members who knew him. He was well-mannered, well-educated and well-informed regarding Iraqi and international issues. In 1959 when Saddam Hussein joined the Ba'ath Party, Abdul-Khaliq was a high ranking party member and in 1968 he was a member of both the regional command and Pan-Arab national command of the Ba'ath Party. In 1973 the first major schism in the Ba'ath, post 1968, arose when it was alleged that Nadhim Gizar, the Director of Iraq's security service, and a few other party members had planned to assassinate Ahmed Hasan Al-Bakr and Saddam Hussein at Baghdad's airport on the arrival of the former from a visit to Bulgaria. Abdul-Khaliq was accused of being one of the conspirators. Whether because the evidence was not solid or because members of the Pan-Arab National Command interceded on his behalf, he was saved from the death that befell Nadhim Gizar and other co-conspirators. Abdul-Khaliq was confined to house arrest instead. It was Saddam's first attempt to remove Abdul-Khaliq. The 1973 schism consolidated Saddam's control over the party and removed some of the people whose support he had needed prior to 1968, but who had since become his adversaries.

The second major schism in the party took place in 1979 when Saddam Hussein concluded that he had sufficiently established his authority so as to assume full control over the party and the state. Saddam Hussein faced Ahmed Hasan Al-Bakr with some difficult decisions including a proposed confrontation with Iran to rescind the 1975 Algiers agreement with the Shah of Iran. When Al-Bakr refused to oblige Saddam, the latter advised him that his tenure was up and he had no option but to hand over the Party and the State. Al Bakr, who himself was one of the most notorious conspirators in the history of the Party, realized that Saddam's control had become ubiquitous and irreversible. On July 16, 1979 Al Bakr made the announcement through television and radio handing over the Party and State to Saddam Hussein. It seems to us that no one in the Party seriously had any doubt that Saddam Hussein was in control, or felt that he should not be, having by then built the Party and the State machinery. Saddam had also elevated his supporters to the second line in the party hierarchy, which guaranteed their loyalty to him.

However, certain members of the Ba'ath leadership, some of whom had been party members earlier than Saddam Hussein and whose loyalties to the Ba'ath were never questioned, discussed the need to have an arrangement whereby Saddam Hussein was to become leader with one of them as deputy, in the same way that Saddam Hussein had been deputy to Al-Bakr. Saddam Hussein saw in this the beginning of a plot that was intended to curtail his authority and consequently derail his plans. Saddam summoned the Party Congress on July 22, 1979; presented an alleged confession of a plot against him supported by his archenemy, Hafidh Assad of Syria; expelled some fifty original members of the Congress and set up a shadowy Party Tribunal. Those sentenced to death were executed at the hands of party members, and others were sentenced to long-term imprisonment. By August 8, 1979, twenty one members of the Party top leaders were executed and twenty other members were imprisoned with lengthy sentences. Some of those imprisoned died later in jail—prominent among them was the competent former Minister of Foreign Affairs, Murtadha Saed Abdul-Baqi.

This time Saddam Hussein ensured that Abdul-Khaliq As-Samarrai' was among the executed conspirators. We have yet to hear an explanation from any Ba'athists as to how Abdul-Khaliq, who had been confined to one building without any contact with the outside world since 1973, could be a conspirator.

What has come to be known by many Ba'athists as the 'Party Massacre' of July-August 1979 was a watershed from which the Party never recovered. For all practical purposes, the Ba'ath Party of the 1950s and 1960s ceased to exist. The state's party turned into the party's state with Saddam Hussein controlling everything. To us that was the first chapter of doom in Iraq, irrespective of all the economic development and prosperity achieved by the regime. Reading a transcript of Tayih Abdul-Karim's interview with Al-Baghdadiya Channel, one wonders how the party operated. Though he was a member of the National Command, Tayih did not seem to know much about what happened. He claims that Nadhim Gizar's alleged coup attempt was never discussed nor were any detailed revelations given to them.[48] The same applies to the 1979 Party massacre, even though he was a member of the special Tribunal established to try and convict the suspects. He states that the only one who spoke during the sessions was the head of Tribunal, Naeem Haddad, while the others kept quiet. He said the rulings were decided elsewhere and came in paper slips to the head of the Tribunal to declare.[49] We believe he was telling the truth and that they were merely puppets doing what they were ordered to do.

By the end of August 1979, Saddam Hussein had eliminated all his potential opponents. His cousin and protégé, Ali Hasan Al-Majeed, rose like a star to top party and state functions. By 2003 not even ministers could get access to Saddam Hussein without having to go through a Tikriti gatekeeper.

The Ill-conceived Invasion of Iran Leads to Ba'ath Decline

It is always easy in retrospect to blame others for your misfortune. Thus it is widely accepted among the apologists for Saddam Hussein that he was persuaded, or encouraged by the Saudis to invade Iran. Although we have no doubt that this did take place, we still think Saddam Hussein was responsible for the blunder which eventually cost him his life and rendered Iraq beyond repair. Saddam Hussein was responsible because it was unintelligent reckless to walk into the trap set for him by the Bedouin, who saw in the war the best way to weaken both Iran and Iraq to their advantage, and that of their controllers in the West. Even worse would have been if he had indeed seen through that conspiracy against Iraq and Iran and still gone to war. It remains a mystery to us how Saddam Hussein convinced himself that he was going to proceed on these grounds and stay faithful to the Ba'ath ideals. One explanation may be found in his overconfidence which was enhanced by the success of the development plan. He might have thought he could enter into agreement with the Bedouin of Arabia to defeat Iran which would have secured the West's general support and, once that was achieved, he would dominate the area and subdue them. If he thought that was possible, which clearly the calamity of Kuwait indicated later that he did, then he had never understood imperialism. It seems that, even though he listened well, his overconfidence, coupled with an incredible peasant naiveté, complicated matters further.

The Shah's officers shared their king's vision of a grand imperial army that could one day re-establish the Persian Empire which was eradicated by the invading Muslim army in 637 AD. Thus no sooner had the Iraqi army crossed the border, than most of the Shah top army officers united behind Khomeini to protect the fatherland.

Khomeini, on the other hand, opposed the Arabs for a different reason. He is one of the Shi'a clerics who believe that Islam is universal and thus the Arabs have no automatic right to rule the Muslim *Umma*. He would cite, along with others, the fact that the Ottomans ruled the Arab in an Islamic Empire for centuries to which the Arabs acquiesced quite normally. This last question has not been addressed by Arabs of today who speak of an impending Persian threat.

Khomeini's appeal to the oppressed masses was phenomenal. Thus when Khomeini promised them paradise in martyrdom, they had nothing to lose and perhaps everything to gain. These masses were used to pin down the Iraqi army at whatever cost to life while the regular army was being rebuilt in the depths of Iran away from Iraqi air and missile attacks.

One year into that bloody war, and realizing that not only was Iraq losing, but the bitter experience was threatening the very existence of Iraq, Saddam Hussein tried all he could to stop the war. But Khomeini was not going to let Saddam Hussein off the hook after all the cruelty, suffering and damage of that war, which included his use of banned chemical weapons—not now that he had him and the Ba'ath ideology on the run. The West, whether upon Saudi's request or through their own realization of what a Khomeini victory would have meant to their plans and interests, rallied to support Iraq. Britain exported high technology, France flew fighter aircraft for Iraq and the US provided Iraq with intelligence and flew the US flag on Kuwaiti oil tankers.[50] There was a clear understanding that all this was being done to enable Iraq, if not to win, then at least not to lose. The price should have been clear to any observer—the falling of Iraq in line with US strategy for the Middle East, including the recognition of Israel.

One look at where Iran and Iraq are today suffices to conclude that Iran won the war. The eight years of bloodshed and destruction ended with Iraq's infrastructure having suffered greatly, with development almost stalled; by 1986, Iraqi oil revenue had declined to $6.9 billion from $26.3 billion in 1980[51] and Iraq was left with a large debt. This was in spite of the fact that both Saudi Arabia and Kuwait had agreed to produce and sell some 300KBD of oil from their own oilfields on behalf of Iraq.[52]

A measure of the magnitude of the cost of the war to the Iraqi economy is to relate it to oil revenue. Between 1931, when the government received its first payment for oil export from the oil companies operating in Iraq, and 1988, the cumulative oil revenue amounted to $179.3 billion. Relative to the $462.6 billion of war losses, this means that in its eight years of war with Iran the Ba'ath regime succeeded in spending 254 percent of all the oil revenue Iraq received in fifty-seven years.[53] Another measure of the extent of the loss is to relate the economic cost of the war to Iraq's GDP during the period 1980-88. During this period, Iraq's GDP amounted to $433.3 billion, or $48.1 billion per year. Since the economic cost of the war is estimated to be $452.6 billion, or $50.2 billion per year, the annual cost of the war amounted to 104 percent of Iraq's GDP during the nine-year period 1980-89.[54] The simple fact of Iraq being in debt was alien to Iraq's economy in general, and it was this debt that was the cause of the Kuwait fiasco. But the most devastating result of the Iran-Iraq war is that it weakened Iraq sharply and took it out of the Arab-Zionist conflict which to most Arabs is the only war worth fighting because it is a matter of survival.

The First Consequence of the Iraqi Invasion of Iran

Saddam Hussein did not seem to understand that while he was planning to defeat Iran and subdue the Bedouin, the latter were, at the same time, doing everything they could to ensure that Iraq would never again be a strong country with the power to subdue them. It was to that end that they paid billions in support for Iraq's war effort.

In 1988 Kuwait found its best opportunity to humble Iraq and Iraqi expectations that its natural outlet to the Gulf should one day be restored to it. It was able to do so because it had some leverage over Iraq through the money it had paid for Iraq's war effort. The imperialists had just clearly indicated the beginning of their campaign to unseat the Ba'ath in Iraq. Iraq was on antagonistic terms with its main neighbors in Iran and Syria and not so friendly with the NATO member, Turkey.

What Kuwait did or did not do is not being argued here. What needs to be emphasized though is that Saddam Hussein took Iraq into the trap set for it—the trap from which Iraq has not been released twenty one years later. We find two indications sufficient to convince us that that was all planned. The first was revealed in Ambassador April Glaspie's statement to Saddam Hussein that the dispute with Kuwait was not a matter in which the US was going to be involved.[55] It is inconceivable that she did not know what the real position of the US was on this matter, which made her statement a clear attempt to entice Saddam Hussein to cross into Kuwait and thus create the excuse to disarm Iraq. The second indication that the plan to topple the Ba'ath in Iraq was being put in motion was manifested in the emergence of many of the regime's opponents who lived in Europe, who would not have dared to speak out previously for fear of retribution. We are able to name a number of them but it would be of no service to do so here. However, we have assurances from one such opponent in London, who had never dared to criticize Saddam Hussein, that the US had informed opposition groups that they would persist until the regime had been toppled by war or other means.

It is undoubtedly true that the imperialists would have found a cause to attack Iraq in 1991, but equally true that Saddam Hussein could have limited the damage and neutralized many actors in the conflict. For example, some Arab regimes which would have found it difficult to join in the attack, had the Iraqi army withdrawn from Kuwait having made the point that Kuwait and others would not be allowed to treat Iraq with such contempt after all that it had done for them. Furthermore, the US initiative at the UN could not have argued a case of Iraqi aggression, which enabled states being coerced to sign on as allies to convince themselves that they were acting on a sound international legal footing.

The Zionist plot against Iraq started in London with the Bazoft case[56] as all Zionist activities have started in London since Balfour.[57] [Farzad Bazoft was a convicted criminal sent to Iraq as a journalist by *The Observer* of London. He was caught spying on Iraq's military industry, accused of spying for Israel, convicted and executed. He was a college dropout with no education who had only been in the UK for two years, one of which he spent in jail.] It was Margaret Thatcher who in 1990 convinced George Bush that a plan to change the regime was opportune. Thus a campaign was started slowly and cleverly maintained through Western media in which Saddam Hussein, his regime and all of Iraq was demonized. It was so successful that it did not need much persuasion for world opinion to either join in or acquiesce in the destruction of Iraq in 1991. The attack on Iraq in 1991 had little to do with getting the army out of Kuwait and replacing it with US units which have since been stationed in Kuwait. It was meant to weaken Iraq to a point where it would collapse from within, allowing for a regime friendly to the imperialists to be installed. The massive assault, which targeted Iraq's infrastructure as far away as the Turkish border some 1000km from the Kuwaiti border, clearly supports this contention.

The Iraqi attempt to reclaim Kuwait was undertaken in the worst possible year of the 20th century. In 1990, the Soviet Union not only dissolved but the survival of Russia was at stake. The US was the only power capable of effectively dictating whatever it chose. By virtue of that reality, the UN became a rubber stamp for US decisions. Resolutions on

Iraq were drafted in Washington, and sometimes in London, and passed by the Security Council with little or no discussion. Their number, their contents, and the speed of their adoption between August 1990 and January 1991 (and after that into 2003) clearly show that. The only possible country to object would have been China, but China was busy building its economic and military base. Iraq was a small price to pay for consolidating that power without antagonizing the Americans. If Saddam Hussein had tried to find a worse year to move into Kuwait, during his 35 years in power, he could not have found one.

The Security Council remained almost in continuous session handing down resolution after resolution. One cannot but pause to ask how many resolutions were passed when the Israeli tanks reached Beirut in 1982 and why not? Why has every resolution on Iraq since 1990 been under Chapter VII of the UN Charter and not a single resolution against Israel under Chapter VII despite the latter having staged a war every decade since its inception? Chapter VII enables the Security Council or some of its powerful members to impose their will on a state against which a resolution has been passed using all means available from economic sanctions to the use of military force. It should be remembered here that Iraq until the writing of this chapter in 2012 is still under Chapter VII despite having been 'liberated' and enjoyed 'democracy' for more than nine years.

It is clear that the imperialists found in the ill-timed retaking of Kuwait by Iraq an opportunity to implement a plan for the Middle East that had been touched upon on many occasions, no more clearly than during Henry Kissinger's days in power.[58] The plan was to mold the Middle East into a US designed confederation of small sectarian based statelets with Israel being consequently a legitimate sectarian entity and by far the most powerful and dominant element of that confederation. The unholy alliance of Zionists and fundamentalist Christians found its natural habitat in the Bush dynasty. We would like to cite two examples as to why we believe that what happened in 1991 had little to do with Kuwait but much to do with implementing the new plan for a Zionist dominated Middle East.

The first such proof can be seen in the shifting of the aim of sanctions resolutions from ousting Iraq from Kuwait to seeking a level of disarmament that was clearly in breach of the sacred right of every state to arm itself for self-defense. It was this new decision that had used Kuwait as an excuse to enforce total sanctions against Iraq and enabled maintaining sanctions against Iraq until such time as Iraq could prove that it had no weapons. This was an impossibility because it demanded that Iraq should prove that it had none, instead of the Security Council having to prove Iraq had these weapons. It presumed guilt and required proof of innocent in contradiction to all legal norms. We will see later how this led to genocide through sanctions. The second proof is clear even today. We were told that Iraq was put under Chapter VII of the UN Charter because it had committed an act that threatened peace and security of the world. If that is the case, then why is Iraq today, years after the US brutal elimination of the Ba'ath, still under Chapter VII of the UN Charter?

Where the Ba'ath Failed: Some Conjectures

As careful observers, there is no doubt in our minds that the battle for survival between Arab Nationalism, spearheaded by the Ba'ath, and Zionism has been at the heart of every conflict in the Arab Middle East since WWII. Iraq was destroyed to serve the Zionist design to fragment the Arab world by disarming it and subduing it. Students of history and politics could not avoid noticing that the Ba'ath in Syria, which shares the same ideals as the Iraqi Ba'ath, had until 2011 survived such a fate despite having fought Israel three times during its reign. However, since the Islamists in Turkey, allies of Zionist imperialism, managed to convince the Zionists of their version of political Islam, a new campaign against Syria was initiated in which the Syrian Salafis (most of whom were indoctrinated while working in Arabia) were financed, armed and organized to take up arms against the Ba'ath.

When Michel Aflaq, the Orthodox Christian Syrian and founding member of the Ba'ath movement, attempted in the early 1930s and 1940s to present some hazy view of what the Ba'ath stood for, he was careful to indicate that the Ba'ath derived its legitimacy from Arab Islam while not being Islamic, thus maintaining its Arab Islamic identity while remaining secular.[59] It was not an easy balancing exercise, but it worked and the Ba'ath remained secular and fought Islamic fundamentalists both in Syria and in Iraq.

Saddam Hussein, like most members of the Ba'ath Party, did not grow up as a devout Muslim. He was born into a Muslim family and understood Islam, as most Arabs do, as a fact of life that is rarely questioned. It is thus a fallacy to attempt to portray Saddam Hussein as a fanatical Sunni who was out to persecute the Shi'a. For him loyalty to the Party, which later became loyalty to himself, was the yardstick by which people were measured. Thus he had Shi'a Arabs, Sunni Arabs, Sunni Kurds, Alawites, Shi'a Kurds, and Christians around him without distinction so long as he believed they were loyal. This was the success of the Ba'ath especially amongst minorities which saw in it protection from the excesses of Muslim fundamentalists.

Iraq had been ruled by the Sunnis for centuries before the

Ba'ath assumed power, going back as far as the Ottoman and Abbasid empires. The Shi'a, who gradually became the majority in Iraq, by and large believed that an injustice had been imposed on them in denying them the opportunity to rule Iraq. This sense of injustice was underlined by the fact that successive governments in Iraq had not genuinely tried to rectify the situation. However, the Shi'a had also voluntarily excluded themselves from government and the army in the 1920s and therefore left it almost exclusively in the hands of the Sunnis. It is equally wrong to allow this sense of injustice to turn into anti Arab nationalism sentiment, which can only serve Persian ambitions in Iraq directly and Zionism indirectly. The first could be seen in the Da'wa Party having been created or at least supported and financed by the Shah of Iran. The service to Zionism clearly materialized in the unfortunate Shi'a support for the invasion and occupation of 2003.

Saddam Hussein's inability to comprehend the nature of Iraq and the potential forces working within it prevented him from understanding or appreciating the significance of the Shi'a sense of injustice. But Saddam was also surrounded by advisers, some of whom were Shi'a, who must have played down this sense of injustice. Whether the Ba'ath as a Party failed equally is difficult to assert because by allowing Saddam Hussein to act alone in every measure of policy since 1979, the Party was an accomplice in that failure whether it liked or not.

The Marji'ya was used very effectively, in part as anti Arab Nationalism, and in part as simply capitalist interest, affiliation and benefit. In addition to the economic deprivation, the imperialist agents within the Marji'ya appealed to basic sentiments of the Shi'a masses in Iraq, highlighting the fact that the regime had prevented the Shi'a from observing their religious days of sorrow which occur throughout the year. For a Shi'a, even those brought up in secular families, the tragedies of the death of Imam Ali and his son, Hussein, are at the heart of the faith, fundamentally rather than peripherally. Denying the Shi'a the right to exercise these rituals amounted to denying them their faith.

Instead of denying the Shi'a this right, Saddam Hussein should have defused this ticking time bomb by not only allowing people to practice these rituals but by supporting them and facilitating them. He would have disarmed his enemies of one lethal weapon and won the sympathy of the Shi'a masses who constituted more than 60% of Baghdad on the eve of the invasion.

To add insult to injury, Saddam Hussein allowed a dangerous campaign to be launched in 1995 under the slogan 'Campaign of Faith'. Under this campaign, some fanatical semi-literate Sunni clerics launched a drive towards reviving old Sunni beliefs and making them the heart of the State. We cannot think of a worse scenario. How could Iraq, run by the secular Ba'ath ideology, with a Shi'a majority feeling an extreme sense of injustice both economically and religiously, allow its functions to be determined by a bunch of Shi'a hating Wahabi influenced clerics!

When a leader loses the support of the masses around him, he finds it difficult to rule. But when the masses become agitated against him, then he cannot rely upon them when he is invaded. Thus when the American tanks rolled through Baghdad on 9 April 2003, many Shi'a in Baghdad felt it was not their battle. The failure of the Ba'ath to understand the realities of Iraq and deal with them properly was the main reason why it failed to stay in power in Iraq when their comrades across the borders in Syria managed against all odds to survive.

THE BA'ATH PURSUES THE ECONOMIC DEVELOPMENT OF IRAQ

Whatever one's opinion regarding the Ba'ath regime, no one can deny that between 1968 and 2003, Iraq had been transformed from a non-developed country to a semi-industrialised one.

Despite the 1958 Revolution promise to carry out development in Iraq all attempts were derailed by the ten year struggle for power among rival leaders and groups. It was only after the political system became fairly stabilized after 1968 that the Government laid down a consistent policy correlating political, economic and social affairs and took steps to carry them out, the ultimate objective of which was to establish a socialist society.[1]

When the Ba'ath assumed power in July 1968, the last development plan had one year left. The new leadership let it run while it set out to prepare the most ambitious development plan Iraq had witnessed since its new birth as a nation state in the 1920s.

There may be arguments for and against what the priorities in development ought to have been or how successful this plan reflected the actual needs of the country and the nation, but we doubt that there are many who would dispute the following three facts relating to the development plans.

- The Ba'ath was genuinely keen on developing Iraq into an industrial state.
- The Ba'ath was the only regime in Iraq of the 20th century which completed not just one five year plan (1970-74), but two (the

second from 1975-1980). Development slowed down in the 1980s and stopped completely in 1990 because of the wars and the sanctions.

- The Ba'ath realized from the outset that such development needed massive resources and the only way to secure that was to concentrate on the oil industry.

Planning: The Cornerstone of the Ba'ath Strategy for Iraq's Development

Between the 1950s and late 1960s, different Iraqi Governments attempted to set up Development Boards with the intention of undertaking real evaluation of the nation's needs and the preparation of development plans. For many reasons none of these attempts led to much by way of tangible results and in 1968 Iraq's economy was anything but healthy. Even before coming to power in 1968, the Ba'ath seemed to have realized the importance of evaluation and strategy.

After the Revolution of 1958, there was increased awareness of the need to direct planning toward a more balanced development and social objectives. Between the July Revolution of 1958 and the July Revolution of 1968, development plans concentrated on agrarian reform, slum clearance (especially in the Baghdad area), and the improvement of working conditions, education and health services. Between 1958 and 1965 several economic plans were set up but achieved little.[2]

The social and economic policies following the 1968 revolution marked a significant departure from those of previous regimes. The new rulers not only set out to transform the economic system from free enterprise to collectivism, but also to achieve the country's economic independence, without which political independence cannot be long sustained. While the 1958 Revolution had asserted the country's political independence and achieved some economic independence, it did not succeed in correlating social and economic developments to fulfil those assertions nor did it pursue them to their logical conclusions.[3]

The main objectives of the economic policies of the 1968 revolution were:

1. To achieve economic independence and free national assets from imperialist monopolies;
2. To set up policies in the oil field that would grant Iraq greater flexibility in managing its oil production;
3. To increase national wealth and raising agricultural and industrial output;
4. To decrease the level of unemployment;
5. To raise the share of the public sector in all economic activities;

6.   To achieve material advances in major economic sectors through adopting major investments;

7.   To achieve centralized control of foreign and domestic trade.

The Planning Board was reorganized in 1968 and given real power by making the President of the Republic its head. This mini cabinet employed experts in all fields, who were soon gathering and collecting data in a way that had never been seen in Iraq. The collected data were used later to prepare the two five-year development plans.

The Ba'ath had been accused, unfairly at times, of not recognizing the class struggle, of having an ideology which lacked a coherent political, social or economic program, and of having recognized private ownership of the means of production thus allowing a national bourgeoisie to flourish.[4] The charge of not recognizing the class struggle is refuted in the political report of the sixth national congress of the party of 1963 in which the class struggle was acknowledged, albeit in a slightly different form, reflecting the differences between an underdeveloped Iraq of the 1960s and industrialized Britain of the 1840s. As to the charge of allowing the bourgeoisie to flourish through allowing private ownership of the means of production, we believe that the development plans show that the Ba'ath, in actuality controlled all means of production. It was then in turn criticized for not allowing the private sector to flourish and keeping everything under the tight control of the central Government.
It is not uncommon to read criticism about Third World leaders and Governments being unable to produce coherent economic programs. Such an accusation automatically assumes that Governments in the "First World" do. But do they?

Economics in our opinion is not an "absolute" science, and as such no one could be accused of failure simply because some ideas and theories did not achieve the intended results. This is the nature of theoretical disciplines, especially since economic theories are always related to and follow political ideologies and thoughts. The failure of the "great economist minds", including the Nobel laureates, to explain the recent economic collapse let alone warn of it beforehand supports our above belief. Furthermore, and in fairness to the leaders of the Ba'ath in Iraq and other leaders of the Third World—putting corruption aside and realizing that the Ba'ath regime may be charged with many failures, corruption never being one of them—it must be acknowledged that most of these leaders repeatedly stated that they were novices and experimenting with policies. That is an admirably forthright stand and they should be commended on it, provided it can be shown they did their best to achieve their goals. We believe that the Ba'ath was sincere in its aspirations.

It is with the above in mind that we believe it to be fair to accept Khadouri's conclusion on the robustness of planning procedure of the Ba'ath as he explained how the development plan came into being.

> The projects are usually formulated on the basis of the specific proposals submitted by the various Ministries which take part in the formulation of plans, such as the Ministries of Agriculture and Industry. These proposals are then submitted to the Steering Committee of the Planning Board and, before scrutinizing them, they are first referred to the various units and technical departments' committees of the Ministry of Planning which correlate and fit them together within a general plan for development. It may take a long time before the general plan is ready for scrutiny, but it is always the Steering Committee, composed of experienced and highly technical men, which lays down the framework and the specific projects of the plan. When final formulation is completed, the plan would be taken up by the Planning Board for final scrutiny and approval. For a formal action, the Revolutionary Command Council, presided over by the President of the Republic, enacts a law for implementation. Upon becoming a law, the plan would be entrusted to the Planning Board for distribution of the projects among the departments concerned for implementation. The Ministry of Planning undertakes the supervision of implementation.[5]

The Ba'ath party based its development policies on its ideological visions and its socialist objectives, which aspired to end human exploitation in all its forms and build an egalitarian society. Development could be divided into two clear phases: the first phase from 1968 until 1980, and the second from 1980 until the early 1990s.

Six measures were laid down by the Ba'ath Government to achieve these goals:

1. planning and research
2. agrarian reform
3. nationalization of the oil industry
4. industrialization

5. irrigation

6. social and cultural development.[6]

The first task the Ba'ath Government faced was dealing with the projects laid down under the former regime. The first Five Year National Development Plan of the Ba'ath Government of 1970-1974 clearly showed a definite qualitative departure from the plans of previous regimes. To begin with, the Ba'ath Party's commitment to socialism made it formulate the plan along socialist lines. To achieve this objective, an increase in agricultural and industrial production was considered a primary step in the process of development. The Ba'ath Government possessed a clear understanding of the meaning of development and reached for social and cultural development and a higher standard of living by increasing production. The ultimate aim of the Ba'ath Government's development was to achieve social justice for all and not merely for a particular group or class.[7]

The plan also aspired to balance the structure of the economy and diversify production by reducing dependence on oil exports and introducing other domestic resources. The Ba'ath Government realized from the beginning that even though dependence on oil income would increase in the first stage in order to be able to improve agricultural production and expand industry, Iraq would eventually depend on domestic resources and capital to carry out social and economic programs. This initial or transitional stage was stressed in the First Five Year Plan (1970-74), but the long-term objective was made clearer in the Second Five Year Plan of 1976-80.[8]

The National Development Plan (NDP): The Most Ambitious Plan in the History of Iraq

The National Development Plan 1970-1974[9] was the most successful in implementation, insofar as this Ba'ath development plan was implemented and allowed to run its full course under the same political power structure. The planners of the NDP had the advantage over their predecessors of being able to capitalize on the wealth of collective studies, planning and technical experience, and administrative competence Iraq had been able to attain over the previous two decades. This advantage was recognized in the preamble to the plan's strategy, which described the NDP as a comprehensive plan for economic and social development founded on clear strategy, well-defined goals, and adequate implementing structures.[10]

The plan was divided into eight chapters: Agriculture, Industry, Transport and Communication, Buildings and Services, Follow up, Loans, International Obligations, and Miscellaneous Investment Expenditures, with projected grand total allocations of some 540MID (equivalent to some $1.8 billion). Law No. 70 of 1970, which gave effect to the 'National Development Plan for the Fiscal Years 1970-1974', included in addition to the detailed tables for each of the eight chapters, an explanatory note on the plan. It is worth looking at parts of the note as it explains the economic principles underpinning the whole of the Ba'ath thinking and expectations.

The planners established a series of specific growth rates for each sector in order to achieve the Plan's objectives. The following tables show these rates:[11]

Table 3.1

NDP: Projected Total Increases in Certain Economic Indicators, 1970-1974

Indicator	Projected Increase Percentage
National income indicators (1969 prices)	
Gross domestic product	34.6
Gross national product	39.2
Gross domestic investment	89.8
Personal income	37.6
Private Consumption	33.7
Public consumption	27.6
Imports of goods and services	26.2
Exports of goods and services	14.2
Other indicators	
Employment	24.3
Worker Average Annual Income	13.1
savings	62.9
Per Capita Income	19.6

The plan's explanatory note sets out the objectives as follows:

(a) Economic Objectives:

(i) National income growth at a rate of 7.1%, which is double the annual population growth rate and achieving a rate of growth per capita equivalent to the maximum set out by the UN Economic and Social Council for the next decade.

(ii) National exploitation of untapped mineral resources.

(iii) Paying special attention to development in Northern governorates, which had been damaged during fighting of previous years.

(iv) Coordinating with other Arab States with view to integrating Arab economies in the future. [12]

On economic policy the explanatory note[13] advises that the Plan sets out to establish the following four aspects:

- Enhance the role of the public sector to participate in major projects, which the private sector will shy away from because of no quick profit.
- Create favourable circumstances for the private sector to play a part in achieving development while still maintaining that the public sector owned the principal means of production.
- Strike an economic balance between the available material resources and the requirement of the Plan's projects.
- Secure monetary stability by preventing a rise in prices, which might lead to redistribution of income detrimental to the low income groups.

But these four aspects require proper financial, commercial and Monetary and Credit policies to be drawn up. A summary of these is as follows.[14]

Financial Policy

The financial policy aimed at:

1. Redistribution of the financial resources available to the State to ensure most is spent on development.
2. Extending beyond the State's resources: relying on loans from friendly countries.
3. Controlling government consumption expenditure.
4. Reorientation of government consumption.
5. Realization of just distribution of tax burden to reduce the disparity in the distribution of income and wealth.
6. Coordination of the financial decisions in the State's ordinary budget with the investment decisions in the development plan.

Commercial Policy

This policy aimed at:

1. Promotion of exports and improvement of marketing efficiency of agencies.
2. Correlation of import policy with the requirements of economic development through prioritizing import of investment commodities.
3. Planning foreign trade geographic distribution to ensure maximum number of states, especially Arab, for import and export relations.

Monetary and Credit Policy

This policy aimed at:

1. Achieving economic stability by regulating flows of money in such a way as to conform with the volume of transactions,
2. Expanding of banking and saving facilities to the whole country to ensure mobilization of the greatest possible amount of personal savings.
3. Participation of the banking system in financing the Plan through increasing funds available to specialized banks and expanding their credit activities.

The NDP gave the following general objectives for different economic sectors.

Agricultural Sector[15]

1. Development at an annual rate of 7%,
2. Satisfying the industrial sector's need for agricultural raw material,
3. Replacing imported agricultural products by those locally produced through cultivation,
4. Increasing water storage for irrigation purposes.

The Plan suggested many procedures to be adopted in order to achieve these objectives. These included: flood control, irrigation and drainage, desalination, agricultural cooperatives, maintenance and repairs stations, fostering the Agricultural Bank, and coordination of all Government agencies towards better implementation of the Plan.

Industrial Sector[16]

1. Development at an annual rate of 12%.
2. Raising levels of productivity.
3. Proper utilization of available and untapped capacities.
4. Proper account for geographical distribution of new industrial projects.
5. Aiming at self-sufficiency in concentrating on producing goods.
6. Aiming at industrial integration with other Arab states.

The Plan suggested many procedures to be adopted in order to achieve these objectives. These included: prioritizing production of goods to reduce imports, expanding the food industry, expanding petrochemical industries, and reinforcing the Industrial Bank.

Transport and Communications Sector

The Plan considered this sector to be the backbone of the national economy and thus it concentrated on its development. The Plan projected increasing the network of land transport by an extra 600km of motorways and 1330km of rural roads in addition to improving some 3000km of existing local roads. Baghdad International Airport was planned to be completed and equipped. The limited sea access facilities at Um Qasr and Ma'qil were to be improved and equipped.[17]

Building and Services Sector

With respect to the Building and Services Sector, the Plan took into consideration the need for social planning alongside economic planning. It thus projected spending on many vital services such as education, health, and potable water. It projected that by 1980 every child reaching the age of compulsory primary school education ought to have a place in a school. Construction of schools was planned to allow for this projection. Vocational education was seriously considered in the Plan with the aim of setting up a number of vocational schools training young people in the fields of agricultural and industrial fields.

The Plan detailed the targets as follows:

Income Targets: After having considered the results of the previous development plan, the Plan projected the income targets as follows: If the national economy in the previous plan realized a compound growth rate of per capita income of about 2.2% annually, a compound growth rate of per capita income of around 3.6% annually may be considered a rate that reflects the progress aimed at in the Plan. At the same time, however, this rate imposed an increase in the national income, during the next five years, equivalent to the increase achieved by a compound rate of growth of 7.1% annually, which is precisely the rate that has to be achieved in order that national income may be doubled in ten year's time.

The projection as compared to the base year of 1969 which is the year in which the last development plan ended is given in the following table:

Table 3.2
Per Capita Gross National Product 1969-1974[18]

	Base Year 1969	**Fifth year 1974**	**Percentage Increase over the Base year**
Gross National Product (Million Dinars)	879.5	1234.5	40.36
National Income (MID)	826.8	1162.6	40.61
Population	9205185	10827596	17.62
Per Capita Gross National Product (ID)	95.5	114.0	19.37
Per Capita Income (ID))	89.8	107.4	19.60

The Plan aimed at creating a structural change in the economic set-up that would lead to a decrease in the relative importance of the mining and quarrying sector from 32.6% of gross domestic product in 1969 to 26.4% in 1974; while achieving an increase in the relative importance of the manufacturing sector from 9.1% to 11.4% of the gross domestic product and from 19.1% to 19.7% for the agricultural sector. The service sector was projected to be maintained at the same level as the previous plan.[19]

Production Targets: The Plan projected that after considering the increase in the value of production and the additional increase in production as a result of the expected rise in the level of productivity as well as the utilization of the unused capacities, it was expected that the value of production would increase from 1517.6 million Dinars in the base year 1969 to 2131.2 million Dinars in the fifth year 1975, i.e. an increase of 614.6 million Dinars, and a rate of increase of 40.4% during the Plan period. [20]

Employment and Wages Targets: The Plan estimated that the ratio of labour force to the whole population would rise from 27.7% in 1969 to 29.2 in 1974. It aimed at increasing the labour force from 2546.2 thousand employed persons in 1969 to some 3165.7 thousand employed persons in 1974 which represented an increase of 24.3% over the base year. It also aimed at increasing the average annual income per employed person, from 324.72 Dinars in 1969 to 367.25 Dinars in 1974 which represented an increase of 42.53 Dinars and a rate of increase of 13.1% during the Plan period.[21]

Hers is a summary of allocations and expenditure of the NDP:

Table 3.3
Revised Allocations, Actual Expenditures, Original Allocations and Revenue, 1970-1974 (ID Millions)

	Revised Allocation	Actual Expenditure	Original Allocation
Expenditures			
Agriculture	366.2	208.5	185.0
Industry	391.0	329.7	132.0
Transport & Communication	219.3	177.5	60.0
Building & Services	283.0	171.3	67.0
Other	672.5	293.8	92.91
Total	1932.0	1180.8	536.9
Revenue			
Oil	1554.4	1389.1	425.0
Non oil	172.6	150.3	111.9
Total	1727.0	1539.4	536.9

The Second Development Plan 1976-1980

The 1970-74 NDP, which covered the five-year period, ended in March 1975, which marked the end of fiscal year 1974-75. A nine-month investment program to cover the period April-December 1975 followed this Plan, and it was intended to accommodate the change in the fiscal year from April through March to January through December.

Two investment programs followed the 1975 investment program: one for 1976 and another for 1977. In 1977, the Revolutionary Command Council (RCC) adopted the National Development Plan, 1976-1980. Upon the launching of this Development Plan, the percentage of imported capital goods was raised to 80%, while consumer goods, which included mainly essential material such as flour, sugar and tea and only limited luxury items, were confined to only 20%.[22]

In introducing the 1976-1980 Development Plan, it said:

> The ultimate objectives of the plan are to achieve full employment, increase wages and narrow the disparity of income between rural and urban areas, and raise the standard of living. It is hoped that greater prosperity and welfare would be achieved and Iraq would become a truly socialist state among the "developed" countries of the world.[23]

Table 3.4
Sectoral Allocations under Annual Plans, 1976-1980 (ID Millions)

Sector	Allocations ID Millions	Share of Total Percentage
Agriculture	2157	13.7
Industry	4490	28.5
Transport and Communications	2318	14.7
Buildings and Services	2458	15.6
Other Allocations	4312	27.4
Total	15735	100.0

The following table sums up the allocations of GDP for the period between 1970-1990. This is important as it gives indications, when a comparison is made later, as to what happened after the imposition of the total blockade on Iraq:[24]

Table 3.5
Allocations of GDP for the period between1970-1990

Period	Oil	Agriculture	Water & Electr,	Mfg	Bldg
1970-74*	72.3%	9.7%	0.2%	3.1%	1.8%
1975-80**	68.3%	6.3%	0.2%	4%	5.6%
1981-85***	30.3%	7.1%	0.6%	5.3%	7.8%
1986-90****	42.6%	7.1%	0.8%	4.1%	5.8%

* The success of oil nationalization led to oil constituting 70% of the GDP.
** This period witnessed a limitation of growth in manufacturing and agricultural sectors.
*** This period was characterized by a reduction in oil revenue caused by the Iran-Iraq war. Most resources were directed towards the military. The war had one positive aspect. It forced the authorities to pay more attention to agriculture.
**** This period witnessed further deterioration due to the effects of war.

After having covered the main features and objectives of the development plans between 1969 and 1980 we shall now look at the real achievements in different sectors, starting with the Oil Sector.

The Development Plan and the Oil Sector

Although the Ba'ath intended to build an economy less reliant on oil, it was inevitable that reliance on oil was going to increase initially until the stage was reached where agricultural and industrial products were going to minimize the reliance on oil to carry out social and economic programs. When General Qasim promulgated in 1961 the most revolutionary measure of 20th century Iraq in Law 80, he envisaged that Iraqis were to develop the oil in the 99% of Iraq's land that was removed from the control of the foreign oil companies. But Qasim had neither the money nor the personnel to do this. More importantly, he did not have the time as he was overthrown and executed in February 1963 after the first Ba'ath led coup. Although the Iraqi National Oil Company (INOC) was set up in February 1964, it was not provided with a strategy or the resources to develop Iraq's oil fields. It was the Ba'ath regime which 'put into effect policies that would attain the original goals of the INOC by providing it with enabling legislation and funds'.[25]

Oil and the Rise and Decline of the Iraqi Economy

On cessation of the military activities of WWI, the American Oil majors were very livid about the Treaty of Sèvres of 1920, and thus they joined forces and persuaded the U.S. Senate to launch an investigation, which eventually found that American interests were indeed being systematically excluded from foreign oil fields by the European powers. As a result of this, negotiations began in July 1922, under substantial American government pressure, for USA Majors' entry into the Iraq Petroleum Co. Mr. W. C. Teagle, the president of Standard Oil of New Jersey, represented the companies, in these negotiations.

After six years of haggling, the USA Majors succeeded on 31 July 1928 in getting a combined 23.75% share in the Iraq Petroleum Co. (IPC). This was to be held by the Near East Development Corporation (NED Corp). [26]

The finalized IPC was incorporated in the UK not to operate as an independent profit-making company, but as a cartel for producing and sharing crude oil among the individual oil corporations who owned it. Accordingly, each company lifted, transported and marketed its own proportionate share of the produced crude.

By 1961 the IPC had explored only 0.5% of the whole concession and the remaining 99.5% was just held idle by the company as unexplored and unproductive reserve. The Concessionary Agreement between Iraq and the IPC did not contain any provisions for a Government buyback. This led to an increased sense of resentment among Iraqis and their institutions, which were unanimous in supporting the demand that this imbalanced concession agreement must go. This feeling of resentment was further fuelled by the hostile and loud opposition in the West, led by the United States, to the establishment of OPEC. Iraq had had a major input in OPEC's creation, and many Iraqi oil officials had justified suspicions of any cooperation with the Western oil companies and their political backers.[27]

With this as a background, the Iraq National Oil Company (INOC) was created in February 1964 to develop the concession areas taken over from the foreign-owned IPC. But it was not until 1967, after three years and two laws, that INOC was given the exclusive rights to exploit the country's oil resources.[28] INOC was eventually granted exclusive rights by law to develop Iraq's oil reserves, but it was forbidden to grant concessions to other oil companies, although INOC could permit IPC and other foreign companies to participate in the further development of existing concessions.[29]

In 1967 INOC concluded a Service Agreement with the French Government-owned Entreprise des Recherches et des Activites Petrolieres

(ERAP), covering exploration and development of a large segment of southern Iraq, including off-shore areas. The service agreement with ERAP was used as a model for other service contracts to French, Italian, Japanese, Indian, and Brazilian oil companies,[30] and allowed these companies to explore for petroleum in Iraqi concessions areas under INOC control. Any petroleum discovered and developed would thereafter be surrendered to the full control of INOC, which would sell the produced petroleum to these parties at an agreed discount in exchange for their bearing the full costs and the risks of the total activity.

Backed by a highly successful management and efficient technical practices, INOC succeeded in increasing oil production capacity from 1.5 million bpd in the early 1960s to 3.5 million bpd by 1979, accompanied by an increase in the discovery rate of new oil exceeding 6 billion b/year between 1972 to 1977, a rate that is equivalent to global levels. The Iraqi oil industry was very profitable, making it the envy of the international oil industry because of the low costs of discovery and development which were about $0.5/B and $0.5- 1.0/B respectively.

The evolution of some of Iraq's important oil indicators are shown in this table.

Table 3.6
Oil Revenue, Oil Output, Gross Domestic Product and Population
1960-1995[31]

Year	Oil Revenue ($ billion)	Oil Output (million bpd)	GDP ($ billion in 1980 prices)	Population (million)
1960	.3	.97	8.7	6.9
1970	.6	1.5	16.4	9.4
1980	26.3	2.6	53.9	13.2
1985	10.1	1.4	31.7	15.3
1990	9.5	2.1	16.4	18.1

The Nationalization of Oil and its Consequences

As a new organization, OPEC lacked the power, the means, or the unity of purpose to force the oil companies to change their pricing policies, even though the reason for creating OPEC was the unilateral price reductions by the oil companies. OPEC passed many resolutions calling upon the companies to restore prices to their August 1960 levels, but the companies simply ignored such calls. This forced OPEC by 1963 to give up the price issue and concentrate on other means to raise per-barrel revenue for member countries. The price issue was not revived until 1970 when Libya succeeded in negotiating an increase in its posted oil prices and a rise in the tax rate from 50% to 54%, upon which the companies unilaterally announced an increase in Middle East posted prices, as well as an increase in Governments' share of the profit from the traditional 50% to 55%.[32]

The Tehran price agreement of February 1971 stabilized prices over the next five years, causing an increase in per-barrel revenue for the key 34-degree API Arabian Light crude from 91 cents in 1970 to $1.53 by 1975.[33]

The decision by the U.S. Government in August 1971 to suspend convertibility of the dollar into gold led to depreciation in the value of the dollar against other currencies. This was immediately reflected in the oil prices, because the dollar was the currency of trade and calculation of oil and Government revenue. This new crisis prompted OPEC to go back to the companies to seek upward price adjustments to offset the loss in the dollar purchasing power, a loss that the companies offset in part.

Concurrent with these fiscal changes, OPEC sought a change in the concession system that would allow member countries to purchase equity interest in operating companies such as Aramco, KPC, IPC, and others. By the end of 1972, an agreement was reached according to which Governments were allowed to acquire a 25 percent interest in 1973, which was to rise to 30 percent in 1978 and then gradually to 51 percent by 1982.

The Ba'ath Party had called for nationalization of the oil industry, epitomized in the slogan "Arab oil for the Arabs" even before it came to power in 1968. With that background, the Ba'ath Government started in 1970 taking measures whose aim was the eventual nationalizing of oil. Some of the measures taken towards that end were:

- Signing a major agreement with the Soviet Union in 1969 in which the Iraqi National Oil Company (INOC) agreed with Machinoexport for the latter to provide Iraq with machines for drilling and exploration and with a loan to purchase such necessary equipments.
- Agreeing with the Hungarian Kimocomplex for the latter to drill four oil wells in North Rumayla and to provide a loan of 15 MID to purchase equipment and pay for technical skills.
- On 15 July 1970 the drilling of the first well in Rumayla started and its first oil shipment was delivered on 7 April

1972.[34]

Long and protracted negotiations took place between Iraq and the oil companies before final nationalization was achieved. These may be summarized as follows:

- Demand in 1970 from the oil companies to increase oil production;
- Demanded the payment of an accumulated amount of royalty expensing since 1964, when the principle of expensing was agreed on at a meeting of OPEC in Jakarta in 1964. Though the IPC agreed in negotiations to pay the royalty from 1971, it withheld retroactive payments pending settlement of the IPC demands relating to Law 80.[35]
- Oil production was reduced by oil companies from 4.75 million tons per month in February 1972 to 3.39 in March and to 2.5 million tons in April of the same year. These measures caused a reduction of 30% in Iraq's revenue amounting to some 110 million pounds.[36]
- In 1972, IPC promised to increase its production in Iraq and to raise the price it paid for Iraqi oil to the Libyan level. In return, IPC sought compensation for its lost concession areas.[37]
- Iraq promulgated Law 69 on 1 June 1972 with which it nationalized the British owned Iraqi Petroleum Company operations.
- A national company called the Iraqi Company for Oil Operations (ICOO) was established to operate the fields taken over from the IPC and to be responsible for all the rights and assets transferred to it in accordance with Law 69.
- An agreement with the French Government on June 18, 1972, allowed the French partner in IPC to receive its share from the nationalized oil under the same conditions prevailing before nationalization for a period of 10 years.
- Oil companies imposed an embargo on the purchase of Iraqi oil and pushed the French Government to suspend its oil agreements with Iraq
- The Government of Iraq imposed austere measures and was finally partially successful when it managed to sell some 20M tons of oil to Italy in addition to deals with Brazil, Sri Lanka, and several socialist states in direct purchase or barter terms. It also managed to purchase a few oil tankers and rented a few others.

The oil companies were forced to the negotiation table. In March

1973 an agreement that the Ba'ath Government, rightly in our mind, called 'The Victory Agreement' was reached. Its main elements were:

1. The oil companies relinquished their rights in the Mosul Petroleum Company to Iraq.[38]
2. IPC agreed to pay the equivalent of nearly US$350 million to Iraq as compensation for revenue lost to Iraq over the years when IPC was selling Iraqi oil
3. The oil companies agreed to sell the pipeline passing through Syria and Lebanon and the loading terminal in Tripoli to the Iraqi Government.
4. Iraq agreed to give the oil companies 15 million tons of crude oil delivered from the Mediterranean ports, 7 million to be delivered in 1973 and 8 million in 1974 in full settlement of all claims by the oil companies and for the cost of the pipeline and loading station.

The October 1973 Arab-Israeli War led the Iraqis to take complete control of their oil resources, and Iraq became one of the strongest proponents of an Arab oil boycott of Israel's supporters. Iraq immediately passed a law on October 7, 1973, to nationalize the concessionary rights of two American companies in BPC—the Standard Oil of New Jersey (Exxon) and Mobil Oil Corporation—and the Royal Dutch Oil Company that possessed 60 per cent of Shell Oil Company in the BPC. Iraq also nationalized the Gulbenkian five per cent interests in the BPC.

The final step to nationalize foreign oil interests was undertaken in 1975. Iraq's confidence in the world markets' demand for its oil and in its competence to explore and operate the oil industry led it to nationalize the remaining foreign interests in the BPC and to promise to pay compensation in accordance with its net book value. With this step, Iraq became master of its oil industry. Fifty-three years after the humiliating San Remo agreement, Iraq had finally gained complete sovereignty over its most valuable natural resource.

During 1974 and 1975, the oil production was increased considerably and new fields were explored. During that time Iraq had a conflict with Syria over the Euphrates water. Thus in 1975 Iraq began to construct the so-called strategic pipelines connecting the pumping station at Haditha, west of the Euphrates, with the newly constructed Mina' al-Bakr loading facility situated on the Iraqi coast of the Gulf. These pipelines, which were completed toward the end of 1975, were designed to pump oil not only from the northern fields to Iraqi ports in the south but also from southern fields to Haditha, thereby relieving Iraq from pressures to increase transit duties on oil pumped through the Mediterranean pipelines. In 1976 Iraq completed the construction of a pipeline to the

Turkish Mediterranean terminal at Ceyhan.

In September 1985, construction of a spur line from Az Zubayr in southern Iraq which connected to the then existing pipeline to the Red Sea port of Yanbu' in Saudi Arabia was completed. The line's capacity was 500,000 bpd. A second phase of this project, that of an independent parallel pipeline to the existing one, with a capacity of 1.15 million bpd, was begun by a Japanese-South Korean-Italian-French consortium in late 1987, to run 1,000 kilometres from Az Zubayr to Yanbu and its own loading terminal, and was completed in late 1989. Iraq negotiated with the contractors to pay its bill entirely in oil at the rate of 110,000 bpd, and also negotiated special legal arrangements with Saudi Arabia guaranteeing Iraqi ownership of the pipeline. Iraq had plans for the construction of a 1-million bpd pipeline through Jordan to the Gulf of Aqaba, but this project was shelved in 1988.[39]

Before the Iran-Iraq war, Iraq's refining capacity was 320,000 bpd: 140,000 barrels of which were produced by the southern refinery at Basra, and 80,000 of which were produced by the Dora refinery, near Baghdad. In the opening days of the War, the Basra refinery was damaged severely, but the Dora refinery remained in operation. New installations, such as the 70,000 bpd Salah ad Din I refinery and the 150,000 bpd northern Baiji refinery, boosted Iraq's capacity beyond 400,000 bpd. Domestic consumption amounted to 300,000 bpd, most of which was used to sustain the war effort.

The development, with Soviet assistance, of a major new oil field gave a boost to Iraqi oil policy in the late 1980s. In September 1987, during the eighteenth session of the Iraqi-Soviet Joint Commission on Economic and Technical Cooperation, held in Baghdad, Iraq's State Organization of Oil Projects (SOOP) signed an agreement with the Soviet Union's Techno-Export to develop the West Al Qurnah oilfield. This oilfield was regarded as one of Iraq's most promising, with an eventual potential yield of 600,000 bpd. Techno-Export planned to start by constructing the degassing, pumping, storage, and transportation facilities at West Al Qurnah's Mishrif reservoir, and expected to produce 200,000 bpd.[40] Prior to the invasion in 2003, the West Al Qurnah oil field was producing 250,000 bpd.

Among the major projects in the Oil Sector which Iraq executed in the period between 1970 and 1990, excluding the rise in production of oil, are:

- Completion of deep Mina al Bakr port in Khawr al Amayah in Basra with a capacity of 80 million tons annually, capable of being raised to 120 million, and capable of handling tankers of 350 thousand tons at a cost of 101 MID.

- Completion of the strategic pipeline for oil and gas shipment between Haditha and Fao of 667 Km length and capable of shipping 850 thousand barrels in 1975. This was later raised to 1 million barrels in 1988 at a cost of 73 MID.
- Completion of the Iraq–Turkey pipeline, 1500 Km long, between Kirkuk and Cehan on the Mediterranean with a capacity of 700 thousand bpd.
- Building Basra oil refinery of 3.5 million tons.
- Building Mousil oil refinery of 1.5 million tons.
- Building the Petro-chemical complex in Basra for the production 120 thousand tons of ethylene.
- Discovery and exploitation of the new oil field of Zarkan that went into production in 1976 with an initial capacity of 50 thousand bpd.
- Discovery and exploitation of the new oil field of Majnoon that went into production in 1976 with an initial capacity of 350 thousand bpd.
- Increasing Kirkuk production from 1.2 Million barrels to 1.8 Million barrels in 1988.
- Acquiring a fleet of 17 oil tankers, 7 of which were built by Spain, 4 by Sweden, 5 by Japan.
- Completion of strategic pipeline between Az Zubayr to Yanbu in SA with a capacity of 500mbpd.
- Completion of Salah ad Din refinery with a capacity of 70,000 bpd.
- Completion of Baiji refinery with a capacity of 150,000 bpd.

Any observer might question why Iraq, which managed from 1975 until 2003 to explore, produce, market and export its oil efficiently, needed foreign companies to take control of most of Iraq's oil since the invasion and occupation. This leads one to question to what extent the reason for the invasion and occupation of Iraq has always been the restoration of the foreign imperialist control over Iraq's oil. The following are examples of what has happened in the newly democratised Iraq:

In November 2009, the Iraqi Oil Ministry awarded a consortium led by Exxon Mobil Corp. and Royal Dutch Shell PLC the right to develop the West Qurna-1 oil field, representing the first American-led team gaining access to the country's oil patch. BP and the China National Petroleum Corporation (CNPC) were awarded the contract to expand production from the Rumayla oilfield. In December 2009, a joint venture between the UK's Shell and Malaysia's Petronas oil companies won the right to develop Iraq's giant Majnoon oil field, with reserves of 13 billion barrels of oil; it currently produces just 46,000 bpd.

Industrial Development under the Ba'ath

The Ba'ath inherited a weak industrial base concentrating mostly on textile and food industries, whose contribution to the national gross product did not exceed 9%. The industrial sector suffered from many shortcomings, among which were:

1. Low production efficiency due to low technical skills.
2. Lack of necessary funds for investment.
3. Lack of balance between the size of industrial expansion and the availability of infrastructure in roads and communications, warehouses and other necessities for distribution and marketing.
4. The hesitation of private sector to enter the field of conversion industries.
5. The lack of proper administration and weakness in supervision and accountability adversely affected national production and led to the tendency of the people to seek foreign produce.[41]

After 1969, the Ba'ath Government continued with the implementation of the industrial program of the previous regime, before laying down new programs of its own. More important, the Ba'ath regime realized that, in spite of its emphasis on industrialization, the economic development of Iraq would not advance properly without taking into consideration the need to increase agricultural production and improve conditions in the countryside. Agriculture was the country's most important asset after oil, and the majority of the people still lived in rural areas. For this reason, the Government, in the two five-year development plans of 1971-75 and 1976-80, stressed almost equally the projects for industrial and agricultural reconstruction.[42]

The extent of its planning, it has been rightly held, distinguished the Ba'ath programs from the programs of former regimes. [43] It was also deemed necessary that, before the industrial projects were completed, the various industrial centers should be linked with domestic and foreign markets by an efficient system of transportation. This was, in our opinion, a farsighted vision and reflected the Ba'ath's comprehension of the needs of development.

The ultimate objective of industrialization was to achieve self-sufficiency and insure the country's economic independence. For that reason, the Five Year National Development Plan of 1970-74 stressed possible expansion only in such industries as cement, vegetable oils and petrochemicals, which Iraq might be able to export to its neighbours. [44] In the early 1970s, Iraq made capital investments in large-scale industrial facilities and plants such as steel plants. Many of the facilities and equipment were purchased from foreign contractors and builders on a turnkey basis. But Iraq did not pay attention to developing the next stage in the industrial process— the transformation of processed raw materials into intermediate products, such as construction girders, iron pipes, and steel parts.

The Government invested heavily in the public sector industry in an attempt to strengthen it. According to official figures, annual investment in the nonpetroleum industrial sector increased from 39.5 million ID (about $130 million) in 1968 to 752.5 million ID (about $2.5 billion) in 1985. As a consequence of these investments, the industrial output in 1984 was almost 2 billion ID ($6.6 billion), up from about 300 million ID (about $990 million) in 1968, and up more than 50 percent from the start of the Iran-Iraq War in 1980. But productivity relative to investment remained low. [45]

The following table shows the most important industrial projects completed by the public sector in Iraq between 1969 and 1980. It is worth noting that this list includes only part of the major projects that have been completed. [46] It is not intended to be an exhaustive list.

Table 3.7
Most important industrial projects completed by the public sector in Iraq between 1969 and 1980

Item	Project	Total cost MID	Capacity
1	Sulaymaniya Sugar Plant	8.9	75 000 tons
2	Fruit Canning Plant in Duhok	1.2	1.1 million can and 1.5 million ton of concentrates
3	Expansion of Baghdad Dairy Plant	2	100 tons of products
4	Spinning and Cotton weaving in Diwaniya	17	45 million meters of textile and 350 tons of yarn

5	Spinning and weaving plant in Nassiriya	4	1.5 million meters of textile, 450 000 blankets and 250 tons of yarn
6	Spinning and worsted in Arbil	4	45 million meters of textile and 25 000 tons of yarn
7	Textile plant in Duhok	1	86 tons of yarn and 160 000 meters of textile
8	Expansion of Mousil Fabric Factory	4.2	1.8 million yards of sheets, 42000 yards of curtains, 2.5 million yards of textiles
9	Falluja Cement Factory	3.8	200 000 tons
10	Quick lime plant in Hammam Alil	1	30 000 tons
11	July 14 Brick Factory Baghdad	1.3	30 million units
12	Lime Brick Factory Basra	1.5	40 million units
13	Lime Brick Factory Nineva	0.9	20 million units
14	Kerbala Brick Factory	0.9	30 million units
15	Babylon Brick Factory	0.9	30 million units
16	July 30 Brick factory	2	60 million units
17	Asbestos Pipe Factory in Kirkuk	1.1	20 000 tons
18	Fibre Board Factory	2.8	60 000 tons
19	Asbestos Boards Factory Baghdad	0.6	295 tons
20	Expansion of Ramadi Glass factory	0.9	21 tons of glass
21	Concrete Block Factory Mousil	0.8	150 000 units
22	Concrete Block Factory Basra	1.5	340 000 units

23	Plastic Pipes Factory Baghdad	1.26	12 000 tons
24	Petrochemical Complex Project	60	120 000 tons
25	Iron and Steel Factory	40.5	1.6 million tons
26	Heavy Machinery Assembly Plant	2.5	
27	Iskendariya Project - expansions	4	
28	Lamp Factory	1.4	2.5 million lamps
29	Expansion of Chemical Fertilizers Plant	28	590 000 tons
30	Bicycle Rubber tires and tubes	1.1	120 000 units
31	Car Rubber tires and tubes	7.8	1.9 million units
32	Rubber Sponge Factory	1.1	120 000 tons
33	Agricultural machines and tools Iskendariya	30	Different products
34	Samarra Medicine factory	7	Different medicines
35	Cotton Textile Factory in Kut	10	30.5 million meters of textile
36	Paper factory in Hartha	34	30 000 tons
37	Sulphur recovery from Natural Gas Plant	10.7	210 tons
38	Expansion of Samarra Medicine Factory	12	
39	Mousil Refinery	13	1.5 million tons
40	Rayon Plant in Hindiya	20	8500 tons
41	Cane Sugar Factory	17.5	100 000 tons
42	Al Misharq Sulphur Factory	11	1.5 million tons
43	Chemical Feretlizer Factory in Basra	38	197 000 tons
44	Basra Refinery	25	3.5 million tons

The following is a summary of industrial achievements of the Public Sector for the period 1974-1983 from the available data. It neither represents the full picture for that period nor for the period up to 1990. It should always be borne in mind that many of Iraq's records were destroyed after the invasion or removed by the USA. The USA took custody of over 2 million Iraqi documents and moved them to Qatar after the occupation of Iraq.[47] Quite a number of important documents and reports relating to achievement of the Ba'ath Government or the effects of sanctions, including those by UN organizations, are not available on the Internet anymore. It seems clear that this extinguishment of its positive record was part and parcel of the US effort to erase not just the Ba'ath Party (and thereby Iraqi nationalism), but also of any notion of Iraq's capacity to industrialize, per se.

1. Increasing investment in industrial sector. Actual investment in the years 1968-74 rose to 365.4 MID and in the years 1975-81 to 3832.3 MID amounting to a growth of 123.6% per annum.
2. Entering new and ambitious industries such as steel, electrical and phosphate and Sulphur.
3. Increasing production level especially in the conversion industries. Production rose from 266.509 MID in 1968 to 594.9 MID in 1974 to reach 1797.9 MID in 1981 equivalent to 14.3% growth between 1968-74 and 14.2% growth between 1975-81.
4. Conversion industries grew from 94.6 MID in 1968 to 187.8 MID in 1974 and to 594.8 MID in 1981 amounting to a yearly growth 13.2%.
5. Raising the capital invested from 36.4 MID in 1968 to 123.7 MID in 1974 and to 676.5 MID in 1981 equivalent to 20.4% annual growth.
6. Increasing the share of wages in the public sector to total industrial sector from 56.6% in 1968 59.3% in 1974 and to 71.9% in 1981.
7. Increasing the share of number if workers in the public sector to the total industrial sector from 47.5% in 1968 to 69.5% in 1974 to 78% in 1981.[48]

Infrastructure Development under the Ba'ath

The nationalization of oil and the big hike in the prices of oil in the mid-1970s generated huge income to Iraq. The Ba'ath Government funnelled much of this revenue into expanding and improving the infrastructure. The investments were not limited to the oil sector, but covered all sectors of the economy and greatly improved the living standards of Iraqis.

Developing the Generation and Supply of Electricity

The Ba'ath Government invested heavily in electric power generation in the 1980s, contracting with Britain, West Germany, France, Italy, South Korea, the Soviet Union, and Yugoslavia to build or expand thermal and gas generating plants, hydroelectric facilities, and transmission lines. By 1990, Iraqi society became highly dependent on the national electricity grid for many of its basic needs, as this serviced, inter alia, telecommunications, industry, agriculture, education, housing, health, water, and sanitation. Apart from the most remote rural areas, all of Iraq relied on this system. This explains how the US destruction of Iraq's generating capacity in 1991 led to life coming to a halt.

In the twenty-two-year period between 1968 and 1990, consumption of electricity had increased by a factor of fourteen, and it was expected to double every four to five years. During the same period, over 7000 villages all over the country were supplied with electricity, and rural electrification contributed to the increased demand. In December 1987, following the completion of power lines designed to carry 400 million kwh of power to Turkey, Iraq became the first country in the Middle East to export electric power. Iraq was expected to earn $15 million annually from this arrangement. Long-range plans entailed exporting an additional 3 billion Kwh to Turkey and eventually providing Kuwait with electricity. The combination of hydroelectric, thermal and gas turbine generators provided an installed capacity of 9,500 megawatts (MW). At that time the reserve capacity was estimated to be 40%. [49]

Developing the Transportation System in Iraq

Transportation was one of the Iraqi economy's most active sectors in the 1980s; it was allocated a large share of the domestic development budget because of its importance to the economy. The Government recognized that transportation bottlenecks limited industrial development more than any other factor. The Government also believed that an expanded transportation system played an important political role in promoting regional integration and heightening the central Government's presence in the more remote provinces.

The total length of Iraq's network of paved roads almost doubled between 1979 and 1985, to 22,397 kilometres, complemented by an additional 7,800 kilometres of unpaved secondary and feeder roads. In the late 1980s, Iraq's major road project was a 1,000 km long segment of a six-lane international express highway that was completed in 1989. The program to build 10,000 km of rural roads was also progressing. [50]

The greatest era of the Iraqi railway was during the 1970s. Iraq imported new trains at that time and developed a new international schedule, with trains leaving Baghdad as part of the Orient Express and heading to Istanbul, Berlin, Paris and other destinations in Europe. The Soviet Union helped extend the standard gauge system to Basra, and by 1977 fully 1,129 km of Iraq's 1,589 kilometres of railroad were standard gauge. In the 1980s the Orient Express was used intensely by the Iraqi Government for military purposes, to transport military equipment for the Iraqi Army during the Iraq-Iran war. By 1985 the total length of railroad lines had been extended to 2,029 km, of which 1,496 km were standard gauge. In 1985 440 standard-gauge locomotives that moved 1.25 billion tons of freight per km were travelling the railroads.

After five years of work, South Korean contractors completed a 252-km line linking Kirkuk and Al Hadithah in 1987. A 550-kilometer line built by a Brazilian company and extending from Baghdad to Husaybah on the Syrian border was completed in 1983. In 1987, Indian contractors completed the line between Al Musayyab and Samarra.[51]

By 1990, the Iraqi railway system had five major routes; a northwest route links Baghdad with Mousil and the Turkish border. A second runs north from Baghdad to Kirkuk and Arbil. The third runs south from Baghdad to Basra and Umm Qasr. A fourth line stretches from Baghdad west to Husaybah at the Syrian border and continues west to link the industrial complex at al-Qaim with the phosphates mines at Akashat. A fifth line connects this route at al-Hadithat with Kirkuk, thus linking the minerals processing complex at al-Qaim with sulphur mines in the country's northern region.[52]

Iraq's main port is at Basra, about 50 miles inland from the Gulf along the Shatt-al-Arab waterway. Before the oil boom of the 1970s, it was a relatively small port, most trade being handled overland through Syria and Jordan. Since then, the Gulf port of Basra has been expanded many times, and a newer port was built at Umm Qasr to relieve pressure on Basra. Oil terminals were located at Khawr al Amayah, and Mina al Bakr, Al Faw, and a port was built in conjunction with an industrial center at Khawr az- Zubayr. In the 1980s, port activities were severely restricted during the Iran-Iraq War because these facilities were Iranian targets. After the war, the Shatt al Arab waterway was full of wreckage and explosives, and it would have had to be cleared of these before it could be used for shipping, which was not done until after the 2003 invasion.

In 1990 Iraq had two international airports, one at Baghdad and one at Basra. In 1979 a French consortium was awarded a $900 million contract to build a new international airport at Baghdad, and this new airport was in use by the end of the 1980s. The Basra airport was also being upgraded with an extended 4,000- meter runway and other facilities at a cost exceeding $400 million.[53]

Significant Development of Telecommunications in Iraq under the Ba'ath

In the late 1980s, Iraq had a good telecommunications network of radio communication stations, radio relay links, and coaxial cables. Iraqi radio and television stations had always been under the Government's control through the Iraqi Broadcasting and Television Establishment, which was responsible to the Ministry of Culture and Information. The domestic service had one FM and nine AM stations with two program networks. The domestic service broadcast in Arabic, Kurdish, Turkoman, and Assyrian from Kirkuk. The short wave Foreign Service broadcast in Arabic, Azeri Turkish, English, French, German, Hebrew, Kurdish, Persian, Russian, Spanish, and Urdu. Television stations were located in the major cities, and they carried two program networks.

In 1990 Iraq had almost a million television sets; the system was connected to both the Atlantic Ocean and Indian Ocean systems of the International Telecommunications Satellite Organization (INTELSAT) as well as to one Soviet Intersputnik satellite station.

It also had coaxial cable and radio relays linking it to Jordan, Kuwait, Syria, and Turkey. Before 1991, there were approximately 37 landlines per thousand residents. Iraq was one of the first Arab countries to provide direct dialling for international calls in the mid-1970s, in addition to its having built a national microwave network that linked all counties.

The Ba'ath Plans for the Development of the Agriculture and Irrigation Sector

In the late 1950s, Iraq was self-sufficient in agricultural production, but in the 1960s about 15% of its food supplies were imported, and by the 1970s that figure rose to about 33%. Food imports only increased in spite of the large investments in the agricultural sector, and by the early 1980s, food imports accounted for about 15% of total imports, rising to about 22% of total imports in 1984. This was due to decrease in total cultivated area and fluctuations in harvests caused by variability in the amount of rainfall. Almost all experts agree that Iraq had the potential for substantial agricultural growth, but shortages in water supply caused by Syrian and Turkish dam building on the Tigris and Euphrates rivers might have restricted that growth.[54]

On the eve of the 1958 revolution, more than two-thirds of Iraq's cultivated land was concentrated in 2 percent of the holdings, while at the other extreme, 86 percent of the holdings covered less than 10 percent of the cultivated land.

Agrarian Reform Law 1958 Enhanced and Enforced by the Ba'ath

The Agrarian Reform Law issued on December 30, 1958 limited

the maximum amount of land an individual owner could have to 1,000 dunams (in Iraq, the dunam is 2,500 m² / 26,910 sq ft) of irrigated land or twice that amount of rain-fed land. The law empowered the Government to take away excess lands from landlords and distribute to peasants who were to cultivate their newly acquired lands and enjoy the fruits of their work.

However, bad management and unavailable capital in the hands of peasants led to only two thirds of land taken away from landowners being distributed among peasants over a period of ten years. The agricultural production did not improve and the country began to import crops it used to export before the land reforms.

When the Ba'ath came to power in 1968, 1.7 million hectares had been expropriated, but fewer than 440,000 hectares had been distributed. A total of 645,000 hectares had been allocated to nearly 55,000 families, but that was only because several hundred thousand hectares of Government land were included in the distribution.

The Ba'ath Government's most important achievement was perhaps abolishing exploitative feudal relations and ending the influence of feudalists permanently. The promulgation of the Agrarian Reform Law No. 117 of 1970[55] and Law No. 90 of 1975[56] under which the reorganization of land tenure and the final liquidation of feudal property for the benefit of the farmers were accomplished, provided new production relations that changed the structure of the sector and its development.

The Government's stress on agrarian reform as one of the primary objectives of the Five Year Development Plan could be seen in the increasing amount of expenditure after proceeding with the projects. When the plan was first laid down, only 180 million ID (about $595 million) were allocated for agricultural projects. In the fiscal year of 1974-75, the estimated expenditure had been raised to 420 million ID (about $1.4 billion), which was more than double the original figure set for agricultural development.[57]

By the end of the five-year period, the Government declared that with the taking over of the rest of the lands from landowners in accordance with the Agrarian Law of 1970, feudal relations had been liquidated. Under the law of 1958, only 4.2 million dunams had been taken over, and with the new law, another 5.8 million dunams were taken over, bringing the total of lands taken over to about 10 million dunams. By 1975, some 8 million of these were distributed, which the farmers can claim to have possessed (approximately some 411,000 families).

Parallel to the distribution of lands, the Government encouraged the establishment of cooperative societies. The purpose of cooperative societies was to arrange loans from the Agricultural Cooperative bank, marketing of products, supplying farmers with seeds, fertilizers, pesticides, tools and machine, establishing animal farms, cattle, poultry, fish farms, providing advice and guidance to farmers, etc..

Before 1968, there were only 433 cooperatives (consisting of some 58,000 families). But in 1974, the terminal year of the 1970-74 development plan the number had increased to 1330; in 1975 the number reached 1600 cooperatives (consisting of over 200,000 families), and 1992 in 1980 with 388,000 members covering an area of about 23.5 million dunams. In addition to that, the Government provided all possible means to encourage farmers to develop and increase the quality and quantity of production. But in spite of all measures taken, agricultural production did not match the pace of the increasing demands of a rapidly growing population and the measures taken to curb the continuing migration from rural to urban areas did not succeed. [58]

The 1976-80 period also witnessed the emergence of agricultural collective farms for the first time in the history of the country, bringing the number of the farms to 28 in 1981, occupying an area of 76,700 dunams, with 1,346 members. The collective farms were farms established on the principle of collective ownership of the means of production, and work was organized through production teams.

At the same time, the number of state farms reached 23 occupying an area of 143, 000 dunams. The period witnessed an increase in the contribution of the social sector in the agricultural production from 1.4% in 1974, to 43.4% in 1981.[59] In 1983 the Government enacted a new law encouraging both local and foreign Arab companies or individuals to lease larger plots of land from the Government. By 1984, more than 1,000 leases had been granted.

The Ba'ath Government concluded that developing the agricultural sector and increasing production in order to feed Iraq's growing urban population could only occur through changing the pattern of production from that of a family owned or small commercial unit to the pattern of large high-production units.

The following table shows the most important agricultural projects of the state farms and their total areas:

Table 3.8
The most important agricultural projects of the state farms and their total areas

Project	Total Area
Dijayla	390 000 dunam
Hawija	35 918 dunam

Latifiya	25 000 dunam
Shahrazur	37 782 dunam
Al-Wahda	53 000 dunam
14 Ramadhan	8 624 dunam
30 July	114 000 dunam
Al Dalmaj	400 000 dunam
17 July	60 000 dunam
7 April	60 000 dunam
Abu Bshout	33 403 dunam
Ash-Shihaymiya	60 000 dunam
Al-Khalis	480 000 dunam
Nahr Sa'ad	90 000 dunam
Al-Muthanna	75 000 dunam
Al-Musayyab	335 000 dunam

Here are some examples of agricultural production under the Ba'ath rule:

• Cereal production increased almost 80 percent between 1975 and 1985, in spite of the wide variations in the yield from year to year which was effected by the amount and timing of rainfall. Between 1980 and 1985, the area under wheat cultivation increased steadily for a cumulative growth of 30 percent, to about 1,566,500 hectares. In 1984, a drought year, Iraq harvested less than half the planted area for a yield of between 250,000 and 471,000 tons, according to foreign and Iraqi sources respectively. In 1985 Iraq harvested a bumper crop of 1.4 million tons of wheat. The north and central rain-fed areas were the principal wheat producers. Between 1980 and 1985, the total area under barley cultivation grew 44 percent. By 1985 barley and wheat production were virtually equal in terms of area cultivated and of total yield.

• Rice, grown in paddies, was Iraq's third most important crop as measured by cultivated area, which in 1985 amounted to 24,500 hectares. 1985 production totalled almost 150,000 tons, which indicates that the area under cultivation did not grow. Iraq also produced maize, millet, and oil seeds in smaller quantities.[60]

• Dates, for which Iraq is famous, have long been a basic part of the local diet. The most productive date groves were along the Shatt al Arab in the south of Iraq. In the early 1960s, Iraq had more than 30 million date palm trees. In the mid-1970s, that number had declined to about 22 million, and production of dates was 578,000 tons. The Iran-Iraq War affected the date palm groves, and in 1985 the number of date palms was less than 13 million. In 1987, date production was only 220,000 tons, of which 150,000 tons, or 68 percent of the harvest, was exported, primarily to Western Europe, Japan, India, and other Arab countries. Iraq produced a variety of other fruits as well, including melons, grapes, apples, apricots, and citrus. Production of such fruits increased almost 30 percent between 1975 and 1985.[61]

The Ba'ath Government paid special attention to increasing livestock. In the 1970s, the Government started to emphasize livestock and fish production, in an effort to add protein to the national diet.

But red meat production (about 93,000 tons) and milk production (375,000 tons) in the mid 1980s were, respectively, about 24 and 23 percent less than in the mid 1970s, although other figures indicated that total livestock production remained stable between these periods. From 1981 to 1985, total production of processed chicken and fish almost doubled, to about 20,000 tons apiece, while egg production increased substantially, to more than 1 billion per year. [62]

General Increase in agricultural products

The value of agricultural products increased from 200.8 million ID in 1968 to 354.9 million ID in 1974 and 1280 million ID in 1981, with an average annual growth of between 1968-1974 9.9%, and 22.1% between 1975-1981. The overall domestic product of the agricultural sector increased from 167.9 million ID in 1968 to 278.4 million ID in 1974 and 977 million ID in 1981, showing an average growth of 8.8% between 1968-1974 and 20.9% between 1975-1981. The fixed capital in the agricultural sector also witnessed a good growth increasing from 16.8 million ID in 1968 to 468.3 million in 1981 ID at an average annual growth of 27.2%.

Understanding the Surface Water Resources

Water resources in Iraq are controlled by the Twin Rivers, the Tigris and the Euphrates. Both are international rivers originating in Turkey. The Tigris river basin in Iraq has a total area of 253,000 km², or 54% of the total river basin area of the Tigris in the three countries where it passes. The average annual flow of the Euphrates as it enters Iraq is estimated at 30 km. Unlike the Tigris, the Euphrates receives no tributaries within Iraq's borders.

The Euphrates and the Tigris are subject to large and possibly disastrous floods, and in the Tigris water can rise over 30 cm/hour. In southern Iraq, huge areas are regularly flooded, floodwalls often collapse, and villages and roads must be built on high embankments. One of the reasons why the Tharthar reservoir was planned in the 1950s was to protect Baghdad from the periodic flooding of the Tigris and the destruction it caused.[63]

A number of new watercourses were constructed, especially in the southern part of the country, whose purpose was to increase water transport efficiency, minimize losses and water logging, and improve water quality. The Third River was completed in December 1992, at a length of 565 km, with a total discharge of 210 m³/s; it is a vast drainage canal that flows midway between the Tigris and the Euphrates from Mahmudiyya to Qurna, functioning as a main drain collecting drainage waters of more than 1.5 million hectares of agricultural land north of Baghdad to the Gulf. An American consultant who was seeking ways to reclaim the vast tracts of Iraq's agricultural land that had become barren through salination designed this river, with its channels and drainage pipes. Other watercourses were also constructed to reclaim new lands or to reduce water logging.[64]

The Ba'ath Achievements in the Construction of dams, irrigation projects and land reclamation

Like in all projects of all fields, the Ba'ath Government deemed it necessary, in the Five Year Development Plan of 1970-74, to complete first the dams that had already been under construction before embarking on new projects. Experts understood correctly that some of these dams could be utilized to store water to be used for irrigation in areas where water is scarce in the summer. The dams that had already been completed to control flooding were: The Dukan Dam (the River Upper Zab), the Darbandikhan Dam (River Diyala), the Samarra Dam (River Tigris), the Ramadi Dam (River Euphrates). Other dams, like the Hindiya and Kut dams, were designed for the distribution of water for irrigation. Most of the flood control dams were in northern Iraq, and funds were provided for the exploration and construction of dams in other areas, such as the projects at al-Haditha and al-Razaza over the River Euphrates.[65]

Two new dams were completed in 1984 and 1987 respectively: Saddam Dam on the Tigris at Mousil and Al Qadisiyah Dam at Al Hadithah on Euphrates. In addition to that, a Turkish-Yugoslavian joint venture began in 1987 constructing a $2 billion dam at Bekhme on the Great Zab River, a Tigris tributary in northeastern Iraq. By June 1990, the first stage of the construction was complete, but works were halted in the late 1990s because of the UN sanctions. Additional dams were constructed at Badush (an unfinished multi-purpose dam on the Tigris River 16 km northwest of Mousil where construction began in the 1990s and was halted prior to the 2003 invasion of Iraq) and Fat-hah (north of Baji between the Jebel Makhal and Jebel Hemrin ridges). In Hindiyah on the Euphrates and in Ash Shinafiyah on the Euphrates, Chinese contractors built a series of barrages in the mid-1980s.[66]

In the early 1970s, both Syria and Turkey completed large dams on the Euphrates and filled vast reservoirs. Iraqi officials protested the sharp decrease in the river's flow, claiming that irrigated areas along the Euphrates in Iraq dropped from 136,000 hectares to 10,000 hectares from 1974 to 1975.

In 1986 Turkey completed tunnels to divert an estimated one-fifth of the water from the Euphrates into the Atatürk Dam reservoir. The Turkish Government reassured Iraq that in the long run downstream flows would revert to normal. Iraqi protests were very low level, because Iraq had not yet exploited fully Euphrates River water for irrigation. There was also the political factor as the Government did not wish to disturb its relationship with Turkey in the midst of the Iran-Iraq War.[67]

In 1970, waterlogging and salinity caused half the irrigated areas in central and southern Iraq to be degraded. The main causes for these problems were the lack of drainage facilities and flooding. In 1978, a land rehabilitation program was undertaken, comprising concrete lining for irrigation canals, installation of field drains and collector drains. By 1989, a total of 750,000 ha had been reclaimed at a cost of around $2,000/ha. The total water-managed area equipped for full or partial controlled irrigation in 1990 was about 3.5 million ha. The areas irrigated by surface water were estimated at 3.305 million ha, of which 105,000 ha (3 %) are in the Shatt Al-Arab river basin, 2.2 million ha (67%) in the Tigris river basin, and 1 million ha (30%) in the Euphrates river basin. It should however be remembered that a part of that area was abandoned due to waterlogging and salinity. The areas irrigated from groundwater were about 220,000 ha in 1990, with some 18,000 wells.[68]

The following table shows the most important irrigation projects completed between 1968 and 1980:

Table 3.9
The most important irrigation projects completed
between 1968 and 1980

Item	Project	Irrigated area	Project length / cost
1	Al Mughaishy Canal / Basra	60 Dunam*	18 km

2	Ad-Dawwaya Canal (with housing for 7500 families)	114 000 Dunam	56 km
3	Hay Al Jadeed Watercourse	245 000 Dunam	
4	Eski Kalak / Arbil	40 000 Dunam	
5	Ad-Dumluj / Wasit	400 000 Dunam	
6	Mandili irrigation	50 000 Dunam	
7	April 7 and Salman Pak	200 000 Dunam	
8	Sa'ad River / Misan	90 000 Dunam	
9	Upper Yousufiya weir	220 000 Dunam	
10	Joint upper part (Diyala)	37 000 Dunam	
11	Kirkuk irrigation project	1 165 000 Dunam	ID 260 million
12	Abu Ghraib and Yousufiya leaches project	900 000 Dunam	
13	Dujaila leaches project	400 000 Dunam	
14	Hilla-Diwaniya-Daghara leaching project	206 000 Dunam	
15	Ramadi leaching project	150 000 Dunam	
16	Mousil Dam /Eski Mousil		ID 200 million
17	Tharthar Canal Project	Multi-purpose	ID 125 million
18	General Estuary	156 Km	ID 10 million
19	Al Bashra River	Multi-purpose	ID 19 million
20	Himrin Dam	4 Billion m^3 capacity	ID 21 million

21	Haditha Dam	8.2 Billion m³	ID 180 million
22	Abu Ghraib Irrigation	1 million Dunam	ID 150 million
23	East Gharraf	1 million Dunam	150 million dunam
24	Al-Ishaqi Irrigation	687 000 Dunam	ID 100 million

The Impact of the Iran-Iraq war on Development

This is not intended to be a political analysis of the Iran-Iraq war. The purpose of this section is to summarize the effect of that war on the development plans and the building of Iraq so as to enable one to evaluate the damage caused later by the sanctions by having taken into consideration the damage caused by this war.

Following the 1968 revolution, Iraq's government pursued a socialist economic policy and the economy prospered. Despite a quadrupling of imports between 1978 and 1980, Iraq continued to accrue current account surpluses in excess of $10 billion per year.[69]

The Iran-Iraq War of 1980-88 greatly damaged Iraq and reduced it from prosperity to economic difficulty. The United States and the UK (as well as France and the Soviet Union) supported Iraq in that conflict, the longest conventional war of the twentieth century. The support included weapons sales, military advisors and intelligence sharing. The United States provided, among other things, economic assistance, political support, arms, satellite intelligence and the assistance of a USA naval battle group. Iran proved a resilient foe, however, and the war dragged out at great cost in life and material infrastructure. The war, which the Iraqi government undoubtedly thought would be short and successful, lasted eight years, with disastrous human and economic consequences from which the Iraqi society suffered. In addition to great damage on the Iranian side, the Iran-Iraq War caused destruction in several Iraqi cities and much of Iraq's oil production and refinery system was damaged and halted. The war also caused several hundred thousand Iraqi casualties, and environmental damage, stripped the government of cash, halted infrastructure building and government welfare programs, and caused large human displacement.[70]

In 1979, Iraq was OPEC's largest oil exporting country after Saudi Arabia. Its export in that year amounted to 3.3 MBD, 11.4 percent of OPEC's total export. Iraq's oil revenue amounted to $21.4 billion, 10.5

percent of OPEC's. When the war with Iran began in September 1980, the Iraqi economy was on the threshold of another decade of economic growth, with the immense increase in oil revenue having enabled the government to increase spending simultaneously on infrastructure, goods producing sectors, social services, imports, and the military. Iraq held reserves estimated at $35 billion.

According to one study, the value of contracts with foreign enterprises for non-military projects increased by 64 percent from $14.8 billion in 1980 to $24.3 billion in 1981.[71] This was seen as a political strategy; an attempt by the government to lessen the impact of the war on living standards by making consumer goods available in large quantities, and thus to show that business was as usual.

The war-caused destruction of oil facilities such as loading terminals, pumping stations, refineries, and pipelines forced oil output to decline sharply from 3.281 million barrel per day (MBD) in August 1980 to .926 MBD in 1981. This in turn resulted in the collapse of Iraq's oil revenue from $26.1 billion in 1980 to $10.4 billion in 1981 or by 60%.[72] However, Iraq succeeded in repairing the damages to most of its oil installations (except of course those in the immediate area of military operations) and by 1990 production was again up to 2.1 million bpd, with more investments and expansions projected.

Military Expansion and its Effects on the Economy

Between the 1970s and the 1980s, there was a massive shift of labour from the civilian economy to the military and a sharp increase in military spending and military imports.

In 1975, there were 82,000 persons (or 2.9% of Iraq's labour force) in armed forces. In 1980 there were 430,000 persons (13.4% of the labour force) in the armed forces. And by the time the war with Iran ended in 1988, the government was employing 1 million persons (or more than 21% of the labour force) in the armed forces.

This expansion in the armed forces was accompanied by a sharp rise in the military's claims on Iraq's fiscal resources. Thus in 1975 military expenditures amounted to $3.1 billion or 13.8% of the GDP—a high ratio by world standards. By 1980 military spending was increased by more than six fold to $19.8 billion or 38.8% of GDP. Another way of measuring the burden of military spending is to relate it to the country's oil revenue. In 1975 the government spent 38% of its oil revenue on the military compared with 75% in 1980. Such spending increased sharply afterward to absorb between 117% and 324% of the oil revenue between 1981 and 1988. In other words in the decade of the 1980s, the government spent several times the country's entire oil revenue on the war effort.

In relation to GDP, the government spent between 23% and 66% of the country's GDP between 1980 and 1988 on the war with Iran. [73]

In 1981, foreign expenditures not directly related to the war effort, reached at an all-time high of $23.6 billion, as Iraq continued to import goods and services for the development effort, and construction continued. Iraq was also paying an estimated $25 million per day to wage the war. Although the Gulf States contributed $5 billion toward the war effort from 1980 to 1981, Iraq raised most of the money needed for war purposes by drawing down its reserves over several years.[74]

Imports also changed in favour of military imports, for while military imports in 1980 amounted to 17% of total imports, the ratio reached 83% by 1984. The economic burden of arms imports in the 1980s may again be understood if these arms imports are related to Iraq's GDP during the same period when arms imports were between 5% and 19% of Iraq's GDP. Saddam Hussein acknowledged the enormous burden of military imports at the May 1990 Arab Summit Conference in Baghdad, saying:

> However, the war dragged on and its cost rose to unprecedented levels. The value of military hardware alone which Iraq purchased and used in the war amounted to $102 bn in addition to other enormous military and civilian expenditure in a devastating war which lasted eight years along a front which extended 1,200 kms.[75]

Understanding the Economic Costs of the Iran-Iraq War

Iraq's losses as a result of the war with Iran were estimated to be $452.6 billion. These were explicit or quantifiable losses which included lost oil revenue, decline in GDP, military expenditure and arms imports and the cost of damaged and destroyed assets; and included implicit losses such as the cost of inflation, loss of income from destroyed assets, lost opportunities for growth and disorganization of development. Iraq's losses included these elements:

1. $91.4 billion in potential GNP losses: losses incurred in the oil sector, industry, agriculture, energy, telecommunications, housing, and health.
2. $197.7 billion oil-revenue losses.
3. $78.8 billion losses in foreign exchange reserves due to the loss of $35 billion in original reserves plus accumulated interest earnings for the duration of the war.

4. $80 billion potential losses in foreign exchange reserves resulting from high military spending.[76]

The easiest way to comprehend the scale of this loss is to relate it to Iraq's oil revenue. Between 1931, when the government received its first payment for oil export, and 1988 when the war with Iran ended, the cumulative revenue from oil amounted to $179.1 billion. This means that the war-inflicted losses were about 254% of all the oil revenue which Iraq received over a period of fifty-seven years. Another way of measuring the scale of the war loss is to relate it to Iraq's GDP. Iraq's GDP during the period 1980-88 amounted to $433.3 billion, and by relating the war cost of $452.6 billion to this figure, it would be clear that the economic loss due to the war exceeded the war period GDP by $19.3 billion.[77]

In 1986, the petroleum sector had revived enough to contribute about 33.5% of GDP, while the nonpetroleum sector, including services, manufacturing and agriculture accounted for the remainder. The largest component of nonpetroleum GDP, business services, amounted to about 23% of GDP. Agriculture accounted for about 7.5% of GDP, mining and manufacturing for slightly less than 7%, construction for almost 12%, transportation and communications for about 4.5%, and utilities for between 1 and 2%. The total estimated GDP for 1986 was equivalent to $35 billion.[78]

Experts estimated that Iraqi debt in 1986 totalled between $50 billion and $80 billion. Of this sum, Iraq owed about $30 billion to Saudi Arabia, Kuwait, and the other Gulf states. Most of this amount was derived from crude oil sales on Iraq's behalf. Iraq promised to provide reimbursement in oil after the war, but had expected that the Gulf States would waive repayment.

The authoritative Wharton Econometric Forecasting Associates estimated in 1986 that Iraqi debt guaranteed by export credit agencies totalled $9.3 billion, of which $1.6 billion was short-term debt and $7.7 billion was medium-term debt.

In the area of government debts, Iraq's debts to Western governments for its purchases of military materiel were considerable. Iraq owed France more than $1.35 billion for weapons, which it was repaying by permitting two oil companies affiliated with the French government, Elf-Aquitaine and Compagnie Française des Petroles-Total (CFP), to lift 80,000 barrels of oil per day from the Dortyol terminal near Iskenderun, Turkey. Finally, Iraq owed money to the Soviet Union and to East European nations. Iraq's debt to the Soviet Union was estimated at $5 billion in 1987.[79] [Iraq was not buying weapons and arms from the US/UK at that time and thus no debt].

It is with this in mind that we should look at how the sanctions went on to devastate Iraq. Sanctions would damage the healthiest of economies but would undoubtedly do immense damage to an economy already affected by eight years of war.

Perhaps the best way to understand development in Iraq is to hear how the enemies of the Ba'ath regime evaluated it. Writing under the pseudonym Samir Al-Khalil, Kanan Makiya, who was a staunch critic of the Ba'ath regime, could not but acknowledge the developments that had been achieved between 1968 and 1990, regardless of his harsh criticism of the regime. He cites Hanna Batatu's *Social Classes* and Joe Stork's *State Power* as sources that show that a substantial real increase in the standard of living must have occurred. Perhaps his words are the best end for this chapter:

> A regime of terror actually presided over an across-the-board increase in the standard of living in Iraq, and it significantly improved the lot of the most destitute layers, furthering the leveling of income differentials that began after 1958. The changes are impressive: the prices of most basic necessities were stabilized by state subsidy; the minimum daily wage was greatly increased over the rate of inflation, which was kept low; new labor laws provided complete job security; the state became an employer of last resort for all graduates; free education and health care was provided; and per capita national income increased from 195 ID in 1970 to 7,564 ID in 1979.[80]

4

THE BA'ATH'S PROGRESSIVE SOCIAL AND POLITICAL POLICIES

After 1968, the Ba'ath Government viewed social reform through the perspective of the Ba'ath ideology and attempted to transform society in such a way that workers, peasants and other poorer classes would enjoy the benefits of development.[1] There is no dispute, in our opinion, that the Ba'ath Government was truly committed to building a strong nation with a strong economy and a strong army. Whether or not they succeeded in doing that is a matter for historians to judge.

However, it is fair to say that before the Gulf Crisis of 1990, Iraq was a mostly urbanized nation with a modern social infrastructure and had been steadily industrializing. Its investment in its own social and economic infrastructure was evident in the services it provided to its population. Prior to the 1990 Gulf war, 93% of Iraqis had access to health care and safe water. Education was free, calorie availability was 120% of actual requirements, and GNP per capita was more than double its 1976 value.

On assuming power in 1968 the new Ba'ath Government had to address two major problems—the future of oil exploration and the Kurdish problem. Both issues needed a solution if the rebuilding of the nation was to succeed. Revenue from oil was necessary to pay for the development plans, but stability and security was fundamental before the government could consider embarking on any development.

The Kurdish problem had taken a turn for the worse during Arif's rule with intensified fighting, some of which coincided, not by chance, with the Arab-Israeli war of 1967. The Ba'athists, contrary to what the media in the USA/UK has made us believe, genuinely wanted an amicable solution to the Kurdish problem. After months of negotiation between both sides, the Law of Autonomy for the Region of Iraq's Kurdistan No. 33 was promulgated on 11 March 1974. The law was revolutionary by any standard. It granted the Kurds of Iraq, the second biggest ethnic group, rights that were light years ahead of what the Kurds had received in neighboring countries such as Iran and Turkey where the majority of Kurds lived.

It is worth noting here that, almost 40 years later, Turkey, a NATO member and a contender for EU, still refuses to recognize the Kurdish language, which Iraq made official in 1974.[2]

In fact, Iraq's Kurds had continuously enjoyed more national rights than in any other host country. Iraqi governments allowed Kurdish language use in elementary education (1931), recognized a Kurdish nationality (1958), and implemented Kurdish autonomy (1974).[3] Having said that, we believe that the Kurds have generally been oppressed and denied their national rights in varying degrees in their national homeland.

The Progressive National Front (PNF)

The Ba'ath Government sought to provide a forum for non-Ba'athist political participation and thus created the Progressive National Front (PNF) in 1974 to ally the Ba'ath with other political parties that were considered to be progressive. The basis for this cooperation, was the National Action Charter proclaimed by President Al-Bakr in 1971, where the Ba'ath invited "all national and progressive forces and elements" to work for the objective of a "democratic, revolutionary, and unitary" Iraq by participating in the "broadest coalition among all the national, patriotic, and progressive forces."[4]

Discussions between the Ba'ath and the Iraqi Communist Party (ICP) took place periodically over three years before the latter was induced to join the PNF in 1974. Like the Ba'ath, the ICP was an elitist party that advocated socialist programs to benefit the masses and that appealed primarily to intellectuals. The Ba'athists tended to suspect the communists of ultimate loyalty to a foreign power, the Soviet Union, rather than to the Arab nation, even though the Ba'athists themselves regarded the Soviet Union as a friendly and progressive state after 1968.

In return for participation in the PNF, the ICP was permitted to nominate its own members for some minor cabinet posts and to carry on political and propaganda activities openly. The ICP had to agree, however, not to recruit among the armed forces and to accept Ba'ath domination of the RCC. The ICP also recognized the Ba'ath Party's leading role in the PNF: of the sixteen-member High Council that was formed to direct the PNF, eight positions were reserved for the Ba'ath, five for other progressive parties, and only three for the Communists.[5]

It may be debatable how genuine the Ba'ath's intention was in inviting the Communists to be part of the political life in Iraq. However, there is no denying that the PNF was a new era that put an end to decades of enmity between the Communist and the Ba'ath of Iraq which witnessed some sad episodes of bloodshed dating back to 1959 through 1963.

New Labor Laws: A Major Contribution to Social and Economic Justice

New laws were enacted during 1970-71 aimed at improving workers' conditions, through regulating labour relationships and extending the benefits of social security. These laws were derived from principles enshrined in the teachings of the Ba'ath Party and the guidelines embodied in the *Charter of National Action,* which the Ba'ath and the Communist parties had adopted on 15 November 1971. These principles may be summed up as follows:

1. Eradication of unemployment.
2. Social security guaranteed to all citizens.
3. Creation and maintenance of a minimum wage.
4. Provision of free health and medical care.
5. Provision of free education.
6. Eradication of illiteracy.
7. Provision of housing units all over the country equipped with general requirements of health, security, communications and education.
8. Granting equal opportunities to women.[6]

Three major laws were enacted in 1970-71 to facilitate the implementation of some of these principles. The first, issued on October 14, 1970, dealt with labour problems. The second law, issued on October 26, 1970, provided general guidelines and regulations for cooperatives and unions. The third law, issued on March 9, 1971, was related to retirement and insurance for workers. According to the third law, employees would contribute 5% to the general fund, the employers 12 to 15% and the Government up to 30%, out of which workers would be paid for their insurances and eventual retirement. The law also provided insurance payment to workers in case of injury during work.[7]

A Distinctive Contribution to the Liberation of Women in the Arab World

Iraq has had a mixed record in its treatment of women. Under the relatively secular Ba'ath regime, women enjoyed significantly more privileges and opportunities than they did under some traditional regimes that enforce Islamic tenets more restrictively.

The Ba'ath era oversaw a social revolution, which offered women high-level government and industry jobs and gave them added freedoms. The Government strengthened the efficient Western style banking system, created a Western style legal system and abolished the old *Shari'a* law. Iraq was the only country in the Gulf region, which was not ruled according to what they put forward as Islamic Law, that being Law dealing only with family/personal sexual morality but overlooking Islamic principles of justice, human dignity and freedom of choice and expression. The primary underpinning of women's equality is contained in the Iraqi provisional constitution, which was drafted by the Ba'ath Government in 1970.

Article 19 (a) of that Constitution specified "Citizens are equal before the law, without discrimination because of sex, blood, language, social origin or religion."

Enrolment of women and girls in rural areas in literacy centers under the illiteracy eradication legislation of 1979 transferred women in Iraq into a new level of education, labour, and employment. With other employment laws, the opportunities in the civil service sector, maternity benefits, and stringent laws against harassment in the work place allowed Iraqi women greater involvement in building their careers. Women attained the right to vote and run for office in 1980. In 1986 Iraq became one of the first countries to ratify the Convention on Elimination of all forms of Discrimination Against Women (CEDAW).[8]

Though women were not subject to conscription, those holding university degrees in health care could serve in the armed forces within their specialities, and during the Iraq-Iran war of 1980-1988 manpower shortages led the government to allow women in other branches of the military service as well. According to a U.S. State Department report on human rights practices, the government enacted laws to equalize women's rights in divorce, landownership, taxation, and suffrage. Women made strides in education; for example, female attendance in primary schools rose from 34% to 95% between 1970 and 1980. Government programs to improve the status of women helped increase job opportunities for women.

In the 1980s, women constituted 46% of all teachers, 29% of physicians, 46% of dentists, 70% of pharmacists, 15% of factory workers, and 16% of governmental employees.[9]

A Unique Attitude to Religious Freedom in the Arab World

Up until the 2003 invasion, Iraq had been a very tolerant society with very responsible policies on religious freedom. People grew up in mixed neighbourhoods with no segregation between sects or religions.

The authors personally both grew up in an area in Baghdad in which Muslims, Christians and Jews lived side by side without any problem. We both went to a Jesuit Society school run by USA Jesuits and studied in a school which taught Christianity and NOT Islam as the religion and which had mixtures of all three main faiths and other smaller ones. The Ba'ath passed a law which granted every employee the right to enjoy his/her religious holidays fully paid in addition to enjoying the official state holidays.[10] Imagine the reaction in Europe if Muslims there requested to enjoy the Muslim Eid holiday. Christians operated seminaries. Christian children received religious instruction in state schools having a Christian majority, the Vatican had diplomatic relations with Iraq[11] and the Archbishop of Canterbury had sent Reverend Canon Andrew White, an Anglican chaplain, to Baghdad in 1998.[12] We wonder how many European capitals have displayed such tolerance. When Switzerland decided to block the building of a Mosque, they resorted to a referendum to claim that it was a democratic decision, only proving thereby that the majority were intolerant of religious freedom.[13]

Iraq's Christian population stood at around 149,000 after the 1947 census, roughly 3.7 percent of the country's population. In 1987, there were around one million Christians in Iraq out of a population of 18.5 million people, over 5 percent of the population.[14] The Ba'ath enhanced the policy of religious coexistence and tolerance at the expense of subduing fundamentalism.

To demonstrate this, it is important to point out that the Ba'ath Government was the only Muslim state that had a Christian as Deputy Prime Minister for such a long period of time. Tariq Aziz, was a Chaldean Christian, though perhaps as secularized a Christian as Hussein was a Muslim. Avak Asadourian, Iraq's Armenian archbishop, told the *Christian Science Monitor* on 21 April 2003 that: "We enjoyed total religious freedom and there was no religious discrimination" under Saddam's rule.[15] How many European states have had a Muslim as a Minister, despite the fact that in some of these countries the percentage of Muslims equals that of the Christians in Iraq?

The relevance of this fact could be seen since the invasion. The Zionist campaign to demonize the Ba'ath in which the Western media took a very active role has presented the Ba'ath as a blood-thirsty chauvinistic movement which had to be uprooted in order to replace it with a democratic regime. What happened in fact is that the first act the USA took in Iraq was to dismantle the secular Iraqi army and replace it with the religious militia established to fight the Ba'ath on a sectarian basis. This led—as intended—to activating different sectarian forces which might facilitate the planned dismemberment of Iraq, an offshoot of which was the perhaps unintended eventual targeting of Christians leading to massive exodus, the like of which Iraq had never seen.[16]

The real tension in Iraq in the latter 1980s was not between Sunnis and Shi'a, as we are led to believe, but rather between a large part of the population, both Sunnis and Shi'a, for whom religious belief and practice had significant value, and the secular Ba'athists of Sunni, Shi'a and Christian descent. The Shi'a made substantial progress in the educational, business, and legal fields. Observers believed that in the late 1980s Shi'a were represented at all levels of the Ba'ath party in rough proportion to estimates of their numbers in the population. For example, of the eight top Iraqi leaders who in early 1988 sat with Saddam Hussein on the Revolutionary Command Council, three were Arab Shi'a (one of whom served as Minister of Interior), three were Arab Sunnis, one was an Arab Christian, and one a Kurd. On the Regional Command Council (the ruling body of the Ba'ath party), Shi'a were actually predominant. During the war with Iran, a number of highly competent Shi'a officers were promoted to corps commanders. The General who turned back the initial Iranian invasions of Iraq in 1982 was a Shi'a.

The Shi'a made good progress in the economic field as well during the 1980s. Qualified observers note that many Shi'a migrated from rural areas, particularly in the south, to the cities, so that Shi'a became the majority in major cities like Basra and Baghdad, many of whom prospered in business, the professions, industry and the service sector. Even those living in the poorer areas of the cities were generally better off than they had been in the countryside. In the rural areas as well, the educational level of Shi'a was no different to the level of their Sunni counterparts.[17]

Ba'ath Ideology in the Education Sector:
Free Education for All at All Levels

The 1947 Charter of the Ba'ath Party considered education to be of utmost importance for the building of a new Arab generation, one armed with scientific thinking and capable of achieving its development aims. The Party's published report[18] stressed that "the rise of the nation and the realization of its objectives cannot be achieved without giving the citizen a socialist and scientific education that frees him from all the inherited, restricting and backward ties, in order to create the new Arab person who has an open, scientific mind, good socialist ethics, and believes in common values".

After rising to power, the Ba'ath leaders paid considerable attention to educational institutions and tried for the first time to correlate educational plans with the overall national development plans.[19]

Article 27 of the Provisional Constitution of 1970 declared the state's commitment to the following:[20]

- combating illiteracy
- guaranteeing of the right to free education at all levels—primary, secondary and post-secondary, and university—for all its citizens
- making primary education compulsory
- expanding technical and vocational education in cities and rural areas
- encouraging evening schools to allow citizens to work and study
- guaranteeing the freedom of scientific research

In the two five-year development plans of 1970 and 1976, the Ba'ath Government planned for illiteracy to be eradicated in two stages; in the first stage it would be considerably reduced among the young generation and then wiped out within a decade after the launching of the second five-year plan. Educational facilities were increased in quantity, as reflected in the number of schools, teachers, laboratories and other facilities; and in quality, they were much improved on previous standards. Tuition fees in all educational institutions including universities were abolished in 1974, and all students' needs—text books, stationery, etc. were met free of charge in all schools at all levels.[21] Iraq under the Ba'ath must have been, in our opinion, the only state that had achieved this.

Thus this investment in education led to significant advances in adult literacy, school enrolment, and teacher training. In 1978, a law enacting a 'Comprehensive National Campaign for the Compulsory Eradication of Illiteracy' was enacted and was the starting point of a large-scale anti-illiteracy campaign.[22] Every citizen in the age group 15-45 years had to enrol at literacy centers to complete the equivalent of grade 4 schooling in reading, writing and mathematics. The effect was that illiteracy in the age group 15-45 decreased from 48.4% in 1978, to 19.9% in 1987. For the efficiency of this campaign, Iraq was awarded five prizes by UNESCO.[23] Adult literacy rates rose from 52% in 1977 to 89% in 1985.

Government spending on educational development in 1988/89 was 690 million ID (about 2.2 billion USD), comprising 6.4% of total government expenditure, and 238% more than educational spending in 1976.[24] The allocation between sub-sectors was 1% for pre-primary education, 47% for primary, 27% for secondary, 20% for tertiary education.[25]

The sixth national conference of the Ba'ath Party, which convened in Baghdad in 1974, emphasized the intention of reshaping the educational system to suit the objectives of the Ba'ath national educational philosophy. It stated that "the next era will encompass the preparation of curricula for all stages from kindergarten up to higher education. Such curricula should be in line with the democratic and socialist ideals of the Ba'ath and the Revolution. This requires a complete elimination of the old reactionary and bourgeoisie objectives of the old regime."

Before 1990, the educational situation in Iraq was considered one of the best in the region. War with Iran in the 1980s greatly affected available resources, but Iraq continued to maintain an education system that was free at all levels and provided all necessary learning and teaching materials. The gross enrolment ratio at primary level was 100%.[26]

Primary and Secondary Schools

Between 1976 and 1986, the number of primary-school students increased 30 percent; female students increased 45 percent, from 35 to 44 percent of the total. The number of primary-school teachers increased 40 percent over this period. At the secondary level, the number of students increased by 46 percent, and the number of female students increased by 55 percent, from 29 to 36 percent of the total. Baghdad, which had about 29 percent of the population, had 26 percent of the primary students, 27 percent of the female primary students, and 32 percent of the secondary students.

The number of primary schools built rose by 6802 from 4907 in 1968 to 11709 in 2001. The student/teacher ratio was 28 in 1980, 25 in 1991 and 21 in 2000.

Table 4.1
Development of Primary schools[20]

Year	Number of Teachers	Number of students			Number of schools
		Female	Male	Total	
1967-68	45201	292398	698320	990718	4907
1979-80	92603	1174449	1434693	2609142	11324
1989-90	138728	1433641	1804642	3238283	11320

Table 4.2

Secondary schools[21]

Year	Number of Teachers	Number of students			Number of schools
		Female	Male	Total	
1967-68	8602	60952	193081	254033	757
1979-80	27987	629034	627967	897001	1774
1989-90	44664	398343	618527	1016870	2585

Vocational Education

Iraq like many developing countries has always suffered from lack of a technical cadre. There may be enough engineers but only a few skilled technical men to do the middle job between engineering design and unskilled labour. The Ba'ath had a policy to tackle this shortage. Vocational education in Iraq, which was known for its inadequacy, received considerable official attention in the 1980s. The number of students in technical fields increased threefold since 1977, to over 120,090 in 1986.[29]

Higher Education

Iraq under the Ba'ath witnessed a quantum leap in university and higher education. In 1968 there were five universities in Iraq. By 1990 there were 11 universities, spread over the governorates of Iraq. In addition to these universities and colleges, 9 technical colleges were established as well as 38 technical institutes within the Technical Education Commission, in addition to other colleges in Misan, Al-Muthanna, Falluja, Samarra and Teachers preparation colleges.

Further universities and colleges were established to serve the different branches of the armed forces: Al-Bakr University for Military Higher Studies, Air Force College, Air Defence College, Military Staff College, Police College and Military Engineering College.

The number of students seeking to pursue higher education in the 1980s also increased dramatically. The table shows the leap when we see that number of universities increased by over 220% and the number of students increased by over 570% and the number of teachers increased by over 560% for the period 1968-1989.

Prior to the imposition of sanctions Iraq used to send thousands of university graduates to Europe to carry out research and achieve even higher education. However, since the imposition of sanctions and deprivation of Iraq, it had to rely on itself in developing its postgraduate research and studies. This era witnessed some clever innovations when academic life became more linked to industry, agriculture and business.

Table 4.3
Universities and teachers[22]

Year	Teachers	Students	Universities	Students /teacher
1968-69	1879	31086	5	22
1973-74	2669	58351	6	22
1978-79	5207	89197	7	17
1983-84	6934	119028	7	17
1988-89	10548	179542	11	19

The Ba'ath Plan to Provide Free Health Service to All

Article 33 of the Provisional Constitution of 1970 emphasized the state's commitment to the continued expansion of free medical services, prevention, treatment and medicine to all the cities and rural areas.[31]

On medical and health services, the National Development Plan projected an increase of 43% in the number of hospital beds. It also concentrated on preventive remedies by enhancing such projects as the Malaria Eradication Project and The Project for the Fight Against TB.

The Plan projected that potable water availability to citizens would increase by 214% over what existed at the beginning of the development plan.[32] The Ba'ath had embarked on a campaign to improve health services in Iraq by building hundreds of hospitals and health centers and clinics, developing health insurance, establishing public and general and specialized laboratories, pharmacies, maternal and child centers and training and educating thousands of specialized medical staff in all types and branches of medicine, dentistry and pharmacy.[33]

Success in Providing Potable Water

Prior to the sanctions, the population of Iraq enjoyed a relatively high level of water and sanitation services. Urban access to drinking water supply was 95% with an average of 330 liters per person per day in Baghdad, and 250-300 liters per person per day in the other cities and towns. Rural water coverage was 75% with an average supply of 180 liters per person per day.[34] This was achieved by a system of 210 water treatment plants, 1200 mobile plants primarily for rural use, 50 pumping stations and 40,000 km. of pipelines.[35]

The campaign was implemented through the following measures:

1. Providing drinking water networks through water purification plants all over the country.
2. Providing sewage networks in Iraqi cities.
3. Building hospitals and health centers across Iraq.
4. Promulgating the Law for Basic Health Care to provide free health services to the citizens   especially to pregnant women and children, as well as covering the school health program.
5. Promulgating the Law for Health Insurance in the provinces.
6. Promulgating the Law for Peoples' Clinics that provided virtually free services in the centers of the Governorates.
7. Working to raise public awareness of health and the establishment of intensive courses for the health cadres to implement the work.
8. Commencing a campaign to eliminate infectious, communicable and parasitic diseases which had been ravaging the health of Iraqi citizens for decades.
9. The building of laboratories and factories producing drugs and antibiotics.
10. The creation of medical and health cadres through the establishment of medical schools, nursing colleges and institutes of medicine and technical health institutes across the country's governorates.[36]

The health care system in Iraq was based on an extensive and developed network of primary, secondary and tertiary health care facilities. These facilities were linked among themselves and with the community by a large fleet of ambulances and service vehicles, and by a good communications network facilitating referral to the next level of the health care system. It was estimated by the Government of Iraq (GOI) that 97% and 79% of the urban and rural populations, respectively, had access to health care. While the system tended to emphasize curative aspects, it was complemented by a set of public health activities that included, among others, malaria control, an expanded program of immunizations (EPI) and tuberculosis control activities.[37]

Specialty surgical care, laboratory testing and comprehensive treatment options were available to the Iraqi population at most levels of health care. Doctors received their training in one of twelve medical schools in the country and often had the opportunity to undertake part of their training in the USA or Europe.[38]

In 1989, the Government spent over $500 million in foreign exchange for required imports for the health sector. The breakdown of the previous figure was as follows:

- 360 million dollars for imported pharmaceuticals, vaccines, medical appliances and disposable supplies;
- 100 million dollars for raw materials for Samara Drug Industries which supplied 30% of the needs;
- 30 million dollars for replacement parts and maintenance of health services equipment; and
- 10 million dollars for ambulances and logistical vehicles.[39]

Prior to 1990, Iraq had one of the highest per capita food availabilities in the region, low rates of malnutrition, and relatively low infant mortality rates. Large quantities of food were imported, which met up to two-thirds of food requirements. In the late 1980s daily food energy availability was 3,200 kcal/day or on a par with industrial nations. A nutritional survey of children aged 0 to 8 years in the Baghdad area in 1989 found their distribution of weight and height to be similar to that in the international reference population. Reflecting this excellent nutritional status of the population, the infant mortality rate (IMR) had declined from about 120 per thousand live births in 1960 to 40-50 per 1000 by the late 1980s.[40] This was further supported by a community based survey conducted by the Harvard International Study Team in 1991. Their estimate of the IMR was 32.5 per 1000 live births and the Child Morality Rate to be 43.2 per 1000 for 1985 to 1990, the period of time prior to the Gulf War and sanctions.[41]

Table 4.4
Child and Infant Mortality: 1960-1998

Year	Under 5 Mortality Rate	Infant Mortality Rate
1960	171	117
1970	127	90
1980	83	63
1990	50	40

Building and Provision of Hospitals

Emphasis was placed on the development of the then existing hospitals and the expansion of departments and wards, and the building of new and modern hospitals equipped with the latest medical equipment. The government was also keen on providing the public hospitals built in provincial centers and towns with all the medical departments that offered diagnostic, therapeutic and pharmaceutical services. In the major urban centers such as Baghdad, Basra and Mousil, new specialized hospitals (children, maternity, surgery, heart surgery, neurosurgery, psychiatry, dermatology, allergies and eyes) were also built in addition to public hospitals. Furthermore, teaching hospitals were established and began spreading with the increase in the number of medical colleges and universities in other provinces of Iraq, all staffed and supervised by Iraqi professors.

A review of the statistics will show that in 1968, when the Ba'ath took power, there were 149 hospitals, poorly equipped and not very efficient. By 1990, there were 256 hospitals in Iraq with 31227 beds.[42]

Setting up Health Centers

Health centers were distributed across Iraq's provinces in cities and towns, districts and remote villages, and were divided into specialized centers in urban centers, reaching 90 centers in 2003; centers for primary health care; and public health centers. These centers provided general health services and primary screening, diagnosis, treatment and free medicine for all citizens and for all kinds of diseases as well as dental services, in addition to providing drugs for people with chronic diseases such as heart diseases, diabetes and blood pressure. Primary health care centers also provided another important service, and that was the care of pregnant women from the beginning of pregnancy until after birth, and a registry of every pregnant woman with regular follow up. Post-natal care was provided for the mother and child, including child vaccination during the first five years of age against polio, smallpox, measles, tuberculosis, cholera and other possible diseases. For example, Saddam City (formerly Ath-Thawra City, today's Sadr City) alone had 19 health centers, each centre providing medical services as well as dental services, each health centre having from 2 to 4 dental care devices, as well as a major analysis laboratory and modern X-ray equipment. The number of health centers increased from 737 centers in 1968 to 1653 in 1990 [43].

Setting up Peoples' Clinics as Secondary Health Service

Peoples' medical clinics were opened to provide medical services for test and diagnosis, treatment and medicine to citizens in Governorate centers operating evenings from four to eight pm at nominal fees so as to alleviate the burden on the citizens who frequented the private clinics, whose fees were too high for people with low income as were the exorbitant prices in private pharmacies. These clinics were their saviour, and were staffed by specialized doctors whose salaries were subsidized by the State. These clinics did not exist before 1968, and by 1990 they numbered 336 clinics.[44]

Table 4.5
Indicators of quantitative growth of medical establishments and their staff

INDICATOR	1968	1980	1990
No. of hospitals	149	200	256
No. of Health Centers	737	1492	1653
No. of people's clinics	-	133	336
No. of doctors	2145	9366	13621
No. of dentists	743	1200	2093
No. of pharmacists	257	950	1470
No. of medical technicians	5303	20907	35022
No. of hospital beds	-	24784	31227

The data in the following table reflects a modern urban society, in which the wealth it obtained from exporting its oil was channelled, for the most part, into improving the quality of life of the Iraqi people, which at that period of time (1988-1989) was at a relatively "satisfactory" level, with indications of further improvement. At that time, Iraq reportedly had a good health surveillance and reporting system, hence, official data reported during this period are considered to be fairly reliable.

Table 4.6
Selected indicators in Iraq before sanctions, 1988-1989[45]

Health indicators:
<ul><li>Birth rate 43 per I 000 population</li><li>Crude death rate 8.0 per I 000 population</li><li>Infant mortality rate 52 per I 000 live births</li><li>Under 5 mortality rate 94 per I 000 live births</li><li>Maternal mortality rate I60 per I00 000 live births</li><li>Low birth weight 5% (below 2.5 kg)</li><li>Life expectancy 66 years</li></ul>
Socioeconomic indicators:
<ul><li>GNP per capita $2 800 -[The official rate was US$3.2169 to the dinar, although in late 1989, the black market rate was 3 dinars for US$1]</li><li>female literacy 85%</li><li>population with health care 93%</li><li>population with safe water 90%</li><li>pregnant women with maternity care 78%</li><li>pregnant women with trained birth attendant during delivery 86%</li></ul>

THE DESTRUCTION OF IRAQ

When Did the Destruction Really Begin?

On 2 August 1990, Iraq invaded Kuwait. The invasion was a consequence of a series of happenings and developments spanning a century. The historical background to the invasion, and our views of it, have all been dealt with before and we do not intend to repeat them here.

It would however be useful to note that the invasion did not and should not have come as a surprise to the US administration. On 25 July 1990, the Iraqi President, Saddam Hussein, summoned US Ambassador, April Glaspie, and at once told her: "I have summoned you today to hold comprehensive political discussions with you. This is a message to President Bush".[1] For Saddam, the actions of the Gulf States regarding oil policy amounted to a declaration of war. He said: "...while we were busy waging war [against Iran] the state of Kuwait began to expand at the expense of our territory". During Saddam's explanation of Iraq's stance and its grievances towards US policy, he said something remarkable that many have missed: "...I am afraid that one day you will say, "You are going to make gunpowder out of wheat."' But perhaps the most remarkable event in the whole meeting was Glaspie's reply: "...we have no opinion on Arab-Arab conflicts like your border disagreement with Kuwait... James Baker has directed our official spokesman to emphasize this instruction.... All that we hope is that these issues will be solved quickly." That was a clear green-light that the Iraq-Kuwait border dispute was not the United States' business.

On 24 Jul 1990, State Department spokeswoman Margaret Tutweiler, said: "We do not have any defense treaties with Kuwait, and there are no special defense or security commitments to Kuwait." [2]

The next day, Assistant Secretary of State for Near Eastern and South Asian Affairs, John Kelly, prevented a planned Voice of America broadcast that would have warned Iraq against action against Kuwait. There was nothing new in that, because visiting Senate Minority Leader Robert Dole had personally assured the Iraqi leader in April, speaking on behalf of the President, that the Bush administration dissociated itself from a Voice of America broadcast critical of Iraq's human-rights abuses and also opposed a congressional move for economic sanctions against Iraq. [3]

On 31 July, Kelly told Congress: "We have no defense treaty relationship with any Gulf country. That is clear. ... We have historically avoided taking a position on border disputes or on internal OPEC deliberations." When Rep. Lee Hamilton asked if it would be correct to say that if Iraq "charged across the border into Kuwait" the United States did "not have a treaty commitment which would obligate us to engage U.S. forces" there, Kelly responded: "That is correct". [4]

It appears, however, that the US did indeed have an official position on the Iraq-Kuwait border dispute, a matter that came to light after the invasion, when the Iraqis found in a Kuwaiti intelligence file a memorandum concerning a November 1989 meeting between the head of Kuwaiti state security and CIA Director William Webster. [5]

In a speed never seen before nor since, the US called the UN Security Council into session less than 10 hours after the Iraqi army entered Kuwait; a session which adopted resolution 660—the first of a series of resolutions against Iraq that would permanently change the face and future of Iraq—determining a breach of international peace and security under Articles 39 and 40 of the UN Charter, and calling for immediate withdrawal of Iraqi forces from Kuwait.

President George Bush immediately condemned Iraq's invasion stating that the seizure of Kuwait and the potential threat to Saudi Arabia were a direct threat to US strategic interests. He thus issued Executive Order 1272 "Blocking Iraqi Government Property and Prohibiting Transactions With Iraq" declaring that "the policies and actions of the government of Iraq constitute an unusual and extraordinary threat to the national security and foreign policy of the United States and hereby declare a national emergency to deal with that threat." [6]

At a news conference on 2 August in Woody Creek, Colorado, President Bush and Prime Minister Margaret Thatcher of Britain raised the possibility of economic or even military action by the United Nations. [7] Having seemingly decided to take military action, President Bush also began consultations with European and Arab leaders. Immediately after Iraqi troops crossed its border, Kuwait requested US military assistance, to which the US responded within less than an hour and sent a carrier battle group, led by the USS *Independence*, from positions near Diego Garcia in the southern Indian Ocean to a position in the Gulf of Oman, near the Straits of Hormuz. Another carrier battle group, led by the USS *Eisenhower*, moved to the eastern Mediterranean to prepare for deployment to the Red Sea. Two USAF KC-135 tankers that had already been sent to the UAE on July 23 were ordered to stay in the area.[8] The speed of the US response indicates readiness to deploy, and an early intention, perhaps even preparedness, to intervene militarily in the conflict.

In the months between Iraq repossessing Kuwait and the beginning of the attacks on Iraq on 17 January 1991, the Security Council passed no fewer than twelve resolutions, eleven of which were under Chapter VII of the UN Charter. Between 1991 and 2002, there were fifty-three resolutions, forty-eight of which were adopted under Chapter VII.

On 6 August 1990, the UN Security Council adopted Resolution 661, which imposed total and comprehensive mandatory economic sanctions on Iraq, calling on all countries to halt all trade and financial dealings with Iraq and Kuwait, with some exceptions—"supplies intended strictly for medical purposes, and, in humanitarian circumstances, foodstuffs" and "payments exclusively for strictly medical or humanitarian purposes and, in humanitarian circumstances, foodstuffs" were to be permitted. All funds were to be denied to Iraq and its assets abroad were frozen. In reality, the sanctions effectively applied to these humanitarian items too because Iraq, which imported most of its food and medicines, was denied access to funds to buy these items.

The declared objective of the sanctions was "to secure compliance of Iraq with paragraph 2 of resolution 660 (1990)" which demanded the immediate and unconditional withdrawal of Iraqi forces from Kuwait and "to restore the authority of the legitimate Government of Kuwait". The real objectives came to be something completely different, as we shall see.

Resolution 661 also set up a committee of the Security Council (known as the Sanctions Committee), representing all member states, to monitor implementation and compliance with the sanctions by the UN members. Resolution 661 affirmed in its Preamble "the inherent right of individual or collective self-defense, in response to the armed attack by Iraq against Kuwait, in accordance with Article 51 of the Charter," but did not provide for any military enforcement of the sanctions, leading to the assumption that it was issued under Article 41, rather than under Article 42.[9] It is worth noting here, that Article 41 of the Charter relates to sanctions imposed by the Council, but not to their enforcement through military force, whose authorization is provided for in Article 42. It might even be possible that the Resolution was drafted intentionally in such a vague and loose way so as to make it subject to different interpretations. Thus when the Resolution stated that foodstuffs were exempted from the sanctions regime "in humanitarian circumstances", the US interpreted it to mean that foodstuffs would be exempted *only* if the Council would determine that its exemption had become detrimental to the livelihood of the population. In the opinion of most legal scholars, this prohibition of foodstuffs is itself in breach of customary international law.[10] It is generally accepted that US officials drafted every Security Resolution imposing and enforcing the sanctions on Iraq for the first several years of the sanctions regime.[11]

On 8 August 1990, the Council of the European Communities passed a regulation, the declared purpose of which was to ensure uniform implementation of the sanctions resolution and regulate which medical products and foodstuffs were to be exempted from the boycott. The Regulation [12] exempted hormones, antibiotics, glands, blood, vaccines, bandages and some pharmaceutical products, but did not exempt any surgical instruments and equipment, nor anesthetics, disinfectants and other basic medical supplies. The consequences of such resolutions and regulations had a devastating effect on the people of Iraq.

It could be easily seen that these actions and other matters relating to the lack of attention by the UNSC to the issue of human rights is what prompted the Centre for Economic and Social Rights (CESR) to accuse the UNSC of "failing to acknowledge its own legal responsibility to protect the rights of Iraqi civilians suffering under sanctions". The CESR also pointed out that "the Security Council has not created a commission or devoted funding to monitor the human rights impact of sanctions, instead occasionally taking note of reports by other UN bodies and independent research groups."[13]

Regardless of what explanations and justifications were given for the military assault on Iraq in January 1991, in reality, the destruction began on 6 August 1990, the day the Security Council adopted resolution 661 which imposed the most brutal total blockade against Iraq. Never before has a state been subjected to such collective measures, a blockade, not dissimilar to the sieges of the Middle Ages, which prevented everything from going in or out of the country.

Planned Incremental Destruction:
Dividing the Sanctions Regime into Distinctive Phases

Because of the changing context of US policy towards Iraq, it seems most logical in our opinion to separate the sanctions regime into more than one phase. The primary reason for this separation of the sanctions is that the stated primary objective of the sanctions before the military attacks (the unconditional withdrawal of Iraqi forces from Kuwait), had nothing at all to do with the new objectives of the sanctions imposed after the end of military attacks (the removal of Iraq's WMDs), let alone with what followed those two objectives—regime change. These phases can be outlined as follows:

1. The first phase, which began on 2 August 1990 and ended on 15 January 1991: the pre-attack sanctions;
2. The second phase, which followed the military attacks, began on 3 April 1991, seeking to achieve compliance with Security Council Res. 687: the post-attack sanctions;
3. The shift to 'smart sanctions' through the Oil-for-Food program whose aim was to deflect criticism of the sanctions regime, while maintaining it;
4. The continuing imposition of partial sanctions after the occupation through maintaining Iraq under Chapter VII of the Charter.

Phase One: Sanctions Preceding the 1991 Attack

In the months following Iraq's invasion and annexation of Kuwait in August 1990, the publicly declared approach of the United States was to endorse Kuwait's right of self-defense, fully restore the sovereign rights of Kuwait, and to make Iraq pay the costs of the harm inflicted, through a combination of diplomacy and sanctions.[14]

Even though the Security Council clearly stated in Resolution 661 that the sanctions were imposed in order to effect the withdrawal of Iraq from Kuwait and, as in Resolution 660, called "upon Iraq and Kuwait to begin immediately intensive negotiations for the resolution of their differences and supports all efforts in this regard", the US and UK thwarted all attempts at finding a negotiated solution. It was quite evident that the US was not genuinely seeking a diplomatic resolution of the dispute. It was quite evident to all that Iraq would respond negatively to the US's unconditional and rigid terms for withdrawal, and the US would have therefore knowingly been setting the stage for war. Even Javier Perez de Cuellar, the then UN Secretary-General, was of the opinion that a more flexible approach might have achieved the stated UN goals without war. But it soon became very clear that the US was moving towards a military solution that would eliminate Iraq as a regional power and as a potential threat to Israel.[15]

All the Iraqi proposals for a negotiated solution to the crisis were rejected by the US and UK, for whom "the nightmare was an Iraqi partial withdrawal, which would have flung the coalition into disarray and delayed the military campaign, perhaps indefinitely".[16] The Presidential spokesman, Marlin Fitzwater, issued a statement at the White House on 4 August, in which he said: "As we have stated before, all U.S. options are under consideration." [17]

On 8 August 1990, and several hours before President Bush delivered his televised address announcing the troop build-up in Saudi Arabia, the US Ambassador to NATO, William H. Taft 4th, informed the North Atlantic Council of Washington's plans and emphasized the importance of a multinational military response to the Iraqi challenge.[18] Even the headlines of *The New York Times* articles changed from 'The Iraqi Invasion' to 'Confrontation in the Gulf'.

In an address to the Los Angeles World Affairs Council on 5 November 1990, Secretary of State James Baker said:

> In the 1930s, the aggressors were appeased. In 1990, the President has made our position plain: This aggression will not be appeased.... We must be clear about our military mission. Our military objectives are to deter an Iraqi attack on Saudi Arabia, protect American lives, and to ensure the effective implementation of the Security Council resolutions. Without such forces, Iraq's neighbors would be subject to attack if they tried to enforce economic sanctions. Our military forces are also there to provide an effective and decisive military response should the situation warrant it.[19]

During the Iran-Iraq war, Jordan had developed extremely good relations with Iraq and became almost fully dependent on trade with Iraq. Iraq was forced by the attacks on its ports to become dependent on Jordan by receiving most of its imports through the Port of Aqaba, in the development of which Iraq had also invested heavily. In order to thwart any attempt by Iraq to evade the effects of sanctions through the Port of Aqaba, and probably in preparation for the coming attacks, President Bush took unilateral measures on 12 August 1990, without any UN mandate, and installed a naval 'interdiction' of all ships going to Iraq or Kuwait.[20]

Here is how *The New York Times* explained the issue:

> The extent of the blockade, which the Administration calls an "interdiction," remained unclear.

> In a briefing for reporters at Kennebunkport, Marlin Fitzwater, the White House spokesman, said that even food and medicines were covered by the quarantine, at least until the Administration was convinced that an exception for materials in those categories was justified on humanitarian grounds. At this point, he said of the embargo, "the President's guidance is the operating one: 'everything.' " [21]

This so-called interdiction was criticised by the UN Secretary General as well as by several members of the UN because in their opinions the sanctions were not given time to show their effectiveness and this interdiction was in reality a 'blockade' under Article 42 of the Charter, which only the Security Council could authorize.

The blockade took effect on 16 August when the Deputy Permanent Representative of the United States to the United Nations notified the Security Council that "military forces of the United States, at the request of the Government of Kuwait, have joined the Government of Kuwait in taking actions to intercept vessels seeking to engage in trade with Iraq or Kuwait...." that "these actions are being taken by the United States in the exercise of the inherent right of individual and collective self-defense...." and that "the military forces of the United States will use force only if necessary and then only in a manner proportionate to prevent vessels from violating such trade sanctions contained in resolution 661." [22]

President Bush also announced a "burden sharing" program whose aim was "to help pay for keeping scores of thousands of American soldiers in the Saudi desert" and to "aid countries that are suffering financially from the economic sanctions because they are losing trade with Iraq, income associated with Iraqi oil exports, or the incomes of their citizens who normally work in Iraq." [23] All oil producing Gulf countries participated in financing this program, as well as Japan, Germany, France and Britain among others. Aid was provided to Egypt and to Turkey, Jordan, Morocco, India, Bangladesh, the Philippines and countries in Eastern Europe. In the joint statement after their summit in Helsinki on 9 September 1990, Presidents Bush and Gorbachev supported the idea of subjecting any food imports to strict monitoring to allegedly ensure that food reaches those for whom it was intended. [24]

Right from the beginning of the crisis, President Bush and his aides, especially Dick Cheney and Brent Scowcroft, began phoning both Western and Arab leaders concerning the situation in the Gulf. As Secretary of State James Baker put it:

If we could get a broad-based international coalition,
it would be Saddam Hussein against the international
community, not a cowboy action by the United States.[25]

President Bush sent his Foreign Minister, James Baker, to each
of the fourteen member states of the UN Security Council to "lay the
foundation" for possible military action against Iraq. In the case of
Finland, the Finnish President Mauno Koivisto had already promised
President Bush during the OECD summit in Paris in November 1990 that
Finland would vote for the resolution.[26] In Yemen, Baker warned Yemen's
President Ali Abdullah Saleh he was risking $70 million in annual US aid by
refusing to cooperate with the United States in the Security Council. But
in a press conference after the meeting, Saleh delivered a resounding no
to the resolution.[27] After its vote, Yemen not only lost that aid, but also
had problems with the World Bank and the IMF; and 800,000 Yemeni
workers were expelled from Saudi Arabia.[28] Baker toured seven countries
on 3 November 1990 to acquire their support for the US plan, and on
November 28 he met with representatives of China, Cuba and the Soviet
Union at the UN.

In two memos dated 10 November 1990, Baker briefed President
Bush on his meetings with British Prime Minister, Margaret Thatcher, and
her Foreign Minister, Douglas Hurd, and with President Francois Mitterand
and his Foreign Secretary, Roland Dumas. In both cases the leaders were
in agreement with Bush's planned Security Council Resolution, though
Thatcher was apparently skeptical of the need for such a resolution.[29]

Resolution 678 (1990) was adopted through a campaign of
bribery, coercion, blackmail and threats. Opposition in the Middle East
to the use of force was wiped out through certain "incentives". Egypt
was bribed with 14 billion dollars in "debt forgiveness". Syria was given
a free hand in Lebanon. Iran was bribed by allowing the World Bank to
approve a loan of 250 million dollars. Bribing the Soviet Union was of
utmost important, and that was achieved through Saudi Arabia whose
foreign minister offered Gorbachev a billion dollars in aid, followed by
3 billion dollars once he agreed to the Resolution.[30] China's incentive
was the ending of the international boycott following its crushing of the
Tiananmen Square protests.

The votes of the non-permanent members of the Security
Council were crucial. Zaire was offered undisclosed "debt forgiveness"
and military equipment in return for controlling the Security Council
when the attack was under way. Hence, as the rotating president of the
council, it refused requests from Cuba, Yemen and India to convene an
emergency meeting of the council, even though it had no authority to
refuse them under the UN Charter.[31]

Resolution 678 takes on an added importance when we look at how it conforms to the UN Charter. Article 27 of the Charter requires that decisions on non-procedural matters receive the concurring votes of the permanent members. In the case of Resolution 678, China (a permanent member) abstained, which means that it did not give an affirmative concurring vote to the resolution. This can only mean that Resolution 678 did not receive the necessary concurring votes for its adoption in accordance with Article 27, and therefore any action based on this resolution is a violation of the Charter. We do not subscribe to the belief among many international lawyers that the Security Council can amend the UN Charter through idiosyncratic interpretation.

Was there a Real Chance for Peace Prior to the 1991 "Allied" Attack?

In his first months in office, President Bush had ordered a review of national security policy, which concluded: "In cases where the U.S. confronts much weaker enemies, our challenge will be not simply to defeat them, but to defeat them decisively and rapidly. For small countries hostile to us, bleeding our forces in protracted or indecisive conflict or embarrassing us by inflicting damage on some conspicuous element of our forces may be victory enough, and could undercut political support for U.S. efforts against them." [32]

On 14 January 1991, France and three Arab countries, Yemen, Algeria and Libya, issued last minute appeals urging President Saddam Hussein to announce Iraq's withdrawal from Kuwait to avoid a war with the US and its allies. In return for such a commitment to withdraw, the appeals wanted the UN Security Council to promise Iraq it would not be attacked and to mount a new drive to resolve the dispute over Palestine between Israel and its Arab neighbors. But a hostile American stance ruled out any chance of the Security Council agreeing to the French plan. Thomas R. Pickering, the US representative, said he did not expect the Security Council to back the French plan, adding: "We do not believe it is an appropriate time or appropriate circumstances for such a statement."[33]

Sanctions Indicate Pre-planning for an Attack on Iraq

The US had ten years earlier established twenty fully operative air bases in existing airfields in Saudi Arabia for the Rapid Deployment Force. Warplanes from all over the world were sent to these bases. US warships used nine naval ports prepared for them. These sophisticated facilities with the most advanced equipment allowed the US to launch the kind of massive attack that it could not have launched elsewhere.[34]

According to the Pentagon, the plan for Operation Desert Storm "envisioned opening the war with a focused, intense air campaign" involving "attacks into Iraq's heartland and against Iraqi forces in the field." The attacks were planned so as to "paralyze the Iraqi leadership's ability to command and control the operations of its forces both offensively and defensively, to destroy Iraqi capability to threaten the security and stability of the region, to render Iraqi forces in the [Kuwait theatre of operations] ineffective, and to minimize the loss of life".[35]

In an interview in the *Washington Post* on 16 September 1990, Air Force Chief of Staff General Michael J. Dugan presented plans for the use of "unlimited air power which could not only destroy Saddam Hussein and his family, but every target in Iraq which the military would find necessary in order to win the war in a short time." Dugan stated that it was not enough to attack Iraqi air defenses, air fields and warplanes, intermediate range missile sites including Scud ground-to-ground missiles, communications and command centers, chemical, nuclear and ammunition plants, and Iraqi armor formations, but that Iraqi power systems, roads, railroads, and perhaps domestic petroleum production facilities should also be targeted.[36] That, we submit, is precisely what happened in the attack that followed.

Washington Post reporter Barton Gellman interviewed several of the war's top planners and carried out extensive research into how targets were determined. On 23 June 1991, he wrote the following:

> Planners now say their intent was to destroy or damage valuable facilities that Baghdad could not repair without foreign assistance. Many of the targets in Iraq's Mesopotamian heartland, the list of which grew from about 400 to more than 700 in the course of the war, were chosen only secondarily to contribute to the military defeat of Baghdad's occupation army in Kuwait. Military planners hoped the bombing would amplify the economic and psychological impact of international sanctions on Iraqi society, and thereby compel President Saddam Hussein to withdraw Iraqi forces from Kuwait without a ground war. They also hoped to incite Iraqi citizens to rise against the Iraqi leader... Because of these goals, damage to civilian structures and interests, invariably described by briefers during the war as "collateral" and unintended, was sometimes neither.[37]

A Planning officer interviewed by Gellman said:

> People say, "You didn't recognize that it was going to
> have an effect on water and sewage. Well, what were we
> trying to do with [United Nations-approved economic]
> sanctions—help out the Iraqi people? No. What we
> were doing with the attacks on the infrastructure was
> to accelerate the effect of sanctions.[38]

Col. John A. Warden III, deputy director of strategy, doctrine and plans for the Air Force, agreed that one purpose of destroying Iraq's electrical grid was that "you have imposed a long-term problem on the leadership that it has to deal with sometime." Saddam Hussein cannot restore his own electricity," Warden said. "He needs help. If there are political objectives that the UN coalition has, it can say, 'Saddam, when you agree to do these things, we will allow people to come in and fix your electricity.' It gives us long-term leverage.[39]

By using bribes, threats and intimidation against member states of the UN and the Security Council to force them to support aggression against Iraq, President Bush had knowingly violated not only the UN Charter but also the US Constitution and Federal law.[40]

Operation Desert Storm:
Extensive Unnecessary Damages Indicate Intent to Destroy Iraq

US forces began an air bombardment of Iraq and Kuwait on 17 January 1991, and between 24 and 27 February 1991 a land offensive drove Iraqi forces out of Kuwait. In this whole operation, the UN was a bystander, watching the US-led coalition armies commit war crimes and crimes against humanity against a defenseless nation.[41]

Altogether, more than 120,000 sorties were flown by coalition air forces, at an average of once every 30 seconds, delivering more than 88,500 tons of explosives, which exceeded the combined allied air offensive of WWII. More than 35,000 combat sorties were flown against targets in the Kuwait-Iraq military theater, while approximately 32,200 attack missions were executed against targets in "Iraq's heartland." Nearly 60 percent of the sorties were carried out by the US Air Force. Of the total number of US air strikes, 23 percent were conducted by aircraft from the US Navy and the US Marines.[42]

B-52s dropped about 30% of the total tonnage of bombs and were used against chemical and industrial storage areas, airfields, troop encampments, storage sites, and they were apparently used against large populated areas in Basrah. These huge bombers were used from the first night of the war to the last. Flying at about 12000 meters and dropping 40–60 bombs each weighing 250 or 350 kilograms, the only function they could have was to carpet bomb entire areas.

The Gulf War of 1991 was the first opportunity for the US and British forces to test their depleted uranium (DU) weapons in combat conditions. It has been reported that the US is known to have fired 14,000 DU shells and 940,000 rounds from airplanes targeting tanks. ... a massive 564,000 pounds of depleted uranium vaporized or was left unexploded. "70% of the shell is vaporized into tiny particles and can be carried down wind for many miles. ... "Iraqis have since extremely abnormal rates of cancer, birth defects, and miscarriages ... particularly around Basrah." [43]

It is widely accepted that US forces used FAEs (Fuel-air Explosive) against Iraqi troops. The *Washington Post* reported on 3 February 1991, "All of the frontline Iraqi troops have been subjected to extensive bombardment, including many detonations of 10,000 pound BLU-82 bombs, containing fuel-air explosives".[44] Eleven of these BLU-82 bombs were used between 7 February 1991 and the commencement of ground hostilities.[45]

In spite of the fact that their use is illegal under international law because of their indiscriminate nature, the US used cluster bombs. Human Rights Watch has calculated that a typical B-52 dropping a full load of 45 cluster bombs, each containing 650 sub munitions, could produce an average of 1,700 unexploded sub munitions, even assuming a low "dud" rate of 5 percent.[46] Cluster bombs and DU rounds were used on the notorious 'Highway of Death' - the road from Kuwait to Basrah in southern Iraq where a 12-kilometer long convoy of fleeing soldiers, civilians, and foreign workers were mercilessly bombed by allied forces. The US army estimated that 25,000 died in these highway attacks.[47]

The most serious report was that of the award-winning Canadian journalist, William Thomas, who reported that a nuclear weapon was detonated 11 miles east of Basrah sometime between 2 and 5 February.[48] The unprecedented attack as summarized above resulted in the following damage and losses:

- 85% of all power generation was destroyed which left only two of Iraq's 20 electric generation plants functioning, generating less than 4% of the pre-war output of 9,000 megawatts.[49]
- Almost half of Iraq's 900,000 telephone lines had been destroyed, with 14 central exchanges irreparably damaged and 13 more put out of service indefinitely.[50]
- Iraq's eight major multipurpose dams were repeatedly hit and heavily damaged.[51]
- Four of Iraq's seven major water pumping stations were destroyed, and 31 municipal water and sewage facilities were hit with bombs and missiles, 20 in Baghdad alone.[52]
- The bombing targets included 139 bridges, 26 in Basrah alone.[53]

- Iraq's baby milk powder factory at Abu Ghraib, the only such factory in the whole region, was attacked three times: on 20, 21 and 22 January 1991.
- Grain silos and farms were attacked across the country, decimating over 30% of the sheep and cattle herds, and destroying the country's poultry production.[54]
- The US bombed 28 civilian hospitals and 52 community health centers.[55]
- A major hypodermic syringe facility in Hilla was destroyed by laser-guided rockets.[56]
- 676 schools were attacked, completely destroying 38 of them, 8 of which were university facilities.[57]
- In Baghdad alone 25 mosques were bombed with a further 31 mosques elsewhere in the country.[58]
- The 900-year-old Church of St. Thomas in Mosul, which is more than 1,600 kilometers from Kuwait, was destroyed as was the old Al-Mustansiriya School, one of the oldest Islamic schools in Iraq.[59]
- The industry sector was specifically targeted, damaging 7 textile factories, 5 engineering plants, 5 construction facilities, 4 car assembly plants, 3 chlorine plants, a major ammonia export facility, 16 chemical, petrochemical and phosphate plants;[60]
- 11 oil refineries, 5 oil pipelines and production facilities were attacked, sinking 3 oil tankers and setting 3 others on fire.[61]

The real purpose of the unprecedented campaign can be seen from US media and official reports some of which are summarized below.

The whole of Basrah was bombed mercilessly. Baghdad suffered no less treatment. The *Los Angeles Times* reported on 5 February 1991:[62]

> The massive allied bombardment of the Iraqi city of Basra has demolished every communications center in that strategic southern city, all major oil refineries, most government buildings, some civilian neighborhoods and hundreds of ammunition depots and food warehouses, according to eyewitnesses.... In the besieged capital of Baghdad, witnesses say, air strikes continue to hit military targets, often for the second and third time, smashing key installations, destroying warehouses full of everything from medicine to the machinery of war—but also leveling some entire city blocks in civilian neighborhoods.

Bernard Debusmann of Reuters reported, "Of at least half a dozen burned or damaged vehicles on the desert highway, only one vehicle bombed was clearly a military vehicle... local residents told me the bombing of the road was frequent, and the targets almost always seemed to be civilian trucks or private cars.[63]

General McPeak told *Defense Week*, "The targets we are going after are widespread. They are brigades, and divisions and battalions on the battlefield. It's a rather low-density target. So to spread the bombs – carpet-bombing is not my favorite expression—is proportionate to the target. Now is it a terrible thing? Yes. Does it kill people? Yes."[64]

Testifying before the Commission of Inquiry (chaired by Ramsey Clark) in Montreal on 16 November 1992, journalist Paul William Roberts, who travelled with Bedouin tribes in Iraq during the bombing, said:

> Three waves of bombings a night. And I experienced bombing in Cambodia, but this was nothing like that... After 20 minutes of the carpet-bombing there would be silence and you would hear a screaming of children and people, and then the wounded would be dragged out. I found myself with everyone else trying to treat injuries, but the state of people generally was one of pure shock. They were walking around like zombies, and I was too, because the disorientating effects of the blasts themselves formed a psychological warfare if you like... but if you've been kept awake every night for the past 10 days as everyone had, you begin to lose your perspective on reality.[65]

Perhaps one of the war's most brutal attacks took place in Baghdad. In the early hours of 14 February 1991 precision bombs dropped by US planes hit the Amiriya civilian shelter. At that time Baghdad was without electricity and the shelter was relying on its emergency generator. The first bomb hit the ventilation shaft and started fires inside. The attack, as intended in the design, caused the doors of the shelter to close immediately. While the firemen were trying desperately to unlock the doors and put out the fires, the second precision attack took place. This time it was more hideous and devastating. The bombs used were special penetrating bombs very probably unknown to the Finnish designer of the shelters.

The bombs penetrated the meter-deep layer of earth, passed through one meter of reinforced concrete slab, through the top floor and through another meter of reinforced concrete floor slab to the lower floor. The impact of the bomb caused all the water, fuel tanks and boiler to explode, filling the lower floor with a mixture of boiling water and fuel to a depth of two meters. All the medical staff were killed instantly and the emergency power supply was destroyed, rendering all life-supporting systems inoperative. On the top floor the bomb generated a tremendous heat estimated to have reached some 4000 degrees. The people were incinerated. At the time of the attack there were over 1500 civilians in the shelter. Out of those people only 11 persons are known to have survived after suffering different degrees of wounds, burns and psychological trauma. Whole families were wiped out, as could be seen afterwards from their locked houses in Amiriya. The bodies of the medical staff were found floating in the water-fuel mixture of the lower floor. The caretakers of the shelter claim that the black, burnt walls still have human skin and flesh stuck to them.[66]

Iraq lost between 125,000 and 150,000 soldiers. The US has said it lost 148 in combat, and of those, 37 were caused by friendly fire.[67] 42 Iraqi divisions were either destroyed or rendered combat ineffective, Iraq's entire navy was sunk, an estimated 50% of the combat aircraft were destroyed or fled to Iran, more than 82,000 soldiers were captured—all in 43 days of offensive operations and with minimal coalition casualties.[68] The Los *Angeles Times* quoted one "knowledgeable source" as having said:

> We probably killed more than 100,000 people without ever occupying the territory. We didn't take the lines and move forward. We passed over them day after day, and that's a different kind of war historically than we've ever fought.[69]

On 18 January 1991, General Schwarzkopf said at a briefing in Riyadh: "I'm never going to get into the body count business".[70] When the war ended, General Colin Powell was ordered by the White House to make an estimate of the number of Iraqi deaths. Powell told reporters that he had "no estimate whatsoever" of how many Iraqi soldiers were killed, adding: "I know there's a great interest in the subject. I don't have a clue and I don't really plan to undertake any real effort to find out".[71]

Lieutenant General William Pagonis is reported by Clark as having said: "This is the first war in modern times where every screwdriver, every nail is accounted for." When it came to human beings, he said: "I don't think anybody is going to be able to come up with an accurate account for the Iraqi dead".[72]

European estimates of military deaths were always higher than those of the US. This is perhaps because there is less censorship in Europe as compared to the media in the US. According to the *London Times* of

3 March 1991, allied intelligence put the number of Iraqi soldiers killed at 200,000. The *Times* reported "Thousands of troops may be buried in bunkers and trenches". A French military intelligence source gave the *Nouvelle Observateur* the same figure.[73]

At the March-April European Parliament hearings at the end of the Gulf War, Mike Erlich, member of the Military Counseling Network, described the execution of defeated soldiers: "Hundreds, possibly thousands of Iraqi soldiers began walking toward the U.S. position unarmed, with their arms raised in an attempt to surrender. However, the orders for this unit were not to take any prisoners ... the commander of the unit began firing. At this point, everybody in the unit began shooting. Quite simply it was a slaughter."[74]

On Saturday morning, 16 Feb 1991, and in the peak of the attacks, a seven-person joint WHO/UNICEF mission entered Iraq through the Iranian border, bringing with it a 12-truck convoy carrying 54 tons of basic medical and health supplies. The Mission's findings were submitted in a report, which was distributed by the Secretary General of the UN to all UN members.[75]

The mission's mandate was "to deliver a shipment of emergency medical supplies to assist in the care of children and mothers, and to ascertain essential health needs", and to look at immediate needs for further medical supplies for protection against communicable diseases; at the status of supplies and sanitation; and at other health needs for children and mothers.

Some of the mission findings are summarized as:

- Normal life has come almost to a halt.[76]
- Fear of waterborne epidemics that could soon result from increasingly widespread public use of the Tigris River and other heavily polluted bodies of water for drinking.[77]
- The stress and anxiety caused by the bombing had resulted in breastfeeding failure.[78] The high incidence of diarrhea and upper respiratory tract infections, coupled with food shortages, would certainly result in outright malnutrition, especially among one-to-three-year-olds.[79]
- A lack of transport tied to the non-availability of fuel was leading to professional and paramedical staff failing to come to work.[80]
- Laboratory services in Baghdad health centers including those for pregnant women such as blood sugar and albumin, as well as hemoglobin tests, were closed.[81]
- Up to 20 children in one health center who were sent away for lack of vaccines. Booster doses and the third shots of DPT and polio had been stopped in order to conserve supplies.[82]

- The conditions of contaminated main water supply and untreated, backed-up sewage had set the stage for the onset of some of the communicable diseases as typhoid, meningitis, measles, poliomyelitis, hepatitis A, and malaria in epidemic proportions.[83]
- All significant electrical power generating plants in Iraq had been destroyed. This in a country where over 95 percent of the water was the product of river water treatment provided by seven electro mechanical plants, all of which operated with electric power and required chemicals for treatment.[84]

After the 1991 Attack: Evaluating the Damage

Before evaluating the damage caused by the sanctions, it would perhaps be useful to give a summarized list of the scale of damage inflicted on Iraq (see Table 5.1, right).

In March 1991 and after the cessation of military activities, the UN Secretary General dispatched a mission "to assess the humanitarian needs arising in Iraq and Kuwait in the immediate post-crisis environment". The mission was led by Under Secretary General Martti Ahtisaari and comprised representatives of UN agencies and programs. The mission submitted its report, which came to be known as the 'Ahtisaari Report' on 20 March 1991, and was distributed to Security Council members.[86] That was the first mission to visit Iraq and see and evaluate the scale of destruction and the catastrophe that had befallen Iraq.

Here are some extracts from the report following the original numbering:

> 8. ... The recent conflict has wrought near-apocalyptic results upon the economic infrastructure of what had been, until January 1991, a rather highly urbanized and mechanized society. ... Iraq has, for some time to come, been relegated to a pre-industrial age, but with all the disabilities of post-industrial dependency on an intensive use of energy and technology.
> 9. ... virtually all previously viable sources of fuel and power are now ... defunct.
> 11. ... Sanctions ... had already adversely affected the country's ability to feed its people.
> 12. ... Distribution of powdered milk, for instance, is now reserved exclusively for sick children on medical prescription.
> 13. ... The sole laboratory producing veterinary vaccines was destroyed during the conflict, as inspected by the mission.

Table 5.1:
Establishments and facilities damaged during the raids on Iraq in 1991[85]

Sector	Number of targets
Higher education (universities, laboratories, student dormitories)	39
Judicial and legal institutions	76
Social care (orphanages, homes for the elderly, correctional institutions)	44
Conscription offices and military hospitals	76
Financial and banking services	272
Union and party offices	117
Mayoralty establishments	23
Military industry establishments	32
Oil (oil wells, refineries, pumping and extraction stations)	145
Planning council centers	19
Education (schools and school services)	3968
Health (hospitals, stores, peoples' clinics)	421
Transport and communication (transmission stations, exchanges, roads, flight, railroads)	475
Housing and construction (buildings, bridges, housing complexes)	260
Commerce (silos, central markets, distribution centers)	251
Religious places (mosques, churches)	159
Industry and mining (factories, mines, stores)	122
Agriculture and irrigation (dams, pumping stations, agricultural services)	205
Culture and information (TV stations, radio stations, museums, antiquities)	90
Public services (sewage stations, municipalities, registration offices, shelters)	833

18. ... sanctions in respect of food supplies should be immediately removed as should those relating to the import of agricultural equipment and supplies[29].

... approximately 9,000 homes were destroyed or damaged beyond repair during the hostilities, of which 2,500 were in Baghdad and 1,900 were in Basrah. This has created a new homeless potential total of 72,000 persons.

Sadruddin Aga Khan, who led the second UN mission to Iraq 29 June-13 July 1991, stated in the summary of the main findings of his 59-page report submitted to the Secretary General the following:

16. ... damage to water-treatment plants and the inability to obtain needed spare parts have cut off an estimated 2.5 million Iraqis from the government system they relied upon before the war.[87]

17. ... Hospitals and public health centers are severely affected by lack of electricity, water, medicines, medical, surgical, dental and laboratory equipment, and the fleet of vehicles that once assured the effectiveness of the health services has been reduced to a few units.[88]

18. ... the position of food supply is deteriorating rapidly in virtually all parts of the country. .... prices show tremendous levels of inflation.[89]

20. Iraq's capacity of power generation had been reduced to a negligible level.[90]

21. ... at least 400,000 of the original 900,000 telephone lines were damaged beyond repair, while additional ones were partly damaged. The main microwave links connecting most of the cities were also damaged.[91]

The report details its findings and recommendations for each sector and ends with concluding remarks which start with the following:

130. None of us on the mission team could overlook a glaring paradox: at a time when the international community is beset with disasters of daunting dimensions around the globe, we continue to appeal to the same donors to fund emergency programs in Iraq that the country could pay for itself. With considerable oil reserves in the ground, Iraq should not have to

compete for scarce aid funds with a famine-ravaged
Horn of Africa, with a cyclone-hit Bangladesh.[92]

In December 1991, the UNICEF estimated that 87,000 children alone
would have died by the war's anniversary.[93]

Phase Two: New Sanctions, New Pretexts

Following the ceasefire, the Security Council on 2 March 1991
adopted Resolution 686, whose purpose was to bring hostilities to an
end, while continuing the sanctions and imposing at the same time
several obligations that Iraq was required to fulfill immediately.[94] On
3 March, and in an attempt to deny the US and its allies any excuse to
inflict further harm on the Iraqi population, Iraq agreed to comply with
the obligations stated in the Resolution which included: rescission of the
annexation of Kuwait; acceptance of liability for loss, injury, and damage
resulting from invasion and occupation of Kuwait; release of all detainees
and prisoners of war, as well as return of the remains of those deceased;
return of Kuwaiti property; an end to all hostile and provocative acts; and
assistance in identifying the location of mines and chemical and biological
weapons in Kuwait and parts of Iraq occupied by the coalition. Iraq also
expressed its hope that the Security Council would ensure the prompt
withdrawal of all coalition forces from Iraqi territory, and a complete end
of the blockade.[95]

On 3 April 1991, the Security Council adopted Resolution 687,
which came to be known as the "mother of all Resolutions", being the
most complex of all the Resolutions issued against Iraq, and set the stage
for the indefinite continuation of sanctions against Iraq as was the original
intention.

Resolution 687 was divided into nine parts, addressing such
issues as:

1. respecting and guaranteeing the inviolability of the international
   boundary and the allocation of islands;
2. deployment of a UN observer unit to monitor the 15 kilometer
   demilitarized zone along the border, establishing the conditions
   for the departure of coalition forces from Iraq;
3. the permanent elimination of Iraq's weapons of mass
   destruction, its ballistic missiles with a range of over 150
   kilometers, and its nuclear weapon capability;
4. the return of all Kuwaiti property seized by Iraq;
5. establishing Iraq's liability for losses, damages, and injuries, and
   establishing a UN Compensation Fund and a UN Compensation

Commission to provide a settlement procedure to compensate claimants, such fund to be financed with a portion of the value of the exports of petroleum and petroleum products from Iraq not to exceed a figure to be suggested to the Council by the Secretary-General;

6. lifting the embargo on imports of foodstuffs and, with the approval of the Sanctions Committee, allowing limited imports into Iraq of materials and supplies for essential civilian needs, as recommended by the Secretary General's fact-finding mission and already endorsed by the Sanctions Committee.[96]

It then concluded that upon Iraq's acceptance of these provisions, a formal-cease fire would be effective.

Other than the exemption of foodstuffs, and the exceptions to be approved by the Sanctions Committee for supplies and materials essential to civilian needs, the ban on imports into Iraq that had been imposed under Resolution 661 was to remain in full force and effect. The ban on exports from Iraq under that Resolution also remained in full force and effect, pending the establishment of an oil export program, with interim exceptions to be approved by the Sanctions Committee when required, to enable Iraq to pay for imports essential to its civilian needs.

Even though the resolution stated that the sanctions could be lifted or "reduced" on the recommendation of the Security Council "in the light of the policies and practices" of Iraq, it soon became clear that the US and UK were going to maintain the sanctions using their veto-power and overwhelming military force.

The Invisible Weapon of Mass Destruction:
Sanctions and the Massive Civilian Death Toll

Perhaps the most sinister part of all this is that the world did not realize that the war had not ended; it had only taken another form. This time the weapon was the blockade, which deprived the people of Iraq of access to food, medicine and the basic needs of a normal life.

In 2007, the former UN director of UNSCOM, Rolf Ekeus, revealed to journalist Andrew Cockburn that in 1997, the US acted to prevent him from certifying that Iraq had complied with UN resolutions regarding its WMD's. Ekeus told Cockburn that in March 1997, "I was getting close to certifying that Iraq was in compliance with [UN] Resolution 687".[97]   To prevent this from happening, Secretary of State, Madeleine Albright, told an audience at Georgetown University on 26 March 1997: "We do not agree with the nations who argue that if Iraq complies with its obligations concerning weapons of mass destruction, sanctions should be lifted," adding that "a change in Iraq's government could lead to a change in US policy." For Ekeus, the message was clear: "I knew that Saddam would now feel that there was no point in his cooperating with us, and that was the intent of her speech." The next day Ekeus received an angry call from Tariq Aziz, Iraq's deputy prime minister: "He wanted to know why Iraq should work with us anymore." Thus the US ensured the continuation of sanctions, even though it had known since August 1995, when Hussein Kamel defected to Jordan, that Iraq had destroyed all its WMDs years earlier.[98]

The deteriorating nutritional and health conditions and the fear of further worsening of the situation of the Iraqi population was putting pressure on the Council members, including the US, to allow Iraq to export limited quantities of oil to finance the costs of foodstuffs, medicines, and materials and supplies required for essential civilian needs. On 15 August 1991, the Security Council adopted Resolution 706, which allowed Iraq to export oil for a period of six months to produce a sum not to exceed $1.6 billion, to be paid into an escrow account to be established by the United Nations to finance the purchase and supervised distribution of humanitarian goods. The costs of other UN operations, with 30% allocated for the UN Compensation Fund, were also to be financed from this sum. On 19 September 1991, the Security Council adopted Resolution 712 containing the guidelines and procedures proposed by the Secretary General, and also approved the basic structure for implementing Resolution 706.[99] Discussions between the UN and Iraq resumed in February 1996, resulting ultimately in the signing on 20 May 1996 of a Memorandum of Understanding.[100]

No sooner had the details of the procedures been negotiated and accepted than the US representative in the Sanctions Committee of the Security Council vetoed the adoption of these procedures. The New York Times reported on 1 August 1996 that the chairman of the sanctions committee, Germany's Tono Eitel, described himself as "troubled and very sad" over the American action, as the procedures had already been revised to meet earlier American objections. The proposals would have to be renegotiated to meet the new American objections.[101]

Eventually, Iraq accepted the new procedures to implement the Memorandum of Understanding, and the Oil-for-Food Programme started in December 1996, with the first shipments of food arriving in March 1997. Out of the $2 billion expected to be generated over the next six months from the sale of this oil, $1.32 billion would be used to purchase humanitarian supplies, $600 million would go into the UN Compensation Fund, and the rest would go towards the costs of various UN programs relating to Iraq.[102]

The Iraqi government was permitted to purchase only items that were not embargoed under the economic sanctions. Certain items, such as raw foodstuffs, were expedited for immediate shipment, but requests for most items, including such simple things as pencils and folic acid, were reviewed in a process that typically took about six months before shipment was authorized. Items deemed to have any potential application in chemical, biological or nuclear weapons systems development were not available to Iraq, regardless of stated purpose. Pencils were prohibited because they allegedly contained graphite; and medicines for *angina pectoris* were refused sales permit by the UK government on the grounds that they contained nitrates, which could be used in explosives.

Since the approval of the Oil-For-Food Program in 1996, Iraq earned about $57 billion in oil revenues, of which it spent about $23 billion on goods that actually arrived. This makes about $170 per person per year, which is well below the $400 per dog per year which the UN spent on food for dogs used in Iraqi de-mining operations.[103]

Nearly everything needed for Iraq's entire infrastructure—electricity, roads, telephones, water treatment, as well as much of the equipment and supplies related to food and medicine—was subject to Security Council review. This meant that the US and Britain decided alone, without the involvement of any other country on the Council, what goods were allowed, and what goods were blocked or delayed, including hundreds of humanitarian contracts. Among the goods that the US blocked were dialysis equipment, dental equipment, fire-fighting equipment, water tankers, milk and yogurt production equipment and printing equipment for schools. The US even blocked a contract for agricultural-bagging equipment, insisting that the UN first obtain documentation to "confirm that the 'manual' placement of bags around filling spouts is indeed a person placing the bag on the spout."[104]

Dual-use goods were the most devious targets of the sanctions. The problem was that many of the goods necessary for a country to simply function could easily be considered dual use. Thus equipment needed to provide electricity, telephone service, transportation, and clean water as well as vehicle tires, respirator masks, bulldozers, and pipes were blocked or delayed at different times on grounds of dual use.[105] (For more on the procedure and delays by the Sanctions Committee see Chapter 8.)

With the increasing suffering of the Iraqi people and open criticism by other members of the Security Council regarding the sanctions, the US put forward a proposal for what it called 'smart sanctions', whose declared objective was to tailor sanctions to affect the military and the political leadership instead of the citizenry. But in reality, nothing would change since everything related to infrastructure was routinely classified as dual use, and thus blocked.[106] In order to get the permanent members of the Security Council to support its proposal, the US announced in June 2001 the lifting of holds on $800 million of contracts, of which $200 million involved business with key Security Council members, followed soon by lifting holds on $80 million of Chinese contracts with Iraq, including some for radio equipment and other goods that had been blocked because of dual-use concerns. When Russia did not go along with the US proposal, it faced US holds on nearly every contract that Iraq had with Russian companies.[107]

In November 2001, the US began lobbying again for a smart-sanctions proposal, now called the Goods Review List (GRL). The Security Council adopted the proposal in May 2002, with Russia's support. The GRL had the effect of lifting $740 million of US holds on Russian contracts blocked as necessary to prevent any military imports.[108] Under the new system, UNMOVIC and the International Atomic Energy Agency make the initial decision about whether an item should appear on the GRL, which included only those materials questionable enough to be passed on to the Security Council.

While researching for this book, the authors noted the amazing lack of UN documents available to the public. It is difficult to comprehend how the UN could have failed to document the effects of sanctions on Iraq and the details of goods allowed or blocked. Of course there is also the possibility that the UK and US did not want such documents to be kept by the UN and have retained them themselves. Most of the UNICEF, WHO, FAO, WFP and other notes that documented the situation in Iraq have been removed from their respective websites. We cannot but join Joy Gordon in her conclusion that what has been hidden are documents that show how the US policy agenda has determined the outcome of humanitarian and security judgments.[109]

Impact of Sanctions on the Destruction of the 80-year-old Infrastructure

As we saw in Chapter 4, the two development plans of the 1970s brought great improvements to the infrastructure in Iraq and Iraqi society became highly dependent on the national electricity grid for most of its basic needs such as telecommunications, industry, agriculture, education, housing, health, water, and sanitation. By 1990 a combination of hydroelectric, thermal, and gas turbine generators provided an installed capacity of 9,500 megawatts (MW).[110] Electrical facilities were directly targeted during the attacks in order to paralyze Iraq by disrupting the electrical generating capacity of the country. This resulted in electricity being available for only a few hours a day, with dire consequences on water quantity and quality, sewage treatment, health facilities, education and overall quality of life for the majority of the population in the center and south of Iraq. The generation capacity in 2002 was only about 4000 MW or 43% of installed capacity. With limited reserves of spare parts and the blocking of imports by the Sanctions Committee, Iraq's ability to repair or replace damaged parts was impeded. Between the adoption of the Oil-for-Food Programme (OFP) in 1996 and the occupation in 2003, only slightly more than $3 billion was approved and funded for rehabilitation of the electrical sector, and only $2 billion worth of parts arrived in Iraq. With the adoption of Security Council Resolution 1409 in 2002, spare parts should have been easier to import. But in reality, some plants waited for parts for over a decade, and in some cases the parts received were the wrong ones.[111] In addition to that, there were delays in Letters of Credit, cancellation of contracts by suppliers, and refusal of technicians to go to Iraq to do the installation and maintenance.[112]

Impact of Sanctions on the Health System Devolved by the Ba'ath

One of the sectors most affected by the power shortages was the health sector, with power cuts occurring several times a day in hospitals, affecting performance. Large quantities of vaccines were destroyed because of inability to provide cold storage for them. Water treatment facilities were also affected, preventing the delivery of clean water to the population and health care facilities.

Although some of these health and water facilities had backup generators, they could only run for several hours per day and they gave out much less power than is required for normal operating conditions—25% for water treatment plants, 50% for sewage pumping stations, and 60%-70% for hospitals.[113]

It was difficult to estimate the real effect of the sanctions, due to four factors clearly outlined by Daponte and Garfield as follows:

- The social disruption that followed the war and the early sanctions have made the Iraqi ability to effectively document mortality and morbidity data limited and inaccurate.
- The effects of sanctions on the Iraqi population may not be direct nor immediate, since they target the capability of the nation to trade, aid, access to goods, and economic activity.
- The chain of events from distal to proximal causes leading to the increase in mortality and morbidity of the Iraqi population as a direct result of the sanctions is not well known. In addition, the effects of resource shortages as a result of the sanctions will be differential based on the educational levels, cultural practices, and resource distribution patterns of the population.
- Sanctions have often been imposed on less developed nations with weak health systems; subsequently the effects of sanctions on health have not been well documented.[114]

With this background in mind, the statistics presented here have been collected from several publications and sources with the aim of giving as clear as possible a view of the effects of sanctions on the health status of the Iraqis from 1990 to 2002.

Primary health care and preventative services essentially ceased, and there was a clear increase in cases of diarrhea, acute respiratory infections, and typhoid in the under 5 population.[115]

The collapse of preventative health services and the consequent increase in communicable diseases was worsened by the interruption in the delivery of essential medical supplies, combined with a 90% drop in imported drugs, affecting the treatment of both acute and chronic illnesses. Prior to the sanctions approximately $360 million in drugs were being imported annually, but that number had dropped by 1996 to $33 million.[116]

Even health care facilities and equipment that were not directly damaged or destroyed during the bombing consequently deteriorated with the lack of maintenance and spare parts. Health care professionals already dealing with a lack of access to drugs, proper facilities and equipment were unable to keep up with new developments in medicine and public health, being prevented by sanctions from even having access to medical and scientific books and journals.

Numerous studies have been conducted on the effects of continuing sanctions on the people of Iraq. Among these were those by the United Nations Children's Fund (UNICEF), World Food Program (WFP), the Food and Agriculture Organization (FAO), the Harvard Study Team and the Centre for Economic and Social Rights in New York. All of those reports and studies have agreed that sanctions have caused severe health and nutritional problems. A survey undertaken by two independent scientists in November 1995 on behalf of the FAO found that "there has been nearly a five-fold increase in mortality among children under the age of five in Baghdad compared to the period prior to the imposition of economic sanctions. The sustained mortality has resulted in *half a million* child deaths related to the war and the sanctions occurring over the past five years."[117] The study concluded. "At this level of malnutrition and excess mortality among children under the age of five, Iraq is increasingly becoming like a concentration camp. The economic pressure exerted on the country by the U.S. and the international community effectively serves as the barbed wire."

The New York Times reported that "As many as 576,000 Iraqi children may have died since the end of the Persian Gulf war because of economic sanctions imposed by the Security Council ... steeply rising malnutrition among the young, suggesting that more children will be at risk in the coming years." [118]

UNICEF concluded in several surveys carried out in 1996-1997 that 32 per cent of children under the age of five, some 960,000 children, were chronically malnourished—a rise of 72 per cent since 1991. Almost one quarter (around 23 per cent) were underweight—twice as high as the levels found in neighboring Jordan or Turkey. All three surveys found that around one quarter of children under the age of five were underweight, with no improvement since the first survey was carried out in 1996. There was little or no improvement in the figures for underweight infants in 1997, with 14.6 per cent of infants underweight in October, compared to 14.7 per cent in April.[119]

Table 5.2 shows the average number of reported deaths among children under five years of age per 100,000, per month.[120] Data from the Iraqi Ministry of Health suggested a rapid worsening of the health conditions of Iraqi children, reflecting the situation of the small portion of the population which continued to rely on public medical care services. Low-weight births, children treated for malnutrition, and the reported number of illnesses which are associated with contaminated water all rose rapidly from 1990 through 1994 and subsequently stabilized at high levels by 1995. Table 5.3 summarizes the finding of the Iraqi Ministry of Health.[121]

Impact of Sanctions on Education/Literacy after Iraq Managed to Eradicate Illiteracy

After the attacks of 1991, UNESCO concluded that: "the education sector experienced a rapid deterioration of educational facilities, a critical shortage of teaching and learning materials, and the loss of qualified teachers (brain drain) due to poor remuneration. Thus, the impressive educational achievements of the past were steadily undermined."[122]

There was a clear imbalance between the substantial population growth and the increasing demand for quality education at all levels, and the development in the education sector. This can be summarized as follows:

- There was a major decline in student per capita spending from $623 in 1989 to $35 in 2003.
- Teacher salaries plummeted from $500 per month to less than $30 per month over the same period with a similar reduction in operations and maintenance costs.
- There was a systematic deterioration and destruction of vital physical infrastructure.
- A wholesale decline in system and administrative delivery took place.
- An overall downgrading of all major aspects of the educational system occurred.[123]

Table 5.2

Average number of reported deaths among children under five years of age per 100,000, per month

Year	1989	1990	1991	1992	1993	1994	1995	1996	1997
Deaths	592	742	2289	3911	4147	4409	4652	4750	4804

Table 5.3

Worsening of the health conditions of Iraqi children

Description	Year								
	1990	1991	1992	1993	1994	1995	1996	1997
Percent Registered Births Under 2.5 Kgs.	4.5	10.8	17.6	19.7	21.1	22.1	22.6	23
(Totals below are in actual figures)								
Children In Treatment Programs for Malnutrition	0	1000	10,600	12,500	13,900	17,900	20,200	20,800
Reported Cases of Cholera	0	0	1217	976	825	1345	1216	831

children aged 6 to 11 were out of school,[124] with a rising number of children begging in the streets or shining shoes or selling paper towels to passing cars in an attempt to earn a living. Repetition rates in the different grades of primary schools reach as high as 22%.[125]

The same decline of primary education was repeated in secondary education too.

Repetition rates were also high, and the shortage of school buildings and the inadequate state of existing buildings were even more acute in secondary than in primary education.[126] The restrictions on exporting up-to-date textbooks and vital teaching materials, language labs, etc. worsened the level of education and frustrated teachers.

The technical/vocational education sector also suffered a setback during the years of sanctions, linked to the decline in economic activity, the falling salaries for teachers and instructors and the difficulties in acquiring materials, teaching aids and spare parts.[127] Enrolment declined dramatically from a peak of 147,942 in 1990 to 65,750 in 2000, a decline of over 55%.[128]

By 1991, Iraq had 19 universities (including 3 in the North), as well as 9 Technical Colleges, and 38 Technical Institutes (including 11 in the North). Major problems that effected higher education institutions and faculty were:

- Insufficient infrastructure and facilities, such as laboratories and libraries.
- Insufficient equipment, for example, in engineering and science faculties, and in technical institutes.
- Lack of channels of communication among faculty both inside Iraq and with foreign scholars.
- Weak relationship between higher education and the labor market.
- Lack of a comprehensive review of the systems of management of higher education, including the adaptation of curricula and course content to the changing economic situation.
- Diminishing state support for students, and other economic constraints, and the need to encourage mobilization of local and private sector resources. [129]

Impact of Sanctions on Water and Sewage Treatment Facilities

In the decades before the sanctions, Iraqis had access to a well-developed sanitation infrastructure. A system of 210 water treatment plants, 1200 mobile plants primarily for rural use, 50 pumping stations and 40,000 kms of pipe guaranteed safe drinking water to residents of

95% of urban areas and 75% of rural areas. But that infrastructure was destroyed by the aerial bombing, decreasing the availability of potable water in the years between 1990 and 2000 from 330 to 150 liters per person/day in Baghdad and from 180 to 65 liters per person/day in rural areas. Attempts to repair the damaged installations, resulted in availability of potable water in 1999 to almost 94% of the pre-1990 level in urban areas but only 45.7% in rural areas.[130]

There were no accurate reports of fecal coliforms and other bacteria, but analysis of samples has shown that water was highly contaminated. In some areas raw, untreated water was added to potable water in order to meet increased demand particularly in the summer. Broken mains and pipes allowed for further water contamination by sewage and accounted for 30-40% of treated water lost.[131] The situation was made worse by the lack of spare parts, operating materials, chemicals, especially chlorine, and by the decrease in the number of employees, which went from 20,000 in 1990 to 11,000 in 2000.

Sewage treatment was equally inadequate and sewage was often poured into rivers without being treated because of lack of spare parts and unreliable electricity supply. It was estimated in 2002 that 500,000 tons of raw sewage were entering the waterways daily for the entire country, 300,000 of this in Baghdad.[132]

Then in 2003, the US launched its campaign of "shock and awe"...

Impact of Sanctions on the Oil Industry:
Running Down Iraq's Economic Lifeline

In 1950 Iraq's oil revenue was just 3% of Iraq's GDP, increasing in 1980 to 56%. But in 1990 the share of oil revenue dropped sharply to 12% percent of GDP and in 1995 further to 4.5%. During the nearly same half century, real per capita GDP (in 1980 prices) increased from $654 in 1950 to $4219 in 1979 as oil revenue rose from a mere $20 million in 1950 to $26.3 billion in 1980. In 1995 it had collapsed to $461 million.[133]

The 1991 attack and the following years of blockade had been so damaging to the oil industry that Iraq was unable to produce enough oil to pay for its Oil-for-Food Programme after it was adopted in 1995. The group of experts dispatched by the UN Secretary General to assess Iraq's capacity to produce enough oil to pay for its food bill reported as follows:

> The group of experts is less optimistic than the Government of Iraq is regarding the Government's capacity to meet the $4 billion target during the period envisaged. Its overall impression is that the oil industry

of Iraq is in a lamentable state and that the developed oilfields have had their productivity seriously reduced, some irreparably, during the past two decades. In its view, the oil processing and treatment facilities, refineries and storage terminals in the country have been severely damaged and continue to deteriorate, and that this deterioration, particularly in the oilfields, will accelerate until significant action is taken to contain and relieve the problems... The two United Nations oil overseers who accompanied the group of experts have also indicated that the Iraqi oil industry is in desperate need of spare parts in order to comply with the provisions of Security Council resolution 1153 (1998).[134]

Although, the Security Council approved later the export of spare parts to the oil industry as recommended by the group of experts, the process met the same obstacles at the hands of the Sanction Committee (see chapter 8) in having some applications on hold indefinitely. Thus on 29 November 2000 the Secretary General had this to say in his report to the Security Council:

I note with concern that the project-based list of phase VIII oil spare parts and equipment, submitted to the Security Council Committee by the Office of the Iraq Programme on 8 August 2000 pursuant to paragraph 18 of Security Council resolution 1284 (1999), has remained on hold in the Security Council Committee despite repeated reminders by the Executive Director of the Iraq Programme.[135]

Needless to say that such mild complaint by the SG was repeated up until the invasion of 2003.

Impact of Sanctions on the Agrarian Sector: Forced Reliance on Imports for All Iraqi Food Needs

The agrarian sector in Iraq witnessed a number of strong measures since the 1970s. These included: land reform, cooperative and collective state farming, central planning and, finally, private ownership. Growing water shortages, especially from the Euphrates, were characteristic of the 1990s. A new estimate based on current population growth indicated that the combined Iraqi water demand on the Tigris and Euphrates in the period after 2020 would range from 70,000 to 90,000

MCM, which could result in a negative balance of 15,000 MCM, mainly on the Euphrates.[136]

In 1999, there were reports of "huge areas of waterlogged lands and white sheets of salt stretching across fields of the main irrigated regions of Iraq". One study estimated that half of the 750,000 ha (hectares) previously reclaimed land had turned back to marshy lands unsuitable for agriculture, while the other faced similar prospects.[137]

By 2002, nearly 20-30% of Iraq's potentially irrigable land had become unusable, i.e. had been converted to desert by salinization of irrigation projects.[138]

A joint FAO/WEP assessment mission to Iraq in June/July 1997 made the following observations on the condition of agriculture in Iraq after the war and years of blockade.

> Iraq's agricultural sector has deteriorated significantly in the1990s, because of lack of investment and shortage of essential inputs, according to the report. Perhaps the most far-reaching recommendation for both agriculture and nutrition concerns the need for economic rehabilitation and development throughout the whole country.[139]

On the condition of food and nutrition the mission made the following conclusion:

> Before the Persian Gulf War in 1990, Iraq imported two-thirds of its food requirements. UN sanctions, imposed in August 1990, however, significantly constrained Iraq's ability to earn foreign currency needed to import sufficient quantities of food to meet needs. As a result, food shortages and malnutrition became progressively severe and chronic in the 1990s. Widespread starvation has only been avoided by a public rationing system that provided minimum quantities of food to the population.[140]

6

SANCTIONS AND INTERNATIONAL LAW

In this chapter, we will look at the way sanctions meet or breach the principles upheld under international law, both humanitarian and human rights law. But before doing so, we will consider briefly the way the Security Council, which is controlled by Western nations, deals with similar issues under international law by employing different standards. We believe this to be relevant when discussing international law, because laws that are not applied universally are not laws or bad laws at best.

UN Resolutions on Iraq vs. Resolutions on Israel:
But One Example of Ongoing Double Standards in UN Application of Punitive Measures

On 6 June 1982, Israeli tanks rolled across Lebanon's border, destroying property and killing thousands of Lebanese before reaching the capital, Beirut.[1] In 2004 Osama bin Laden was reported to have said in a videotape that he was inspired to attack the buildings of the United States by the 1982 Israeli invasion of Lebanon in which towers and buildings in Beirut were destroyed in the siege of the capital.[2] But despite the blatant breach of international law in invading a sovereign state, the Security Council passed Resolution 509 (1982) in which it simply called on Israel to withdraw its forces to the internationally recognized borders.[3] There was no condemnation for the destruction, killing and invasion, but more importantly this resolution, in line with every resolution on Israel since its inception, was not passed under Chapter VII, which enables the Security Council to take punitive measures if not implemented. It is not surprising that Israel, which had failed to abide by previous resolutions without repercussion, did not feel threatened by this new resolution. Furthermore, the Security Council made a mockery of international law when, on 29 July 1982, it passed Resolution 515 (1982) calling on the Government of Israel to "lift immediately the blockade of the city of Beirut in order to permit the dispatch of supplies to meet the urgent needs of the civilian population and allow the distribution of aid provided by UN agencies and by non-governmental organizations, particularly by the ICRC."[4] Firstly, the resolution made no reference as to what the Security Council would do if the invading army besieging the capital of a sovereign member state of the UN failed to comply. Secondly, and more importantly in our mind, it made no mention of the government of the sovereign state of Lebanon. Such omission was not accidental but intended by the Europeans who drafted the resolution, in order to present the matter as a conflict between the State of Israel and some lawless Palestinian organizations. This would eventually mitigate their silence over the crimes committed during and after the invasion.

However, when Iraqi tanks rolled across the desert on 2 August 1990 towards the city of Kuwait, the Security Council in Resolution 660 (1990) treated this action very differently. This merits a careful consideration as it sheds some light on what happened in the decade that followed. In order to understand this distinction it is best to compare the two Resolutions as follows:

Table 6.1
Comparison of Resolutions 660 (1990) and 509 (1982)

Resolution 660 (1990) on Iraq's Invasion of Kuwait	Resolution 509 (1982) on Israel's invasion of Lebanon
Alarmed by the invasion of Kuwait on 2 August 1990 by the military forces of Iraq;	Gravely concerned at the situation as described by the Secretary-General in his report to the Council;
Determining that there exists a breach of international peace and security as regards the Iraqi invasion of Kuwait,	Reaffirming the need for strict respect for the territorial integrity, sovereignty and political independence of Lebanon within its internationally recognized boundaries;

Acting under Articles 39 and 40 of the Charter of the UN [Chapter VII]	[None]
Condemns the Iraqi invasion of Kuwait	[None]
Demands that Iraqwithdraw immediately and unconditionally all its forces to the positions in which they were located on 1 August 1990;	Demands that Israel withdraw all its military forces forthwith and unconditionally to the internationally recognized boundaries of Lebanon;
Calls upon Iraq and Kuwait to begin immediately intensive negotiations for the resolution of their differences and support all efforts in this regard, and especially those of the League of Arab States;	Demands that all parties observe strictly the terms of paragraph 1 of resolution 508 (1982) which called on them to cease immediately and simultaneously all military activities with Lebanon and across the Lebanese-Israel border;
Decides to meet again as necessary to consider further steps to ensure compliance with the present resolution.	[None]
[None]	Calls on all parties to communicate to the Secretary-General their acceptance of the present resolution within twenty-four hours;
Decides to meet again as necessary to consider further steps to ensure compliance with the present resolution.	Decides to remain seized of the question.

Although a careful consideration of the above would reveal issues that would distract us from the purpose of this book, it is clear to any observer that these two resolutions apply different standards, one for offences committed by Europe and its allies and one for those not so lucky to be in that camp. It should not come as a surprise to find that people in the Middle East are cynical when they hear any talk about international law. In fact the only people who talk about international law in the Middle East are the corrupt rulers!

In the six months after August 1990, the Security Council passed no fewer than twelve resolutions which imposed the most brutal blockade known in history. The last resolution before the US-led invasion of Iraq was adopted on 29 November 1990. It is quite a coincidence that it was on 29 November 1947 that the United Nations General Assembly approved the partition plan of Palestine. However, when on 17 January 1991 Iraq was invaded by the US and its allies, the Security Council, although still seized of the matter, remained silent until 2 March 1991.

Four days after Iraq's entry into Kuwait and while attempts were under way by many parties, not least the League of Arab States, to negotiate a peaceful way out, the US had the Security Council adopt one of the harshest resolutions ever passed and whose continuity was to cause the most devastating effects in peace time on any state in the 20th century. Resolution 661 (1990) passed on 6 August 1990 invoked Article 51 of the UN Charter which gives a state under attack the right of individual or collective self-defense, thus setting in place the mechanism for future military action against Iraq. It decided that all States should prevent: (a) Imports of all commodities originating in Iraq or Kuwait; (b) The sale or supply of any commodities or products, "but not including supplies intended strictly for medical purposes, and, in humanitarian circumstance, foodstuffs" to Iraq or Kuwait. There are even indications that the original US intention was to include medicines and foodstuffs, in the blockade.[5]

The Resolution further demanded that no state should directly or through its nationals make any funds or other financial or economic resources available to Iraq or Kuwait. The Resolution called on all states, even non-UN members, to abide by the terms of the Resolution notwithstanding any contract entered or license granted before. The Resolution set up a committee of all members of the Council to monitor the implementation of the Resolution which effectively meant the Council was in continuous session. Ambassador Marjatta Rasi, who was deputy permanent representative of Finland to the UN from 1987 to 1991, was chosen as the first chairman of the Security Council's Iraq Sanctions Committee. In November 1990, she stated that Iraq should not be allowed to receive medicines allowed in Resolution 661 because it could use them in chemical and biological warfare,[6] a claim which was strongly criticized even inside Finland.[7]

The destruction of Iraq in the twelve years that followed was seeded by Resolution 661 (1990). It was the first time that a state was put under total blockade in which nothing was allowed in or out. Even medicine and medical supplies, as we have shown in Chapter 5, were subject to scrutiny and permits. Food was to be allowed but only in humanitarian circumstances. We believe that it would have been impossible for a highly industrialized state, like the UK, to survive even for a short period, if subjected to such a blockade, yet a semi-industrialized state like Iraq was subjected to it for twelve years. Such total blockade meant denying the whole population of Iraq its most fundamental right in life. Furthermore, we believe that no states have such a right to deny another state the right to survive irrespective of the reason that brought punishment upon the guilty party. We shall now look at the meaning of blockades and their position under international law. Although we believe that what the Security Council imposed on Iraq was a total blockade, it seems that Anglo-Saxon wisdom has opted for the sanitized term of sanctions. We shall hesitantly conform and use them interchangeably but only for the sake of clarity.

Invoking Chapter VII: The Abuse of International Law

A point should be forcefully made here that despite all the wars, interventions and aggressions that have plagued international relations since WWII, Chapter VII of the UN Charter, which enables action to be taken against a faulting state, has rarely been invoked and only ever against Third World states.[8]

Before we attempt to examine the position and scope of sanctions under international law, it may be helpful to list the main UN Charter Articles which have been relied upon in adopting the Security Council Resolutions and subsequent action against Iraq:

Article 39

The Security Council shall determine the existence of any threat to the peace, breach of the peace, or act of aggression and shall make recommendations, or decide what measures shall be taken in accordance with Articles 41 and 42, to maintain or restore international peace and security.

Article 40

In order to prevent an aggravation of the situation, the Security Council may, before making the recommendations or deciding upon the measures provided for in Article 39, call upon the parties concerned to comply with such provisional measures as it deems necessary or desirable. Such provisional measures shall be without prejudice to the rights, claims, or position of the parties concerned. The Security Council shall duly take account of failure to comply with such provisional measures.

Article 41

The Security Council may decide what measures not involving the use of armed force are to be employed to give effect to its decisions, and it may call upon the Members of the United Nations to apply such measures. These may include complete or partial interruption of economic relations and of rail, sea, air, postal, telegraphic, radio, and other means of communication, and the severance of diplomatic relations.

Article 42

Should the Security Council consider that measures provided for in Article 41 would be inadequate or have proved to be inadequate, it may take such action by air, sea, or land forces as may be necessary to maintain or restore international peace and security. Such action may include demonstrations, blockade, and other operations by air, sea, or land forces of Members of the United Nations.

Article 51

Nothing in the present Charter shall impair the inherent right of individual or collective self-defense if an armed attack occurs against a Member of the United Nations, until the Security Council has taken measures necessary to maintain international peace and security. Measures taken by Members in the exercise of this right of self-defense shall be immediately reported to the Security Council and shall not in any way affect the authority and responsibility of the Security Council under the present Charter to take at any time such action as it deems necessary in order to maintain or restore international peace and security.

The Questionable Legality of Total Sanctions under the UN Charter

The starting point for the consideration of sanctions under international law is Article 39 of the UN Charter which gives rise to the right of the Security Council to consider taking such measures as sanctions against a member state. Under Article 39, as sited above, the Security Council "shall determine the existence of any threat to the peace, breach of the peace, or act of aggression" before deciding on the measure to be taken. Once the Security Council determines the existence of the conditions under Article 39, then all the measures taken by the Security Council under Articles 41 and 42 ought to be taken only "to maintain or restore international peace and security". *The Security Council is not empowered under the Charter to maintain the measure without determining at each stage that the threat to international peace remains.* It is not empowered to simply extend the imposition of these measures on the grounds that its demands have not been met. The continuous imposition of sanctions on Iraq would have been an unlawful act even if Iraq had not indeed disarmed itself. The Security Council should have determined at each stage of the sanctions that failing to impose them would have created a threat to international peace. It is submitted here that the Security Council never carried out such determination during the twelve years of sanctions. It would have been ludicrous for any state to argue that Iraq, after its destruction in 1991, was a threat to international peace.

It is clear that the clever drafting of Article 39 was intended to prevent the Security Council from acting on the whim of a single state or a group of states seeking to further some political objectives. Sadly that is precisely what the Security Council did in imposing sanctions on Iraq as it served the American plan for the Middle East.

In fact it is submitted here that the *imposition of sanctions on Iraq, when it was no longer a threat to international peace, was itself an act of war or aggression and by imposing the sanctions, the Security Council was itself guilty of breaching international law.*

It has been argued, and we subscribe to such an argument, that the principle under Article 22 of the Hague Convention 1907 which reads: "The right of belligerents to adopt means of injuring the enemy is not unlimited", applies to the right to impose sanctions.[9] Indeed if the right to injure is not unlimited in times of war then it stands to reason that the right to injure in time of peace should be even more limited.

The conduct of the Security Council, especially over the last two decades since the demise of the Soviet Union, has instilled in people's minds, quite wrongly, the idea that the Security Council is entitled to make any resolution it sees fit. People need to be reminded that the

Security Council was created by the United Nations Charter which is itself a contract between sovereign states. It is thus bound by the Charter in addition to the wider principle of its being bound by international law. We will first consider the limitations imposed on the Security Council by the UN Charter before considering the wider limitations imposed by the principles of international law.

The preamble of the Charter declares that the people of the world are setting up the UN:

> ... to save succeeding generations from the scourge of war, which twice in our lifetime has brought untold sorrow to mankind, and to reaffirm faith in fundamental human rights, in the dignity and worth of the human person, in the equal rights of men and women and of nations large and small...

It needs little analysis to see that total sanctions breach, above all, the principles of the Charter. Total sanctions do not stop wars but become themselves acts of war. By denying people the right to work and earn, they deny them the most fundamental right to life. By forcing people to lose their jobs, they take away all their dignity.

Article 1 of the Charter defines the purpose of the UN. It declares that measures taken for the prevention and removal of threats to the peace should be in conformity with the principles of justice and international law. Although we will address later how sanctions breach principles of international law, it is submitted here that sanctions are unjust because the most fundamental principle of justice is that the innocent should not be punished and sanctions are clearly indiscriminate in punishment. Some utilitarians in the Anglo-American world may object to this on the grounds that the innocents may be punished if it could be shown that more good will befall society from such punishments. We believe that they should simply be reminded that most of the world does not subscribe to Locke's views, assuming that Locke was indeed fully understood by Anglo-Saxon writers on philosophy.

Article 1 goes on to declare that among the purposes of the UN is the establishment of relations between nations based on respect for the principle of equal rights and self-determination of peoples. But sanctions lead to internal disquiet and deny the people the right of self-determination by making them a hostage to the Security Council.

Last but not least total sanctions imposed on one nation as in the case of Iraq but not on others such as Israel for ostensibly the same actions is a breach of the purpose as stated in Article 1 for the UN to be the center for harmonizing the actions of nations. Sanctions will only be seen as facilitating harmonization when they are imposed equally upon states found in breach of international peace.

Further support to our contention that the Security Council is bound by the Charter which created it, is found in Article 24 of the Charter which deals with Functions and Powers of the Council. It states that the Council, in discharging its duties, is given powers which are laid out in different parts of the Charter. Article 24 goes on to state that the Council, in discharging its duties, is bound to act in accordance with the Purposes and Principles of the United Nations, which have been set out in the Preamble and in Article 1. We have argued that sanctions are imposed in breach of the principles of the Preamble and Article 1 and thus we conclude that by imposing total sanctions the Security Council acted in breach of Article 24.

Another constraint on the imposition of sanctions can be found in Article 55 of the Charter, which deals with the purpose of the UN in economic and social cooperation, declaring the function of the UN to promote:

> a. higher standards of living, full employment, and conditions of economic and social progress and development;
>
> b. solutions of international economic, social, health, and related problems; and international cultural and educational cooperation; and
>
> c. universal respect for, and observance of, human rights and fundamental freedoms for all without distinction as to race, sex, language, or religion.

We suggest here that total sanctions, which lower standards of living; deny employment; hinder the peaceful international cultural, economic and educational cooperation; and apply different standards in respect of human rights and freedoms to different races are clearly in breach of Article 55.

It is fair to say that the General Assembly has on numerous occasions adopted resolutions on sanctions which clearly uphold the Charter and other principles of international law. But because of the structuring of the UN Charter, which gives the Security Council the powers and makes the General Assembly a spectator, these General Assembly resolutions represent nothing more than a moral stand—albeit speaking on behalf of the world.[10]

The Illegality of Total Sanctions under International Humanitarian Law

The 26th International Conference of the Red Cross and Red Crescent (4 -7 December 1995) held that "Any sanction regime established in the context of armed conflict is governed by international humanitarian law, which requires that the survival and essential needs of the civilian population be ensured".[11] It is clear that the RC Conference was referring to some limited sanctions imposed during armed conflict which it found to be abhorrent if it denied the civilian population its essential needs. What the RC Conference avoided, deliberately in our mind, is *how total sanctions imposed indefinitely on civilians, could possibly conform with International Humanitarian Law* (IHL).

The protection of civilians was developed through the principles of customary international humanitarian law and encoded into treaties and conventions through the Hague Regulations 1907 to the Additional Protocol I 1977 to the Geneva Conventions. The consistent principle has been to apply in times of war the principles of law of civilized nations, of humanity and the dictates of the public conscience. We will not consider the principles of customary international law but adhere to those principles of customary law that have since been incorporated into treaties and conventions of the 20th century.

The Hague Regulations (1907) concerning the Laws and Customs of War on Land is a good starting point.[12] Article 50 of the Regulations provides that:

> No general penalty, pecuniary or otherwise, shall be inflicted upon the population on account of the acts of individuals for which they cannot be regarded as jointly and severally responsible.

It is clear that the total sanctions against Iraq were a breach of this principle because the penalty was imposed on the civilian population who could not be regarded as having been responsible for any of the actions of the Government of Iraq, assuming the latter was at fault, a population who were living under a dictatorship that, as the West itself contended, repressed their freedom of choice and action.

Following WWII Europeans, who were shocked by the atrocities of the war, rushed to incorporate many principles in the Genocide Convention and the Geneva Conventions. We shall deal with the Genocide Convention in chapter 7. Out of the four Geneva Conventions we shall consider here is the Fourth Convention Relative to the Protection of Civilian Persons in the Time of War and Protocol I (1977) that expanded the protection of civilians to apply at times of international conflict.

Although the Fourth Convention [13] deals generally with the protection of civilians, two articles are worthy of note here. Article 8 provides that:

> Protected persons may in no circumstances renounce in part or in entirety the rights secured to them by the present Convention, and by the special agreements referred to in the foregoing Article, if such there be.

This article established a fundamental principle of forbidding the waiving or abrogation of the rights secured under the Convention.

Article 33, on the other hand, expands on the principle stipulated in Article 50 of the Hague Regulation in providing that:

> No protected person may be punished for an offence he or she has not personally committed. Collective penalties and likewise all measures of intimidation or of terrorism are prohibited.

> Pillage is prohibited.

> Reprisals against protected persons and their property are prohibited.

It seems clear that the total sanctions imposed on Iraq were in direct breach of the above principle. They were clearly collective punishment and reprisals against civilians and their property.

Following the adoption of the Geneva Conventions, the world realized that civilians caught in armed conflict needed more protection. Thus two Additional Protocols were adopted in 1977. We shall deal in more detail with Protocol I.[14]

Protocol I, whose title states it as relating to the Protection of Victims of International Armed Conflicts, established many principles of protection for civilians, and incorporated so many restrictions that the US Congress still refuses to ratify it because it limits the freedom of imperialist activities in the world. As the Protocol refers continuously to the term 'attack', a good starting point should be the definition of attack according to the Protocol. This appears in Article 49 as:

> 1. "Attacks" means acts of violence against the adversary, whether in offence or in defense.

> 2. The provisions of this Protocol with respect to attacks

apply to all attacks in whatever territory conducted, including the national territory belonging to a Party to the conflict but under the control of an adverse Party. 3. The provisions of this section apply to any land, air or sea warfare which may affect the civilian population, individual civilians or civilian objects on land. They further apply to all attacks from the sea or from the air against objectives on land but do not otherwise affect the rules of international law applicable in armed conflict at sea or in the air.

We also believe that the main addition to International Humanitarian Law made by Protocol I was the rescinding of the need to weigh military advantage against so-called collateral damage to civilians and civilian objects. Protocol I made it a crime to make civilians the object of attack. This was introduced in Article 85 which provides that:

3. In addition to the grave breaches defined in Article 11, the following acts shall be regarded as grave breaches of this Protocol, when committed willfully, in violation of the relevant provisions of this Protocol, and causing death or serious injury to body or health:

(a) making the civilian population or individual civilians the object of attack;

(b) launching an indiscriminate attack affecting the civilian population or civilian objects in the knowledge that such attack will cause excessive loss of life, injury to civilians or damage to civilian objects, as defined in Article 57, paragraph 2 (a)(iii);

(c) launching an attack against works or installations containing dangerous forces in the knowledge that such attack will cause excessive loss of life, injury to civilians or damage to civilian objects, as defined in Article 57, paragraph 2 (a)(iii);

(d) making non-defended localities and demilitarized zones the object of attack;

(e) making a person the object of attack in the knowledge that he is hors de combat;

(f) the perfidious use, in violation of Article 37, of the distinctive emblem of the red cross, red crescent or red lion and sun or of other protective signs recognized by the Conventions or this Protocol.

...

5. Without prejudice to the application of the Conventions and of this Protocol, grave breaches of these instruments shall be regarded as war crimes'

We submit that Article 85 establishes four facts:

1. Making civilians the object of attack is a grave breach of the Protocol.
2. Grave breaches of the Protocol are regarded as war crimes.
3. There is no scope for introducing the balance of any military advantage that could result from an attack on civilians as a mitigating or annulling factor in determining whether war crimes had been committed.
4. The Security Council would have committed a war crime in imposing total sanctions against Iraq.

We therefore suggest that the sanctions imposed on Iraq fall fully within the above definition of breaches, and thus any reference to an attack in the Protocol covers sanctions as applied to Iraq and all the relevant articles on attack, therefore, apply to sanctions.

The basic rule incorporated in Article 48 of the Protocol provides that:

In order to ensure respect for and protection of the civilian population and civilian objects, the Parties to the conflict shall at all times distinguish between the civilian population and combatants and between civilian objects and military objectives and accordingly shall direct their operations only against military objectives.

It is clear to any reader of the above principle that sanctions make no such distinction between civilian and non civilian and thus pose a questionable issue for defenders of sanctions, to say the least.

The Protocol defines in Article 50 the meaning of "civilian population" thus:

> The civilian population comprises all persons who are civilians.

> The presence within the civilian population of individuals who do not come within the definition of civilians does not deprive the population of its civilian character.

Iraq for the purpose of the above article is clearly a civilian population despite having armed forces within it. The protection of the civilian population as outlined in the articles should apply to Iraq during the sanctions regime, in line with other principles in Protocol I, such as the requirement, where there is doubt, to assume that the target is civilian and that when both the military and civilian use the same facility, then it should be assumed to be civilian. The whole purpose of Protocol I is to raise the protection of civilians in the 4th Geneva Convention to a new level whereby the argument about weighing military advantage against civilian casualties is no longer acceptable. In accordance with Article 50, imposing sanctions on Iraq was an attack on the civilian population irrespective of the fact that there were military people in Iraq, because the sanctions did not target them alone.

Article 51 defines the protection guaranteed by the Protocol to the civilian population in international conflict. Among this protection:

> Indiscriminate attacks are prohibited. Indiscriminate attacks are:

> Those which are not directed at a specific military objective;

> (b) Those which employ a method or means of combat which cannot be directed at a specific military objective; or

> (c) Those which employ a method or means of combat the effects of which cannot be limited as required by this Protocol;

and consequently, in each such case, are of a nature to
strike military objectives and civilians or civilian objects
without distinction.
and
Attacks against the civilian population or civilians by
way of reprisals are prohibited.

We suggest that the sanctions were in clear breach of the
above guaranteed protection. The violence was clearly directed against
the entire civilian population in Iraq and not specifically against specific
military objectives. It was clearly made in reprisal for what was assumed to
be the failure of the Government of Iraq to abide by the Security Council
resolutions. Or perhaps that was just the pretext.

Article 52 covers the protection of civilian objects in international
conflict. It provides that:

1. Civilian objects shall not be the object of attack or of
reprisals. Civilian objects are all objects which are not
military objectives as defined in paragraph 2.

2. Attacks shall be limited strictly to military objectives.
In so far as objects are concerned, military objectives
are limited to those objects which by their nature,
location, purpose or use make an effective contribution
to military action and whose total or partial destruction,
capture or neutralization, in the circumstances ruling at
the time, offers a definite military advantage.

3. In case of doubt whether an object which is normally
dedicated to civilian purposes, such as a place of
worship, a house or other dwelling or a school, is being
used to make an effective contribution to military
action, it shall be presumed not to be so used.

Reminding ourselves that 'attacks' has been defined in Article 48 as *"acts
of violence against the adversary"*, then it is beyond doubt that the total
sanctions imposed on Iraq were attacks in breach of the above principles.

It is imperative to point out the importance of paragraph (3) of
Article 52. We have heard repeatedly from both US and Israeli officials, in
relation to Iraq, Lebanon, Afghanistan, Pakistan, when civilian targets had
been attacked that they were attacked because it was thought they were
being used for military purposes. It is clear from the draft of paragraph
(3) that the drafters anticipated such possible criminal actions and thus

made sure that when such doubt arises the presumption must be that they are civilian targets and not otherwise. The value of this paragraph has been demonstrated repeatedly in recent times especially when pilotless aircraft are sent to attack civilian targets. It has become almost like a mantra to hear US officials acknowledging that civilians were killed in what turned out to be a purely civilian target suspected of having been a military one.[15]

Article 54 deals with protection guaranteed by the Protocol to civilian objects that are indispensible to the survival of the civilian population. Although very much related to Article 52, it furthermore provides that:

> 1. Starvation of civilians as a method of warfare is prohibited.
>
> 2. It is prohibited to attack, destroy, remove or render useless objects indispensable to the survival of the civilian population, such as food-stuffs, agricultural areas for the production of food-stuffs, crops, livestock, drinking water installations and supplies and irrigation works, for the specific purpose of denying them for their sustenance value to the civilian population or to the adverse Party, whatever the motive, whether in order to starve out civilians, to cause them to move away, or for any other motive.

We have treated the effect of sanctions on Iraq's economy and the civilian population in more detail in Chapter 6. However, to state the obvious here, Iraq was starved through sanctions both directly and indirectly. It was starved directly through curtailing the Government's ability to trade freely and forced to purchase only in accordance with the approval of the sanctions committee and under its control, even though Security Council Resolution 661 excluded humanitarian goods from the sanctions restrictions. It was starved indirectly when people lost their jobs because the government, being the main employer and being denied any access to its own money, was unable to pay out salaries. The loss of the purchasing capacity of families led to starvation and unnecessary deaths especially among children.

Preventing Iraq from importing spares for its electricity, water and sewage systems, which were themselves attacked unlawfully during the invasion of 1991, meant that the civilian population had to be denied objects and services indispensable to their survival. One potentially criminal act which followed from the sanctions regime and the unlawful activity of the sanctions committee was the case of the Mosul Dam. It appeared during the 1990s that there was some erosion within the Mosul Dam which, if not tackled, could lead to the dam collapsing and flooding the Tigris basin on a scale larger than that of the biblical flood of Noah. The Government of Iraq pleaded with the sanctions committee to allow some international consultants to inspect the dam in order to get some remedial action, but the request was denied on the grounds that the sanctions did not allow it. Since the invasion of Iraq in 2003, the new ruling cliques, who are there temporarily building their own personal fortunes, have done nothing to rectify this. The Mosul Dam remains a ticking time bomb. In May 2003, the US Department of State's US Agency for International Development reported that:

> USAID/OTI supported the emergency provision of approximately 3,000 tons of special cement that will reinforce the Mosul dam foundation and interior core for up to two months, as well as obtaining a shipment of turbine oil for the generators and sulfuric acid for the control room batteries. Total support needed for Mosul dam is approximately $144,000. Mosul dam, the largest in Iraq, has structural problems that threaten its integrity. Additionally, its generators, which provide power to around 1.7 million people, are in danger of burning out due to a shortage of turbine lubricating oil.[16]

It is clear that these structural problems did not appear only after the occupation. Not allowing Iraq to receive help to prevent a catastrophe, which might still threaten the lives and possessions of hundreds of thousands of people, was a malicious and intentional act. Even though the disaster did not—or should we say, has not yet transpired— it was nevertheless looming. So effectively, the destruction and needless injury and death which might be attributed to the application of sanctions should include those which may occur in future which can be seen as due to the forced interruption of necessary infrastructural maintenance over a period of decades.

Professor Thomas Nagy, who is one of the few American academics who demonstrated integrity beyond the norm, had this to say on Article 54 when he wrote about the genocide committed by the US Defense Intelligence Agency (DIA), which we will treat in chapter 9.

> The language of Article 54 does not permit escape through the semantics of intent, much less specific

intent. Rather Article 54 prohibits rendering useless 'drinking water installations and supplies' ...'whatever the motive' ... 'to starve out civilians ... or for any other motive'. But that is precisely what the US government did, with malice and forethought. It 'destroyed, removed, or rendered useless' Iraq's 'drinking water installations and supplies'. The sanctions, imposed for more than a decade, almost entirely at the insistence of the United States, constitute an ongoing violation of the Geneva Convention.[17]

It is not possible to finish with the provisions of the Protocol I without highlighting the major principle embedded in Article 57 on Precautionary Measures that parties must take in international conflict. Article 57 provides that:

1. In the conduct of military operations, constant care shall be taken to spare the civilian population, civilians and civilian objects.

2. With respect to attacks, the following precautions shall be taken:
   (a) those who plan or decide upon an attack shall:
   (i) do everything feasible to verify that the objectives to be attacked are neither civilians nor civilian objects and are not subject to special protection but are military objectives within the meaning of paragraph 2 of Article 52 and that it is not prohibited by the provisions of this Protocol to attack them;

   (ii) take all feasible precautions in the choice of means and methods of attack with a view to avoiding, and in any event to minimizing, incidental loss or civilian life, injury to civilians and damage to civilian objects;

   (iii) refrain from deciding to launch any attack which may be expected to cause incidental loss of civilian life, injury to civilians, damage to civilian objects, or a combination thereof, which would be excessive in relation to the concrete and direct military advantage anticipated;

We suggest that simply imposing economic sanctions against any civilian population is a breach of the above principle. One need not analyze any legal or moral principle beyond noticing that by imposing sanctions, as attacks against civilian population, the above principles are breached and thus imposing sanctions on civilians in international conflicts is an illegal act even if committed by the Security Council.

It would only be proper to remind ourselves before leaving Protocol I that the breaches through sanctions contrary to Articles 48, 51, 52, 54 and 83 were all committed during the 1991 military attack on Iraq. The attacks of the sanctions were a mere continuation of them.

Human Rights Law and Sanctions

The Universal Declaration of Human Rights (UDHR)[18] adopted on 10 December 1948 is considered the cornerstone of human rights law. It spells out the basic civil, political, economic, social and cultural rights that all human beings should enjoy. The Declaration gave birth to several Covenants which created not just moral but legal obligations on states with regard to respect of human rights. We shall look at how sanctions fit within the UDHR and the following Covenants:

> International Covenant on Civil and Political Rights, (ICCPR)[19]
> International Covenant on Economic, Social and Cultural Rights, (ICESCR)[20]
> Convention on the Rights of the Child (CRC)[21]

The UDHR, when joined with the above Covenants, came to form what is generally referred to as the International Bill of Human Rights.[22]

The UN commissioner for Human Rights underlines the importance of obligations under human rights law in stating:

> International human rights law lays down obligations which States are bound to respect. By becoming parties to international treaties, States assume obligations and duties under international law to respect, to protect and to fulfill human rights. The obligation to respect means that States must refrain from interfering with or curtailing the enjoyment of human rights. The obligation to protect requires States to protect individuals and groups against human rights abuses. The obligation to fulfill means that States must take positive action to facilitate the enjoyment of basic human rights.[23]

In its fact sheet on the International Bill of Human Rights, the UN Office of the High Commissioner for Human Rights highlights the significance of the UDHR and its effect in determining the conduct of states and the adoption of resolutions since 1948. The report states:

> Thus, for more than 25 years, the Universal Declaration on Human Rights stood alone as an international "standard of achievement for all peoples and all nations". It became known and was accepted as authoritative both in States which became parties to one or both of the Covenants and in those which did not ratify or accede to either. Its provisions were cited as the basis and justification for many important decisions taken by United Nations bodies; they inspired the preparation of a number of international human rights instruments, both within and outside the United Nations system; they exercised a significant influence on a number of multilateral and bilateral treaties;
>
> In many important resolutions and decisions adopted by United Nations bodies, including the General Assembly and the Security Council, the Universal Declaration of Human Rights and one or both Covenants have been cited as the basis for action.[24]

Although there may be some truth in such statements, the Commissioner seems in that report to have ignored objectivity in highlighting only the positive effects of the UDHR. It is imperative that such an independent body should equally indicate that the UDHR and the Covenants that it gave rise to at times were breached or at least not taken into consideration by some member states and some Security Council Resolutions.

This is not completely unexpected. It is not dissimilar to the different attitude of Europeans to killing when committed nationally and internationally. The murder of a child in a forest in England is an abhorrent act that shakes the nation, but the killing of thousands of Iraqi children through lack of food and medicine is a debatable matter. Equally the Commissioner, who is of the same European cultural roots, finds the denial of some human rights to Iraqis at the hands of the Iraqi Government an unacceptable breach of Human Rights Law, but is equivocal about the breach of the human rights of all Iraqis through the imposition of total sanctions for more than a decade! We believe that there will not be any change to the mess of international affairs, aggression and wars in whatever guise until people understand that the killing of a child is a crime whether committed in a park in London by a terrorist bomb, or in a street in Fallujah, or a village in Pakistan by a US missile. Moreover people need to understand that abuse of human rights is not restricted to national policies, but may equally be committed by internationally sanctioned policies. Both should be equally rejected.

We shall look at how the total sanctions imposed on Iraq fit within the obligations under Human Rights law, if at all, and if not, how these rights had been violated. In doing so and to avoid repetition any principle is cited only once and reference is given to where it appears in the Declaration or the Conventions.

The UDHR states in its preamble that:

> Whereas recognition of the inherent dignity and of the equal and inalienable rights of all members of the human family is the foundation of freedom, justice and peace in the world,

> Whereas disregard and contempt for human rights have resulted in barbarous acts which have outraged the conscience of mankind,..[25]

It seems reasonable to conclude that any act which sets out to curtail any of these inalienable rights, deny any group of people their inherent dignity, and show contempt or disregard for due process of law, amounts to a breach of justice and peace in the world. If it can be shown that the imposition of total sanctions in fact results in such outcomes as that which the preamble of the UDHR sets out to uphold, then it follows that sanctions themselves are a breach of the principles of justice and peace rather than the enforcer of them which the proponents of their effectiveness have proclaimed. The Security Council, indeed, would be the disturber of the peace rather than its promoter.

The UDHR consists of two parts, although it is not in fact divided as such. Articles 4 to 21 deal with civic and political rights, while Articles 23 to 27 deal with economic, social and cultural rights. These were expanded and elaborated in the later Conventions. Here are some of the rights and prohibitions.

Right to Life

Article 6 of the ICCPR, on the right to life, which is a reiteration of the principle in Article 3 of the UHDR, introduces a very fundamental principle. It provides that:

> 1. Every human being has the inherent right to life.

> This right shall be protected by law. No one shall be
> arbitrarily deprived of his life.
>
> 3. When deprivation of life constitutes the crime
> of genocide, it is understood that nothing in this
> article shall authorize any State Party to the present
> Covenant to derogate in any way from any obligation
> assumed under the provisions of the Convention on the
> Prevention and Punishment of the Crime of Genocide.

But sanctions resulted in denial of the right to life by denying people the opportunity to work through the reduction of the revenue available to the Government, which was the main employer, thereby depriving families of the income needed to sustain life, and were effectively a factor in the starvation deaths earlier cited.

Although we have treated genocide separately in this book (see Chapter 7), it is worth emphasizing that Article 6 above established the peremptory rule of prevention of genocide under international law. The ICCPR clearly denies the right of any party to derogate from its obligation under the Genocide Convention. It follows, thus, once it is established that sanctions cause genocide, that the crime of genocide would be committed whenever they are applied, irrespective of any argument used, such as the legitimacy of Security Council actions.

Prohibition of Torture

Article 7 of the ICCPR reiterates the principle upheld in Article 5 of the UDHR and provides that:

> No one shall be subjected to torture or to cruel,
> inhuman or degrading treatment or punishment. In
> particular, no one shall be subjected without his free
> consent to medical or scientific experimentation.

But the sanctions imposed on Iraq were by definition and through intent a cruel punishment of the total civilian population. The Iraqi nation was subjected to inhumane and degrading treatment in being forced to beg for its survival and suffer malnutrition when it had the wealth to live a decent life.

Right to Work

Article 6 of the ICESCR which reiterates Article 23 of the UDHR provides that:

1. The States Parties to the present Covenant recognize

> the right to work, which includes the right of everyone
> to the opportunity to gain his living by work which he
> freely chooses or accepts, and will take appropriate
> steps to safeguard this right.

But preventing the Government, as the main employer, to access the resources needed (and available) to be able to employ new graduates over a decade resulted in the biggest community of unemployed university graduates in the Middle East despite Iraq being inherently a rich country. Denying the private sector access to raw material, and the opportunity to import and export forced it to close down industry and lay off thousands of workers.

Freedom to Travel

Article 13 of the UDHR which was later reiterated by Article 12 of the ICCPR provides that:

> Everyone has the right to leave any country, including
> his own, and to return to his country.

But for thirteen years the people of Iraq were forcibly denied the right to leave Iraq when air traffic in and out of Iraq was blocked by sanctions and the illegal no-fly zones. The arduous journey of 15 hours or so by land to Amman was impossible for the sick, who most needed to travel. Thousands of Iraqis died because they could not travel outside Iraq for medical treatment, while the medical care in Iraq, once the star of the Middle East, collapsed.

Right to Family and Decent Living

Reiterating Article 25 of the UDHR, Article 7 of the ICESCR provides that:

> The States Parties to the present Covenant recognize
> the right of everyone to the enjoyment of just
> and favorable conditions of work which ensure, in
> particular:
> (ii) A decent living for themselves and their families
> in accordance with the provisions of the present
> Covenant;

and Article 11 provides that:

> 1. The States Parties to the present Covenant recognize

the right of everyone to an adequate standard of living for himself and his family, including adequate food, clothing and housing, and to the continuous improvement of living conditions. The States Parties will take appropriate steps to ensure the realization of this right, recognizing to this effect the essential importance of international co-operation based on free consent.

2. The States Parties to the present Covenant, recognizing the fundamental right of everyone to be free from hunger, shall take, individually and through international co-operation, the measures, including specific programs, which are needed:..

It is obvious that as Iraqis were denied the right to work and earn their living none of the above rights were secured.

Right to Property

Article 17 of the UDHR provides that:

No one shall be arbitrarily deprived of his property.

However, every bank account anywhere outside Iraq that was held by any Iraqi Government organ, Iraqi company or an Iraqi resident in Iraq was frozen for twelve years thereby arbitrarily depriving ordinary people of their property and the right to enjoy it, and imperiling those who lost their means of income by barring their access to private savings.

Right to Education

Article 26 of the UDHR provides that:

Everyone has the right to education. Education shall be free, at least in the elementary and fundamental stages. Elementary education shall be compulsory.

Iraq, which was rewarded by UNESCO for its achievement in eliminating illiteracy, was denied the basic right to educate its people, leaving it to slide to the bottom of the league of world's states in education. One example of what sanctions meant to the children of Iraq is that the import of pencils was refused by the Sanctions Committee on the grounds that the graphite in them had a dual purpose as it could be used in a nuclear reactor! [26]

Right to Self-determination

Article 1 of the ICCPR, which is also common to ICESCR, on the right of self-determination provides that:

> All peoples have the right of self-determination. By virtue of that right they freely determine their political status and freely pursue their economic, social and cultural development.
>
> All peoples may, for their own ends, freely dispose of their natural wealth and resources without prejudice to any obligations arising out of international economic co-operation, based upon the principle of mutual benefit, and international law. In no case may a people be deprived of its own means of subsistence.

We submit that total sanctions breach the above principle as people under them could neither freely pursue their development nor dispose of their natural wealth. In fact Iraq under sanctions was not only denied such right, it could not even import food without the sanctions committee allowing it to do so.

Rights of the Child

The Convention on the Rights of the Child stands as a significant commitment by the nations of the world to extend particular care to the child, following the development of the principles of human rights law since the UDHR. Its preamble emphasizes the principles of the UDHR and the subsequent declarations on human rights including specifically the Declaration of the Rights of the Child of 1924 and the Declaration of the Rights of the Child adopted by the UN on 20 November 1959. Although most of the provisions of the Convention exist in other Covenants and declarations, the need for a separate Convention of the child is stated in the preamble:

> Bearing in mind that, as indicated in the Declaration of the Rights of the Child, "the child, by reason of his physical and mental immaturity, needs special safeguards and care, including appropriate legal protection, before as well as after birth"[27]

The Convention has been ratified by all UN member states except for the US and Somalia. It is insulting to human intelligence and dignity that any US president, member of Congress or politician, can stand up and lecture the rest of the world on human rights when the US cannot get Congress to ratify the most obvious and basic legal commitment protecting the children of the world! And to see the US stand with the failed state of Somalia on that platform can have but one meaning. The US has also failed to ratify the Convention on the Elimination of All Forms of Discrimination against Women, once again side by side with Somalia.

Article 4 requires international cooperation for the implementation of the rights recognized in the Convention on the Rights of the Child in providing that:

> States Parties shall undertake all appropriate legislative, administrative, and other measures for the implementation of the rights recognized in the present Convention. With regard to economic, social and cultural rights, States Parties shall undertake such measures to the maximum extent of their available resources and, where needed, within the framework of international co-operation.

However, the total sanctions on Iraq not only imposed a blockade on such cooperation, but made it unlawful for any State Party to cooperate with the Government of Iraq to implement the rights guaranteed by the Convention. The Security Council's resolutions for total sanctions were a clear breach of this principle.

On taking measures to protect children, Article 19 provides that:

> 1. States Parties shall take all appropriate legislative, administrative, social and educational measures to protect the child from all forms of physical or mental violence, injury or abuse, neglect or negligent treatment, maltreatment or exploitation, including sexual abuse, while in the care of parent(s), legal guardian(s) or any other person who has the care of the child.

However, total sanctions prevented the Government of Iraq from performing its duty under the Convention. If anything, the imposition of sanctions on the children of Iraq was an act of physical and mental violence, neglect and maltreatment.

Articles 24, 27, 28 and 31 are a few examples of the provisions which the States Parties were obliged under the Convention to secure for the child.

On securing health care, Article 24 provides that:

1. States Parties recognize the right of the child to the enjoyment of the highest attainable standard of health and to facilities for the treatment of illness and rehabilitation of health. States Parties shall strive to ensure that no child is deprived of his or her right of access to such health care services.

2. States Parties shall pursue full implementation of this right and, in particular, shall take appropriate measures:

(a) To diminish infant and child mortality;

(b) To ensure the provision of necessary medical assistance and health care to all children with emphasis on the development of primary health care;

(c) To combat disease and malnutrition, including within the framework of primary health care, through, inter alia, the application of readily available technology and through the provision of adequate nutritious foods and clean drinking-water, taking into consideration the dangers and risks of environmental pollution;

(d) To ensure appropriate pre-natal and post-natal health care for mothers;

(e) To ensure that all segments of society, in particular parents and children, are informed, have access to education and are supported in the use of basic knowledge of child health and nutrition, the advantages of breastfeeding, hygiene and environmental sanitation and the prevention of accidents;

(f) To develop preventive health care, guidance for parents and family planning education and services.

3. States Parties shall take all effective and appropriate measures with a view to abolishing traditional practices prejudicial to the health of children.

> States Parties undertake to promote and encourage
> international co-operation with a view to achieving
> progressively the full realization of the right recognized
> in the present article. In this regard, particular account
> shall be taken of the needs of developing countries.

Total sanctions on Iraq, which limited the import of medicine;
prevented even x-ray machines from being imported into the country;
denied import of all spare parts for medical equipment; denied import
of anesthetics needed for operations; blocked even the ability of an Iraqi
pediatrician to have access to medical journals, were in total breach of
the obligation under Article 24.

Article 27 provides that:

> 1. States Parties recognize the right of every child to
> a standard of living adequate for the child's physical,
> mental, spiritual, moral and social development.

But the parties which imposed total sanctions on Iraq denied
the children of Iraq the right to an adequate standard of living by denying
the work opportunity to their parents.

On the right of a child to education Article 28 provides that:

> 1. States Parties recognize the right of the child to
> education,

But the children of Iraq were denied this right through sanctions
which prevented them from having schools, blackboards, books, paper
and even pencils.

Article 31 provides that:

> 1. States Parties recognize the right of the child to rest
> and leisure, to engage in play and recreational activities
> appropriate to the age of the child and to participate
> freely in cultural life and the arts.

It needs little imagination to conclude that when paper and
pencils were denied, these unfortunate children of Iraq did not even
know, for more than a decade, what toys were, let alone have recreational
equipment installed anywhere near them.

In addition to all the above provisions required to guarantee the
basic rights of children, Article 38 provides for another principle common
to adults for the protection of children during armed conflict. It provides
that:

> 1. States Parties undertake to respect and to ensure respect for rules of international humanitarian law applicable to them in armed conflicts which are relevant to the child.

> 4. In accordance with their obligations under international humanitarian law to protect the civilian population in armed conflicts, States Parties shall take all feasible measures to ensure protection and care of children who are affected by an armed conflict.

It is clear from the above Articles that states are not simply asked to abide by the principles of international humanitarian law as developed under customary law, the Hague regulations, and the Geneva Conventions and their Additional Protocols, but makes it obligatory on states to take all feasible measures to ensure the protection and care of children. We submit that states which imposed sanctions on Iraq made it impossible to ensure the protection and care of Iraqi children. In fact the sanctions were devised and executed with the intention of causing maximum damage to Iraqi children. US Secretary of State, Madeleine Albright's infamous comment that the death of half a million Iraqi children was worth it goes to show precisely that.[28] Albright's comment should not be taken lightly as she represented US official policy. Asserting that the killing of Iraqi children was 'worth it' meets the two legs of intent as defined in the ICC Statute for all international crimes. Firstly, it asserted that the USA was engaged in the act of imposing total sanctions on Iraq. Secondly, the USA either meant to cause the consequences of imposing total sanctions or was aware that such will occur in the ordinary course of events.

It seems reasonable to conclude that many of the rights of the civilian population in Iraq as upheld by the UDHR and the later Conventions were breached by member states that had signed the Declaration and held themselves bound by it. We believe that the people of Iraq have a right at any time in the future to seek redress from each and every member state which voted for the imposition and maintenance of sanctions on Iraq on the ground that they had violated their obligations under the UDHR. This is in addition to the reparations which might legitimately be required in response to the crime of genocide, for which there is no statute of limitations, and for which penalties against individuals might also be imposed in accordance with the Nuremberg Principles—to be further addressed below.

We believe that we have shown in this chapter that the total sanctions imposed on Iraq between 1990 and 2003 were in breach of many principles of international humanitarian law and human rights law.

We do not see the matter as one of setting the measures to be taken when imposing sanctions. Sanctions on a 'targeted population' should never be imposed and are not admissible on the ground that they had been 'subject to pre-assessment study'.[29] If sanctions lead, inter alia, to deaths, and particularly to deaths in large numbers, then they should be regarded, effectively, as worthy of the same degree of opprobrium as acts of violence. We believe that targeting civilians with any violence is a breach of international law. If that premise is not upheld, then injury to civilians will have been acceptable and the only problem will become one of where to draw the line. That is unacceptable if we seek to live in a civilized world.

THE GENOCIDE CONVENTION AND THE QUESTION OF INTENT

It is important to remember that the Great Powers that won WWII took advantage of the post-war environment as well as their privileged position as winners of the conflict to codify the crime of genocide in a way that would not constitute a threat to their status quo and their search for power maximization in the years after the war. Thus the text of the 1948 Convention was elaborated in such a way that it would not constrain the behavior of its drafters in the future.[1] Lippman asserts that "both the US and the former Soviet Union, for example, were reluctant in accepting norms that could be used to limit their actions in their pursuit of global hegemony".[2] It was within that environment that the institutions of international law, including the Genocide Convention, were formulated in accordance with the interests of the victors. However as Drumond commented, rightly in our opinion, "the effectiveness of the document [Convention] was jeopardized, since the primary concern of the most powerful countries at the time was not to construct a law that would serve common principles or shared values, but to consolidate their power interests. This explains why the Convention ended up with a very limited definition of genocide and protecting only groups that were defined in the document, instead of every collectivity and, as a result of those flaws, having very restricted effects in international practice."[3] Despite these major flaws, and realizing that the world order is always dictated by the victors, we shall proceed to argue that the Genocide Convention, even as finally drafted, was breached by the total sanctions imposed on Iraq, by the same Great Powers which had won WWII, almost fifty years before.

Background to the Genocide Convention and its Adoption

The Convention on the Prevention and Punishment of Genocide (Genocide Convention, also CPPCG) finds its origin in the request of the delegations of Cuba, India and Panama, dated 2 November 1946, to the Secretary General of the UN to include in the agenda of the General Assembly an item on the prevention and punishment of genocide.[4] Between that request and the unanimous (with the exception of South Africa) adoption by the General Assembly on 9 December 1948 of the final draft of the Convention, the process went through several stages of enthusiasm and retraction. Of significance among these stages was the stage in which the Secretary General requested the Secretariat's Human Rights Division to draw up a draft Convention. The first draft of the Convention drawn up with experts' advice differed significantly from the final adopted draft. Among the main features of the ambitious first draft, which were not incorporated in the final draft, and whose citation here is relevant because it shows the depth of concern of nations post WWII, were the following:

1.   The draft contained in Article I (i) a definition of Protected Groups in stating, "the purpose of this Convention is to prevent the destruction of racial, national, linguistic, religious or political groups of human beings".

2.   In its definition of Genocide, the draft referred to genocide as meaning "a criminal act directed against any of the aforementioned groups of human beings, with the purpose of destroying it in whole or in part, or of preventing its preservation or development." There are two relevant points worthy of emphasis here. Firstly, the above statement went beyond the final draft in extending genocide to cover not just the destruction but also "preventing the preservation and development of the Protected Groups". Even more significant is the fact that the first draft, as opposed to the final draft, did not require these acts to be committed with intent. It is obvious that those who wrote the first draft were convinced that genocide is a crime of strict liability. We suggest that this must be right. Otherwise, if intent had to be proved as the final draft demands, then an aggressor can exterminate an ethnic group even recklessly and argue in defence that intent could not be established.

3.   The first draft, as opposed to the final draft, included in the definition of genocide acts of biological genocide such as restricting births and cultural genocide.

4.   On punishable offences, the first draft included a section defining

the details of preparatory acts to commit genocide and detailed all public propaganda designed to incite the commission of acts of genocide.

5. The first draft included among its provisions that "command of the law or superior orders shall not justify genocide". This is in line with the similar principle upheld under the Geneva Conventions. It is worth pointing out that the final draft is silent on this provision leaving the matter open to argument.

Reaction to the Convention during the Deliberations

The Convention, which was adopted by a UN vote on 9 December 1948, received a mixed reaction ranging from the enthusiastic to the indifferent. Notable among the enthusiasts was Herbert V. Evatt, the then Prime Minister of Australia, who in addressing the General Assembly of the UN in 1948 following the adoption of the Convention, referred to it as an "epoch-making event in the development of international law". His enthusiasm went further in his passionate belief that: "through the Convention we are establishing individual safeguards for the very existence of such human groups.... In the field relating to the sacred right of existence of human groups, we are proclaiming today the supremacy of international law once and for all".[5]

We shall cite two other views of enthusiasts to show the fundamentally different attitudes of the imperialist mind and the minds of ordinary people. The well-known Chilean poetess, Mistral Gaberia, expressing the feelings of millions of people in the world who had witnessed the carnage of two European wars in one century, was reported to have commented that the Convention "commands the respect and support of all. It should never be weakened or circumvented by adverse measures....the success of the Genocide Convention today and its greater success tomorrow can be traced to the fact that it responds to necessities and desires of a universal nature: The word genocide carries in itself a moral judgment over an evil in which every feeling man and woman concurs".[6]

In contrast to this, Philip B. Perlman, the then Solicitor General of the US, is reported to have stated that "the ratification by the USA will afford a measure of protection for those unfortunates who still live in fear of torture and death at the hands of the cruel, ruthless rulers or dictators who are or may become obsessed with the idea either that they belong to a master race, or that they are apostles of a master ideology, dedicated to the extermination of other races and creeds".[7] It is clear that Perlman was alluding to third world dictators and the communist states. He could never admit that the America of today was based on genocide having been committed by his not too distant ancestors!

Such an attitude was highlighted in the ill-informed statement made by John Foster Dulles, the architect of imperialism, who, when addressing the US Senate Judiciary Committee on 6 April 1953, expressed doubt about the possibility of the Convention achieving its purpose as envisaged by its drafters. His alleged cause for skepticism was that the Soviet Union and its satellites had either refused to ratify the Convention or had ratified it with serious reservations.[8] No official in the State Department or Senate bothered to correct this misinformation which Dulles put before the Senate and the world at large. Had anyone bothered to make a telephone call to the UN, they would have discovered the following:

1. Among the 20 signatories of the Convention following its adoption on 9 December 1948 were the Soviet Union and four of its satellites: Czechoslovakia, Byelorussia, Ukraine, and Yugoslavia.
2. By the time Dulles made his statement to the Senate, the following communist states had already ratified the Convention: Bulgaria: 21 July 1950; Yugoslavia: 29 August 1950; Romania: 2 November 1950; Poland: 14 November 1950; Czechoslovakia: 21 December 1950; and Hungary: 7 January 1952.
3. When Dulles made his statement, neither the US nor the UK had ratified the Convention! In fact the UK ratified it in 1969 and the US even later. It may not be public knowledge but we believe it is worth reminding people, that despite all the misinformation of Dulles regarding the resistance of the Communists to the Convention, the US only acceded to the Convention on 4 November 1988 when President Ronald Reagan signed the Genocide Convention Implementation Act,[9] forty years after its adoption and ratification by most of the Communist States. Australia on the other hand, and despite Prime Minister Howard's endless noise about human rights breaches in Iraq and East Timor, only acceded to the Convention in 2002!
4. This casual indifference to the truth did not escape the attention of everybody. Woolsey commented that Dulles's statement was meant to imply that the Convention was unsatisfactory to the US because (1) the treaty's approach was unsuitable for the accomplishment of the goals envisaged, or (2) the field is outside the external interests of the US.[10]

We believe that Dulles was in fact expressing the view that has prevailed since WWII regarding US official policy, namely that any international law instrument is good so long as it serves US external interests, but once it seems not to serve those interests then the US is not interested in even talking about it. The examples of official policies and politicians' statements to support this are too numerous to cite. However, it suffices here to cite what US Attorney General Gonzales said concerning the Geneva Conventions in his memo to the President on 25 January, 2002:

> The nature of the new war places a high premium on other factors, such as the ability to quickly obtain information from captured terrorists and their sponsors in order to avoid further atrocities against American civilians. ... In my judgment, this new paradigm *renders obsolete* Geneva's strict limitations on questioning of enemy prisoners and renders quaint some of its provisions.[11]

We also believe that Dulles was not ignorant of the facts regarding the ratification by the Communist States. His misinformation is part of the campaign of lies and falsehood which had characterized US foreign policy from the Gulf of Tonkin incident used as the justification for the Vietnam War to the WMD excuse for invading Iraq. The success of this strategy is mainly due to the political ignorance and indifference of the gullible masses and many politicians in the US.

It is important to remember that the Geneva Conventions were drafted post WWII by Europeans to safeguard the lives of their people at times of war. The reason for having these Conventions is the fact that military personnel in times of war may be tempted to use the killing machine to its full capacity. There was reason to put some limitation on such possibility. The Geneva Conventions attempted to do that. If the US believes them to be irrelevant, then the commissions of war crimes and genocide by the US military remains a possibility so long as the US believes it is not bound in the heat of battle by legal constraint.

There were also those who saw some merits but also shortcomings in the adoption of the Convention. Notable among those were two academics, Professors Lauterpacht and Kunz.

Professor Josef L. Kuntz, while partly skeptical, saw some fundamental, positive features in the Convention. He stated that the crimes under Article II and III of the Convention are crimes under international law but not crimes against international law. While these crimes are defined by international law individuals are only under a duty if and when the States enact the corresponding domestic legislation. While, therefore, the Convention is, under these aspects, thoroughly old fashioned and traditional, it would be a mistake to assume that the

Convention does not contain real innovations in international law. The innovations consist in the fact that the crimes referred to in Article II and III, which hitherto, if committed by a government in its own territory against its own citizens, have been of no concern to international law, are made a matter of international concern and are, therefore, taken out of the matters essentially within the domestic jurisdiction of any State.[12] Lauterpacht, in his comments on the Convention, and in total apparent agreement with Kunz wrote:

> the Convention obliges the Parties to enact and keep in force legislation intended to prevent and suppress such acts, and any failure to measure up to that obligation is made subject to the jurisdiction of the International Court of Justice and of the UN. With regard to the latter, the result of the provision in question is that acts of commission or omission in respect of genocide are no longer, on any interpretation of the Charter, considered to be a matter exclusively within the domestic jurisdiction of the States concerned. For the Parties expressly concede to the UN the right of intervention in this sphere. This aspect of the situation constitutes a conspicuous feature of the Genocide Convention—a feature which probably outweighs, in its legal and moral significance the gaps, artificialities and possible dangers of the Convention.[13]

The irony here is that while both appreciated the fact that the UN had become entitled to intervene to prevent genocide, they did not envisage the possibility that the UN itself could end up implementing conditions which lead to genocide as we submit it did in imposing total sanctions on the people of Iraq. We are amazed at the incredible phenomenon in which even well-informed Western writers can condition themselves into such states of mind that they lose objectivity. Thus when Paula Drumond wrote her paper on Genocide Convention in 2008, she did not, even once, refer to Iraq as a possible example of genocide having been committed during the thirteen years of total blockade and the years of brutal occupation since 2003. But worse still, willingly or inadvertently, she fell into the trap of the imperialist argument which has dominated world affairs since WWII. She stated that in order to prevent or suppress genocide "there are also some suggestions in international law literature about measures that could help preventing genocide such as economic and diplomatic sanctions".[14] She omitted to mention the possibility that economic sanctions themselves could result in genocide. The presumption here is that so long as the measure is taken by the Security Council, then it must be right. But was it not the main actors of the Security Council who had themselves committed the biggest war crimes and crimes against humanity for the last century?

There were those who denied any significance to the Convention. We chose two notable views representing, as would be expected, the two mothers of colonialism, France and Britain. The French delegate to the UN, J. L. Brierly, described the Convention as being "without any value".[15] Later he was reported by *The Listener* as having stated that "the real danger is if we allow it to go out in the world, as has been done with this Convention, that an important advance has been made when in fact nothing important has happened at all ... the Convention is symptomatic of a tendency to seek a sort of compensation for all that is so terribly discouraging in the international outlook of today by dissipating energies to achieve results which prove on examination to make no real advance."[16] Sir Harley Shawcross, the British Attorney General declared that the General Assembly should not delude people into thinking that, through the adoption of the Convention, a great step forward was taken; in reality, he claimed, nothing had been changed in the existing situation.[17]

Problems with Application of the Convention

One of the main problems with the Convention has been the question of its application under the doctrine of universality (i.e. universal jurisdiction: a principle in public international law whereby states claim criminal jurisdiction over persons whose alleged crimes were committed outside the boundaries of the prosecuting state, regardless of nationality, country of residence, or any other relation with the prosecuting country). The state backs its claim on the grounds that the crime committed is considered a crime against all, which any state is authorized to punish, as it is too serious to tolerate jurisdictional arbitrage.[18] The first draft of the Convention contained such a clause which enabled courts in a State to indict and try a non citizen for a crime committed outside its territory. However, this was not incorporated in the final adopted Convention - unlike the Geneva Conventions. "The United States was the first to dissent, insisting that prosecution for crimes committed outside the territory of a state could only be undertaken with the consent of the state upon whose territory the crime was committed."[19] The main objection had been that since genocide generally involves the responsibility of a State, enabling a court in another State to repress its action would result in making the courts of the second State the judge of the action of the first State, which would lead to a violation of the sovereign rights of the first State.

This view has since been overruled when the crime of genocide was incorporated in the Statute of the International Criminal Court.[20] It could be argued that the same argument, which the US used in 1948 to prevent the universal jurisdiction principle being incorporated in the Convention, had been one of the reasons behind the US refusal to ratify the ICC Statute. It is such a dramatic change that the US, which had already ratified the Geneva Convention, did not simply refuse to ratify the Statute of the ICC but legislated for sanctions against any state that does so.[21] The US went further and intimidated many states not to ratify the Statute of the ICC. We were told by a high ranking official in one of the Gulf States that despite having spent months shuttling to meetings to discuss the Statute, when the time came for signing, the US told us not to do so and we did not.

At the time of writing this book only three Arab States have ratified the Statute of the ICC. One state and its position on the ICC are worthy of note here: Iraq. Following the invasion and occupation of Iraq we were bombarded by new legislations passed by the US occupier, statements by US and Iraqi officials, articles, TV interviews etc. regarding the heinous war crimes which Saddam Hussein and his colleagues had committed. We all witnessed the sham trial that convicted and executed him for such crimes. Every sensible person would have expected Iraq to be in the forefront of ratifying the ICC Statute because the crimes covered by it were the reason for the invasion, occupation and change of regime. However, no sooner had the puppet regime in Baghdad, which might have thought itself independent, issued an order on 15 February 2005 declaring its intention to endorse the treaty on the International Criminal Court (ICC)[22] and informed the ICC of its readiness to sign the Statute, than it withdrew its application and has been silent since!

Lippman, among others, considered the central flaw in the Convention to be the fact that the Convention places primary reliance for the prosecution of violators on States on whose territory the acts of genocide have been committed. But these are the very governments that usually have sponsored, or have been complicit in such acts, and hence are unlikely to vigorously pursue prosecutions. Even following their removal from office, the perpetrators of genocide often possess sufficient support to avoid prosecution.[23]

We, however, believe, contrary to what the Western jurists had decided, that international law, just like domestic law, should have automatic jurisdiction to everybody once the Convention or treaty comes into force, without requiring further domestic action by the state. This would require amending the *Vienna Convention on the Law of Treaties* 1969 to put an end to the system of adding reservations. We believe that a resolution that is passed by the General Assembly should be binding on the nations that voted in its favor just as much as any Convention is binding on the signatories to it. It is alarming that the creators of the UN, post WWII, have decided that the Security Council is not subject to any judicial scrutiny or appeal process despite the fact that it has a judicial duty of passing judgments of life or death. But even more disturbing has been the decision that among the sources of international law should be the opinions of jurists—primarily European, no doubt. Why should the opinion of a Western jurist, however learned he may be, be a source of international law and not resolutions of the General Assembly representing the world community? It would have made some sense had the Statute of the ICJ referred to a consensus opinion among jurists rather than one single opinion as a secondary source of international law.

We are glad that, despite the Western blockage, which still manifests itself in the West refusal to accept the UN resolution on aggression as its definition of aggression for the purpose of its inclusion in the ICC Statute, the world has finally come to accept that international crimes can, as a matter of principle, be tried before an international court including the crime of aggression. It may still be some time before it becomes possible to indict a Western European before such a court, but the first step has been taken.

Relevant Articles of the Genocide Convention to Sanctions

The Convention on the Prevention and Punishment of the Crime of Genocide, which was adopted on 9 December 1948, consists of a Preamble and 19 Articles. The Preamble, as is expected in international treaties, sets out to identify its aims and purpose. Although the Preamble refers to General Assembly Resolution 96(1) of 11 December 1946, the Convention as adopted does not incorporate all its contents. Notably missing from the Convention are any reference to political groups among those to be protected and any reference to cultural genocide, both of which were in the above resolution. The Preamble sets out the purpose of the Convention as that of liberating mankind from the odious scourge of genocide.

The Convention consists of two main parts. The first part made up of Articles I-IX deals with the definition, prevention and punishment of genocide. The second part consisting of Articles X-XIX deals with the procedures under the Convention. As this is not a study of the Genocide Convention per se, we will not consider the second part and deal only with part of the first part.

The Preamble reads:

> Having considered the declaration made by the General Assembly of the United Nations in its resolution 96(1) dated 11 December 1946 that Genocide is a crime under international law...

Article 1 reads:

> The Contracting Parties confirm that genocide, whether committed in time of peace or in time of war, is a crime under international law which they undertake to prevent and to punish.

The reason why we treat both Article I and the Preamble together is because they are concerned with the position of UN resolutions under international law. It has been argued that there was no need for Article I, which seemed to repeat part of Resolution 96(1) if the UN General Assembly resolutions were mandatory for the Contracting Parties. However, it seems that the views of the US and the UK, which have since been supported by the opinion of the ICJ, won the argument 'that resolutions of the GA were not mandatory but simply declaratory statements.[24] It has become one of the greatest anomalies of the so-called 'international law'. The UN General Assembly, which represents the States of the world, having agreed to delegate part of its authority to the Security Council, has lost its authority to overrule the decisions of the latter. It goes against the nature of things that an organization, which delegates its authority to a sub-division, no longer has authority over that sub-division or its ruling. However, as the Charter is silent on the validity of the General Assembly's resolutions and because the European powers which won the war wanted to remain in control, this bizarre ruling by the ICJ has become part of international law.

It appears that such a belief ruled the drafting of the Convention and thus the need to have Article I assert that Genocide is a crime under international law. It also explains why some of the groups such as 'political groups' were omitted in Article II.

The most significant part of Article I is its assertion that genocide is a crime whether committed in time of peace or war, which distinguishes it from 'war crimes' which are intended to apply at time of war only. We believe that it has introduced a new element into international law which makes both the dropping of the nuclear bomb on Hiroshima during war, killing part of the Japanese nation, and the imposition of total sanctions on Iraq, albeit not precisely in time of peace, fall under Acts of Genocide.

Article II reads:

> In the present Convention, genocide means any of the following acts committed with intent to destroy, in whole or in part, a national, ethnical, racial or religious group, as such:
> (a) Killing members of the group;
> (b) Causing serious bodily or mental harm to members

of the group;

(c) Deliberately inflicting on the group conditions of life calculated to bring about its physical destruction in whole or in part;

(d) Imposing measures intended to prevent births within the group;

(e) Forcibly transferring children of the group to another group.

Although it is commonly referred to as the article which defines Genocide, it does not, in fact, do so. The French proposed a definition for the Convention which was not incorporated. Robinson elaborated on this misconception, in saying that: "the Convention defines genocide as the intentional destruction of any national, ethnical, racial, or religious group is thus incorrect; it is also based on a misconception of Article II: actual destruction need not occur; intent is sufficient". Robinson asserted that the Convention does not carry a definition of Genocide but an enumeration of acts which are considered to be Genocide for the purpose of the Convention.[25]

The choice of using such an exhaustive list of the material element (*actus reus*) of the crime rather than using an exemplicative one was, according to Drumond, due to "an insistence on the part of the United States, because a strict and limited definition of the crime would mean that conducts not contemplated by the above mentioned article would not [sic] be considered as genocide and therefore this would not reduce the USA's margin for manoeuvre in actions that intended to maximize its relative power and, as a consequence of that, achieving hegemony." [26]

It is very important to highlight what we believe to be a significant element of Article II. It is natural for ordinary people when hearing the term 'genocide' to think of the heinous crime of killing people en masse. However, paragraphs (b-e) of Article II add to actual killings crimes ranging from causing serious bodily or mental harm to forcibly transferring children. We intend to show that at least the acts in paragraphs (a-d) were committed in Iraq through sanctions.

Intent in Genocide: Its Meaning and Use to Obviate Criminal Liability

The most significant area of dispute concerning the Genocide Convention centers on the element of intent addressed in Article II. There have been some who have latched onto the need to prove intent in order to establish that genocide was *not* committed in imposing sanctions on Iraq. Because of the importance of this defense we shall elaborate a little on intent.[27] But before we explain what intent means, we would like to highlight one important point, namely that, according to the wording of Article II, actual destruction need not happen provided intent can be established.

This issue was partly addressed by the European Court of Human Rights.[28] In 2007 the European Court of Human Rights (ECHR), noted in its judgment on *Jorgic v. Germany* case that in 1992 the majority of legal scholars took the narrow view that 'intent to destroy' in the CPPCG (Convention on the Prevention and Punishment of Genocide) meant the intended physical-biological destruction of the protected group and that this was still the majority opinion. But the ECHR also noted that a minority took a broader view and did not consider biological-physical destruction was necessary as the intent to destroy a national, racial, religious or ethnical group was enough to qualify an event that had not actually happened or process that was not actually taking place as genocide.

In the same judgment the ECHR reviewed the judgments of several international and municipal courts. It noted that the International Criminal Tribunal for the Former Yugoslavia and the International Court of Justice had agreed with the narrow interpretation, that biological-physical destruction was necessary for an act to qualify as genocide. The ECHR also noted that at the time of its judgment, apart from courts in Germany which had taken a broad view, that there had been few cases of genocide under other Convention States municipal laws and that "There are no reported cases in which the courts of these States have defined the type of group destruction the perpetrator must have intended in order to be found guilty of genocide".

Another ambiguity in Article II, which is independent of the actual meaning of intent, is whether it is necessary to establish that the culprit intended to destroy the group or that the destruction happened as a result of an intended action.[29] We believe that this question has not yet been answered fully even after the International Court of Justice considered the meaning of 'intent'.[30]

The issue of intent, what it means and how it applies to genocide is very important because it has been the cornerstone of the defense used by the perpetrators of genocide. We would like to stress one important matter. It is obvious that most of the writing referred to here or relied upon has been drawn from academics or lawyers in the Anglo-American tradition. Without any attempt to discredit any contribution, we emphasize that it remains the view of this tradition. So when someone asserts a view that a certain definition of 'intent' in genocide for example is "widely accepted", it should be qualified as widely accepted in the Anglo-American tradition. Our reading of the literature suggests that the volume of published work available in the international realm does not pay adequate attention to 'intent' in the context of Russian, Chinese,

Japanese, Indian or South American perspectives to name but a few. This is an important issue because we are dealing with an international crime and thus we need an international consensus on its meaning and elements. No one group should claim moral superiority, even if it is the developed Anglo-American legal system.

It could be argued that the meaning of intent is complicated by the fact that it means different things under different legal systems. Although we do not believe that principles under common law have any preference over those of other systems such as civil law systems, we will be concentrating more on intent under common law in view of the fact that the perpetrators of genocide in Iraq are, in our view, mainly Anglo-Americans who operate under the principles of common law, and are thus bound by what intent means in that system. A British jurist may argue that he does not feel bound by what the International Court of Justice or ICC says but he will have difficulty refuting a principle of law upheld by legislation or a high judicial authority in the UK.

We think it is proper to consider what intent means under Anglo-America legal systems in order to appreciate the meaning of the *mens rea* before we are in a position to argue whether or not that requirement was met in the case of Iraq.

In the USA 'intent' is not one of the classifications of mental states. The influential Model Penal Code in North America sets out the following classes of mental states: Purposefully, Knowingly, Recklessly, and Negligently.[31]

It is immediately apparent that while common law in England acknowledges 'intent' there is no such recognized corresponding class in the US. This raises two unavoidable questions. Firstly, what did the USA intend the term 'intent' to mean when it insisted that it should be incorporated in Article II of the Genocide Convention? Secondly, what is the meaning of 'specific intent' in the USA statute on genocide promulgated after ratification of the Convention by the USA forty years after its adoption and what criteria will USA courts apply for its interpretation?[32]

In England the situation is simpler but not all that clear either. Under English law mental states are classified as: Intention, Knowing, Recklessness, Criminal Negligence and Strict liability. Although lawyers and academics in England write about 'basic intent' and 'specific intent' very few authorities have in fact dealt with them as such. The courts in England have been more inclined to discuss the subjective and objective tests when analyzing the *mens rea* than the basic or specific intent.

The perennial problem has been the extent to which the court may impute enough desire to commit the offence in order to move from pure recklessness to intention. The law has witnessed changes on this.

Thus in the case of *R v Maloney* (1985) 1 All ER 1025, Lord Bridge expanded on the difference between foresight and intent and suggested that if there was a need to direct the jury by reference to foresight of consequences, then two questions need to be addressed:

> Was death or very serious injury a natural consequence
> of the defendant's voluntary act?
> Did the defendant foresee that consequence as being
> a natural consequence of his act?

But only if the answer to both above questions was affirmative then an inference could be drawn that the defendant intended the consequences of his act.

Such a test raises another question: what is a 'natural consequence'? Lord Bridge is reported to have elaborated on it as:

> ...in the ordinary course of events a certain act will lead
> to a certain consequence unless something unexpected
> supervenes to prevent it... [and] the probability of the
> consequence taken to have been foreseen must be little
> short of overwhelming before it will suffice to establish
> the necessary intent.

The link between the probability of a consequence and the resulting harm was defined by Lord Scarman in *R v Hancock and Sharland* (1986) 1 All ER 641, where he is reported to have ruled:

> ..the greater the probability of a consequence the more
> likely it is that the consequence was foreseen and if that
> consequence was foreseen, the greater the probability
> is that it was also intended.

In the same year the Court of Appeal summed up the law on intent when it held in *R v Nedrick* (1986) 83 Cr. App. R. 267 that:

> ...if the jury are satisfied that at the material time
> the defendant recognised that death or serious harm
> would be virtually certain (barring some unforeseen
> intervention) to result from his voluntary act, then that
> is a fact from which they may find it easy to *infer* that he
> intended to kill or do serious bodily harm, even though
> he may not have had any desire to achieve that result.

The Law Commission of England and Wales had over the years made several proposals to revise and reform the definition of intention. In its latest such recommendation it suggested:

> We recommend that the existing law governing the meaning of intention is codified as follows:
>
> (1) A person should be taken to intend a result if he or she acts in order to bring it about.
>
> (2) In cases where the judge believes that justice may not be done unless an expanded understanding of intention is given, the jury should be directed as follows: an intention to bring about a result may be found if it is shown that the defendant thought that the result was a virtually certain consequence of his or her action.[33]

It becomes obvious that during the development of 'intent' under Common Law in England 'specific intent' had hardly been discussed. This raises the question as to how did this term suddenly become so important when considering the crime of genocide despite its total absence in the USA jurisdiction and its insignificance in the UK? The explicit use of the term 'specific intent' seems to have appeared only in cases on voluntary intoxication and was first used in 1920 despite the fact common law had been developing for centuries.[34] A distinction between basic and specific intent was provided by Lord Simon of Glaisdale in his judgment:

> The best description of 'specific intent' in this sense that I know is contained in the judgment of Fauteux J in *R v George* (1960) 128 Can CC 289, 301: 'In considering the question of mens rea, a distinction is to be made between (i) intention as applied to acts considered in relation to their purposes and (ii) intention as applied to acts apart from their purposes. A general intent attending the commission of an act is, in some cases, the only intent required to constitute the crime while, in others, there must be, in addition to that general intent, a specific intent attending the purpose for the commission of the act.[35]

It should always be remembered that such 'intent' had only been referred to under Common Law in cases of 'voluntary intoxication'. Now we can move on and look at what has been said about 'intent' under the Genocide Convention. There are two views on intent with regard to genocide that need to be considered. First is the prevailing academic view that 'specific intent' is required as the *mens rea* under the genocide convention.[36] The second view believes that basic intent or no intent is required to satisfy the *mens rea*.[37]

The 'Specific Intent' View and its Argument

Joy Gordon and William Schabas are examples of prominent academics and lawyers who propound the need for 'specific intent'. In his authoritative book on genocide, Schabas asserts that:

> The reference to 'intent' in the text indicates that the prosecution must go beyond establishing that the offender meant to engage in the conduct, or meant to cause the consequence. The offender must also be proven to have a 'specific intent' or *dolus specialis*.[38]

However, in his entry on 'intent' in *The Encyclopedia of Genocide*, Morten Bergsmo criticizes Schabas for having failed to define 'specific intent':

> It would seem that Schabas does not recognize the concept of degree or quality of mental state. He reiterates that the 'offender must also be proven to have a 'specific intent' or *dolus specialis*,' but without elaboration of what this phrase or the language of the intent formulation in the Genocide Convention actually means.[39]

In 2007 genocide and the meaning of intent was considered by the International Court of Justice (ICJ) in *Bosnia Herzegovina v Serbia and Montenegro*. The court found that in the case of the alleged killing of some 7000 Muslim boys and men in the UN safe haven of Srebrenica in July 1995, genocide was committed. It held that:

> ... the acts committed at Srebrenica falling within Article II (a) and (b) of the Convention were committed with the specific intent to destroy in part the group of the Muslims of Bosnia and Herzegovina as such; and accordingly that these were acts of genocide, committed by members of the VRS in and around Srebrenica from about 13 July 1995.[40]

It is clear from the above paragraph that the Court implied the Latin term (*dolus specialis*) when considering the meaning of intent in the Genocide Convention. The ICJ, like Schabas above, only referred to specific intent without defining it.

It also seems that the Court used the terms 'specific intent' and '*dolus specialis*' interchangeably, which raises the question of the link between them. William Schabas explains the difference between specific intent and *dolus specialis* as:

> The *dolus specialis* concept is particular to a few civil law systems and cannot sweepingly be equated with the notions of 'special' or 'specific intent' in common law systems. Of course, the same might equally be said of the concept of 'specific intent,' a notion used in the common law almost exclusively within the context of the defense of voluntary intoxication.[41]

However, the matter becomes slightly confusing when Schabas asserts in his later work that:

> The degree of intent required by article II of the Genocide Convention is usually described as a 'specific' intent or 'special' intent. This common law concept corresponds to the *dol spe´cial* or *dolus specialis* of continental legal systems.[42]

The ICJ left the definition of *dolus specailis* open to interpretation. However, for the sake of making proper comparison between common law and civil law systems, we would like to highlight that, according to Johan D. van der Vyver, there are three different accepted categories of *dolus*.[43] These are *dolus directus* (direct intent), the *dolus indirectus* (indirect intent), and *dolus eventualis*.[44] Van der Vyver goes on to draw his own interpretation of which '*dolus*' is required for the crime of genocide under the convention:

> Special intent as an element of genocide will be confined to *dolus directus*. The 'mental element' of crimes within the jurisdiction of the ICC—which apply '[u]nless otherwise provided'— requires that the material elements of the crime must have been committed with intent and knowledge.[45]

The meaning of intent under the Genocide Convention was

considered by the two ad hoc tribunals, the International Criminal Tribunals for Yugoslavia (ICTY) and Rwanda (ICTR). The general principle upheld in these tribunals has been that held in *Prosecutor v. Clement Kayishema and Obed Ruzindana*—that a 'distinguishing aspect of the crime of genocide is the specific intent (*dolus specialis*) to destroy a group in whole or in part.'[46]

However, there are several dicta in these tribunals that give the impression that such a principle is not restricted to direct physical destruction as it is made out to be. Thus in the *Krstic* case the judgment approved the possibility of foreseeability of consequence as the *mens rea,* stating that:

> [s]ome legal commentators further contend that genocide embraces those acts whose foreseeable or probable consequence is the total or partial destruction of the group without any necessity of showing that destruction was the goal of the act.[47]

This opinion comes close the dictum of by Lord Scarman in *R v Hancock and Sharland* cited above.

In *Akayesu* the Court seems to accept that knowledge was sufficient *mens rea* stating that: "The offender is culpable because he knew or should have known that the act committed would destroy, in whole or in part, a group."[48] It will be shown later that this principle is close to that adopted in the Rome Statute. It is important, however, to iterate that 'knowledge' does not equate to 'intent' under common law. The requirement of 'specific intent' has gripped the minds of some jurists so much so that the Trial Chamber in *Akayesu* case erred in law when it suggested that *'dolus specialis'* is a synonym for *mens rea.*[49]

The 'Basic Intent' View and its Argument

In contrast to Schabas' opinion on interpreting intent, Alexander Greenawalt suggests that "although the opinion of such authoritative sources [requiring specific intent] carries its own weight, there is nothing in the text of the Genocide Convention that requires such a reading"[50] and argues instead that:

> ...traditional understandings of intent in common and civil law jurisdictions have encompassed a broad range of mental states, a trend that has been followed by the recently adopted Rome Statute of the ICC.[51]

We cannot leave Greenawalt's work without engaging one

important and relevant comment. When addressing the meaning of the phrase 'in whole or in part' which is part of Article II of the Convention, Greenawalt concluded by saying:

> To this end, the proposed interpretation of genocidal intent requires that the perpetrator be aware that the campaign of persecution poses a very serious threat to future survival of either the group as a whole, or a clearly defined segment of the group (such as the Kosovo Albanians or the Iraqi Kurds).[52]

It is worth stating that Greenawalt's paper was written in 1999, i.e. nine years after the imposition of total sanctions on Iraq and clearly in support of US policy in the region. Despite the interpretation of intent suggested by the writer and the mounting evidence by then of the destruction of Iraq through sanctions, Greenawalt was totally silent on the biggest genocide that was still ongoing while the paper was being researched.

What happened in Iraq during the thirteen years of total blockade is a unique manifestation of human evil the cataloguing of which, according to Greenawalt, was what the Convention did. It attests to the politicization of the interpretation of law that someone who spent so much time and effort researching a new definition of intent in genocide could be so oblivious to genocide taking place in Iraq.[53] By contrast it took great courage, and deserves our respect and admiration for someone like Professor Thomas J. Nagy to write:

> Many, including the author, recoil from contemplating the possibility that a Western democracy, particularly the USA, could commit genocide. However, it is precisely this painful and even taboo possibility which needs to be examined.[54]

In addition to Greenawalt, there have been others who have suggested a different interpretation of the required 'specific intent' in Article II of the Convention. Leo Kuper offers a purely objective interpretation suggesting that "intent is established if the foreseeable consequences of an act are, or seem likely to be, the destruction of a group" in that it retains the subjective element of knowledge.[55] This is similar to the definition of the ICC Statute and the opinion held in *Krstic* case as sited earlier.

Professor Matthew Lippmann criticized the Convention for apparently requiring specific intent and said that it allowed individuals to evade responsibility by portraying the violence against these groups as having been based on political grounds, or that the violence was incidental to the achievement of non-genocidal purposes.[56] That we submit is precisely what those in favor of sanctions have been arguing, namely that genocide was not intended, but that the large scale deaths that occurred were simply incidental ('collateral damage') to the political purpose of forcing Iraq to disarm—a demand which it has to be re-emphasized, was in itself contrary to international law.

These opinions on the need for an interpretation of the meaning of 'intent' find some support in certain European states applying the civil law system. In France, for example, there seems to be some confusion on the interpretation of 'intent' with courts taking wide-ranging views from strict conception to "...a looser, unrefined notion of *dol general,* understood merely as the conscious and voluntary action to violate the law".[57]

Bergsmo advises us, however, that the German term 'Absicht' used in German Courts' opinion on genocide signifies *'dolus directus'*.[58] Schabas criticizes the European approach as being insufficient to constitute the *mens rea* for genocide arguing that: "at the low end of recklessness, continental jurists speak of *dolus eventualis*, a level of knowledge that must surely be insufficient to constitute the crime of genocide".[59]

The View That Intent May Be Inferred

Schabas in his treatment of 'Proof of Intent' suggests that the prosecution in proving intent 'will rely on the context of the crime, its massive scale, and elements of its perpetration that suggest hatred of the group and a desire for its destruction'.[60] He goes on to argue that as only the accused has knowledge of his mental state, then intent must be inferred.[61] In doing this several factors and circumstances would need to be considered. Among them he suggests that:

> Factors that may establish intent include the general context, the perpetration of other culpable acts systematically directed against the same group, the scale of atrocities committed, the systematic targeting of victims on account of their membership in a particular group, or the repetition of destructive and discriminatory acts.[62]

International authorities have also lent support to this demand. Thus in the *Krstic* case the Trial Chamber held that:

> [a]n examination of theories of intent is unnecessary in construing the requirement of intent in Article 4(2). What is needed is an empirical assessment of all the evidence to ascertain whether

the very specific intent required by Article 4(2) is established.[63]

The ICC View of Intent

Although we have spent some time seeking to expose the arguments about the meaning of intent in the *Genocide Convention* we nevertheless believe that the true definition of intent has been incorporated in the *Rome Statute of the International Criminal Court*. Despite the fact that the Rome Statute only came into force on 1 July 2002 in our opinion it constitutes the best collective *opinio juris* since it was most recently agreed upon by the international community. It is beyond dispute that the definition of intent in the Rome Statute will be the one accepted by courts in the future. However, we submit that it must be the right definition for crimes of genocide committed even before the Rome Statute came into force, and that the Statute merely reflected the evolved customary international law on the subject. To reject this assertion would seem to suggest that the international community gives different meanings to crime and its constituent elements. Furthermore, the definition of intent here is not significantly different to that developed under English law as discussed earlier. It is worth pointing out that this broad definition of intent under the Statute of Rome is analogous the definition of 'knowledge' in the *Model Penal Code* (MPC) of the US.

The Insufficiency of the Current Definition of Genocide

Earlier we referred to the opinion of the ICJ ruling that genocide has been a crime under customary international law since 1951. We suggest that genocide has always been a crime even before the term was coined. Exterminating a group of people on religious, ethnic, racial, national, political or cultural must always be a crime. We submit that the ethnic cleansing of the indigenous peoples of Australia and the Americas could have been and should be considered as genocide.[64]

Despite the International Law Commission opinion that "The definition of genocide contained in article II of the Convention ... is widely accepted and generally recognized as the authoritative definition of this crime ... "[65] we would argue not only intent but the whole definition of genocide under customary international law could and should be different, and not restricted to peoples or national/ethnic/religious groups. It has been argued for example that the prohibition against genocide under customary law extends to the destruction of political groups.[66]

It could be argued that genocide along the lines of these parameters took place in Iraq from the imposition of the sanctions and throughout the invasion and occupation. The US set out to uproot Arab nationalism starting with Nasir of Egypt through the destruction of the Ba'ath in Iraq and the campaign to undermine the Ba'ath in Syria—though the sanctions embraced and impacted the Iraqi people as a whole. The proof of this policy was clearly manifested in the first Order promulgated by the Coalition Provisional Authorities (CPA) after occupation, which carried out the de'Ba'athification of Iraq—a policy that resulted in untold destruction and death among a substantial part of the Iraqi nation. A similar argument was made during the Vietnam War. In his submission in the Russell Tribunal in 1968, Jean-Paul Sartre argued that since "villages burned, the populace subjected to massive bombing, livestock shot, vegetation destroyed by defoliation, crops ruined by toxic aerosols, and everywhere indiscriminate shooting, murder, rape, and looting' then it was 'genocide in the strictest sense: massive extermination".[67] We doubt if anybody would argue that the Iraqis were not being destroyed for being Ba'athist through de-Ba'athification, but because 'they were there' as Hugo Bedau suggested in responding to Sartre's submission. Sartre is mistaken, Bedau suggests, by confusing "the false proposition that the United States armed forces killed Vietnamese peasants *because they were Vietnamese*, with the true proposition that the Vietnamese peasants were killed *because they were in the way, because they were there.*"[68]

Whether or not the Genocide Convention demands 'specific intent', the possibility of genocide having been committed in Iraq should be the subject of some criminal or judicial enquiry. Where there is evidence of a crime there arises a need for investigation. If the ICC could be activated on the basis of unsubstantiated, uninvestigated and later rescinded claims against Muammar Qaddafi in the context of a civil uprising in Libya, why was it not more appropriate to be activated with regard to Iraq, where the death toll dwarfs that of any other mass killing of the twentieth century? It is surely more appropriate, within the context of the definition offered by Israel W. Charny:

> Genocide . . . is the mass killing of substantial numbers
> of human beings, when not in the course of military
> action against the military forces of an avowed enemy,
> under conditions of the essential defenselessness and
> helplessness of the victims.69

The issue of the commission of genocide in Iraq by the Security Council and its Member States in the imposition and maintenance of sanctions even while knowing and being constantly advised of the substantial death toll to which same gave rise is not a matter for academics to investigate and make a judgment upon one way or another in legal or social science journals or advocacy publications, with the issue left to rest there as a matter of academic contention. The enormity of the crime requires that the assessment of evidence should be undertaken by an appropriate international legal mechanism in order to at minimum investigate, (and in our view, as a result of such investigation, to prove) whether genocide was committed with intent.

That such is warranted is indicated by the views of numerous international lawyers who have voiced opinions on genocide in Iraq. While former US Attorney General, Ramsey Clark did not address issues surrounding the definition of 'specific intent' he nonetheless contended that genocide had taken place and that it was intentional:

> There can be no doubt that the sanctions against Iraq intentionally destroyed in major part members of a national group and a religious group, as such, killing members of the groups, causing bodily and mental harm to their members and deliberately inflicting conditions of life calculated to bring about their physical destruction, at least, in part. If this is not genocide, what is?[70]

Writing on sanctions on Iraq, Professor George Bisharat accepts that "knowing pursuit" is sufficient *mens rea* for genocide in Iraq:

> Knowing pursuit of a policy that kills members of a group, causes serious bodily or mental harm to them or inflicts on them conditions of life calculated to bring about their physical destruction in whole or in part constitutes genocide under international law.[71]

Professor Francis Boyle in his petition to the UN on behalf of Iraqi children accepted the need for 'specific intent' in genocide but asserted that:

> Only the "specific intent" of Respondent George Bush to commit genocide against Applicants remains to be proven beyond a reasonable doubt to establish his criminal responsibility under United States municipal law and international criminal law.[72]

However, as this book will now proceed to demonstrate, as it relates to sanctions and the deaths directly attributable to them, the Security Council and then-Member States can be demonstrated to have knowledge of the effects of their actions (the large number of casualties caused), and to have "knowingly pursued" such actions whose specifically intended target was the people of Iraq.

8

THE SANCTIONS COMMITTEE OVERSIGHT

The most distinctive feature of Security Council resolutions on Iraq as opposed to those adopted in other crises has been that all resolutions on Iraq were adopted under Chapter VII, which effectively meant that punitive measures could be used when such resolutions were perceived not to have been implemented. Another important element of these resolutions is the fact that "according to Paul Conlon, a former official of the Iraq Sanctions Committee, US officials drafted every Security Resolution imposing and enforcing the sanctions on Iraq for the first several years of the sanctions regime".[1] It is not difficult to see the implications of such facts. They simply meant that Iraq was left totally at the mercy of the US, and the Security Council was only a tool to legitimize US crimes against Iraq. That does not obviate liability of members of the Security Council who chose to allow such a state of affairs not only to arise, but to continue for over twelve years.

Article 6 of Resolution 661 (1990), which imposed total sanctions on Iraq, set up the Sanctions Committee (the Committee). Article 6:

> Decides to establish, in accordance with rule 28 of the provisional rules of procedure of the Security Council, a Committee of the Security Council consisting of all the members of the Council, to undertake the following tasks and to report on its work to the Council with its observations and recommendations:
> (a) To examine the reports on the progress of the implementation of the present resolution, which will be submitted by the Secretary-General;

(b) To seek from all States further information regarding the action taken by them concerning the effective implementation of the provisions laid down in the present resolution;

The Committee went on to formulate its own Guidelines, after which the same Committee met again, this time as the Security Council, and approved them. This created an unprecedented entity in international affairs as will be shown in this chapter. It usurped the function of the Security Council and by this sleight of hand, went beyond what the Charter permitted the Council to do. This assertion may be seen from the following facts:

1. The Committee consisting of the fifteen members of the Security Council effectively became a shadow Security Council without such authority being available under the Charter.
2. Each member of the Committee had a veto on the import into or export out of Iraq for any item. The veto available to the five permanent members of the Security Council under the Charter was transferred without authority to the entire Security Council under the guise of the Committee.
3. The Committee held its sessions behind closed doors while the Security Council meetings are held in public.
4. While Iraq could claim the right, theoretically at least, to address the Security Council on matters relating to it, it had no right to attend or address the meetings of the Committee.

In its Guidelines, the Committee decided to report at 90-day intervals to the Security Council on the implementation of the arms and related sanctions against Iraq contained in the relevant resolutions.[2] However, while the Committee gave the impression that it was mainly involved in the disarmament of Iraq, the true function of the Committee was to ensure that as much hardship as possible was imposed on Iraqi civilians by preventing the import of items such as children's milk, spark plugs for cars and disposable gloves and syringes. And to appear to spread out the culpability for having done so, as if the more parties to the procedure would alleviate its heinous nature.

There are two distinct phases of these 90-day reports. When looking at them carefully we discover the underlying process of development of the sanctions regime and the indicating its intended use as part of the preparation for the invasion. But there is one clause common to all the reports over the period of thirteen years: the Committee reported in all of them that no breach of the sanctions had taken place.

First Phase of the Committee's Operation 1990-1996

The significance of this period lies in two facts. Firstly, it was the period during which there was little reporting on the actions of the Committee. Secondly and consequently it was during this period that the main irreparable damage was done to Iraq. This was when the damage to the economy, the deprivation of income to individual Iraqis and the slow deterioration of the unmaintained infrastructure took place. By the time the Oil for Food Program came into effect in 1996, it was too late to repair anything in Iraq. One striking indicator of this, as will be shown later, was the deterioration of the oil industry to such a state that Iraq would have been unable to produce enough oil to support itself, even had the sanctions been lifted.

Thus during that period, except for a few minor points, these reports were so identical that we could predict almost exactly what was going to appear in the next report.

Each report had a clause (appearing as clause 4 in most of them) which stated:

> In accordance with paragraphs 13 and 15 of the guidelines, all States and international organizations are required to consult the Committee on the question of whether certain items fall within the provisions of paragraph 24 of resolution 687 (1991), as well as in cases relating to dual-use or multiple-use items, i.e., items meant for civilian use but with potential for diversion or conversion to military use. During the period under review, no States or international organizations have consulted the Committee on these questions.

The significance of this clause lies in the dual-use items which later became the excuse to put on hold any item the US/UK chose to prevent going to Iraq, because theoretically any item can have a dual-use.

The early reports, up to 12 September 1993, included one clause (mostly appearing as clause 6) which typically stated:

> In a note dated [...] the President of the Security Council published the text of the statement made to the media on behalf of the members of the Council. He had stated that the members of the Council had held informal consultations on [...] pursuant to paragraphs 21 and 28 of Security Council resolution 687 (1991) and paragraph 6 of Security Council resolution 700 (1991).

After hearing all the opinions expressed in the course of the consultations, the President of the Council had concluded that there was no agreement that the necessary conditions existed for a modification of the regimes established in paragraph 20 of Security Council resolution 687 (1991), as referred to in paragraph 21 of that resolution.

There are two points worthy of note regarding the above clause recurring in most reports. Firstly, it refers to informal consultation, which means there were no records kept in order to evaluate the seriousness or depth of such consultation or indeed, record any state protest or questioning with regard to the impact on Iraq, especially so since all members knew that it took only one veto to prevent any decision being seriously considered with regard to changing the sanctions regime. Secondly, from the tenth report dated 14 December 1993 until the invasion and occupation of Iraq, there were no references in the 90-day reports to these informal consultations—perhaps to cover up internal dissent, as well as the extent of awareness of the damages and destruction being caused. The continuance of the sanctions program beyond the recorded awareness of its damages would have provided a further (and official) documentation of intent regarding deaths and damages subsequent to that recording, as the parties knowingly persisted. It is obvious that even that façade of consultation was considered unnecessary because there was going to be no change in the sanctions regime in order for it to be considered. Such a belief was summed up by Secretary Albright while speaking at a symposium on Iraq at Georgetown University in March 1997, when she is reported to have said:

We do not agree with those nations who argue that if Iraq complies with its obligations concerning weapons of mass destruction, sanctions should be lifted ..... [3]

Secretary Albright's statement not only exposed the real purpose of sanctions on Iraq, namely regime change in line with the new Middle East the US wanted to build, but also that there were disagreements concerning its imposition. This was highlighted by the Malaysian representative in addressing the Security Council on the Secretary-General report of Iraq in 2000 when he said:

The defenders of continued, relentless sanctions had argued that such measures had prevented Iraq from threatening its neighbors and rebuilding its arsenal. The goal of the sanctions, however, seemed to have changed. The original resolutions had imposed sanctions to pressure Iraq to eliminate its weapons of mass destruction programs. Certain policy statements emanating from capitals had suggested that sanctions would remain in place until certain political objectives had been achieved. Such a policy clearly undermined the original objective of the sanctions around which international consensus against Iraq had been based. Those, thus, made Iraqi children and families virtual hostages in the political deadlock between governments. The continuing demonizing of Iraq must stop if the international community was serious in its professed concern for the plight of the Iraqi people.[4]

Second Phase of the Committee's Operation 1996-2003

By 1995 international pressure on the US/UK started to mount when it became apparent that what was happening in Iraq was unacceptable even to some of Iraq's adversaries. Something had to be done to at least give the impression that there was a political will to change the sanctions regime. The Security Council adopted Resolution 986 (1995), which set up a system by which Iraq was allowed to sell some oil to finance its imports of humanitarian supplies. This came to be known as the Oil-for-Food Program (OFP). It generated two new reports to the Security Council, one 90-day report and one annual report. These two new reports were submitted concurrently with the other report created by Resolution 687 (1991) which had been submitted under phase one above and which lasted until 29 April 2003. These generated reports in accordance with resolutions 687 (1991) and 986 (1995), which lasted until April 2003 give the impression that the Committee was active in its reporting. However, that was slightly misleading because most of them were repetitive and added little information.

As an acknowledgment of the lack of transparency in its function, the Committee decided, in its 28 November 1995 and 23 February 1996 reports, to increase the practice of issuing press releases reflecting important matters discussed at its meetings. It also decided that its chairman should give oral briefings to interested delegations about the Committee's work after its meetings.[5]

Between August 1996 and January 2002 the reports of the Committee, which were submitted in accordance with Resolution 687 (1991), were simply a repetition of previous reports without much deviation. However from January 2002 until April 2003 the contents of the Committee's reports changed markedly.

The first change came on 18 January 2002 where the Committee reported in its 43rd report:

> 3. ... During the period covered by the present report, the Committee continued its consideration of a letter dated 7 September 2001 from the Permanent Mission of the United Kingdom to the United Nations drawing the Committee's attention to some German press articles concerning a reported Iraqi attempt to develop its weapons of mass destruction programs.[6]

This was followed by a series of reports by the Committee. Thus in its 44th report, dated 23 April 2002, the Committee relied on media to allege that Belarus was providing military training to Iraq.[7] In its 45th report, dated 22 July 2002, the Committee investigated another media report that Iraq was developing its WMD with Indian assistance.[8] In its 46th report, dated 18 October 2002, the Committee reported that Ukraine had allegedly provided Iraq with Kolchuga airspace passive radars.[9] In its 47th report, dated 17 January 2003, the Committee reported further investigation of the Kolchuga claim.[10] And last but not least in its 48th report dated 29 April 2003, the Committee closed its reporting after the occupation of Iraq with a comment that the matter of the Kolshuga should remain on the Committee's agenda.[11]

It is not accidental that the Committee seems to have been inactive in its reporting between 1996 and 2002 until it is suddenly roused in January 2002 to investigate reports made by member states who take pride in having excellent intelligence services but chose to pass media reports to the Committee. It is rather baffling to say the least that the Committee found it necessary to investigate these media reports without even asking the accusing state whether it could corroborate such claims. We should remember that it was in January/February 2002 that the US/UK decided to invade Iraq. It was in line with preparing the public for such eventuality that the Committee was put into service making such claims about possible breaches by Iraq of the arms sanctions. As it has been verified since the invasion that none of those accusations was credible, then the question that must arise is: was the Committee not part of the campaign of raising false fears in order to prepare the world's opinion for the imminent invasion?

Annual Reporting After Oil-for-Food Programme

Following the adoption of the Oil-for-Food Programme (OFP) in resolution 986 (1995) the Committee became more active and transparent in its reporting. This was manifested, as stated earlier, in two reports: one every 90 days and one every year. In addition, the UN Secretary-General made several reports in a clear change of the policy from that which had prevailed prior to 1996. We shall concentrate here on the annual reports.

These annual reports summed up the main features of the Committee's operations for the previous year. They made it easier for an outsider to observe some of the reality of what was happening in Iraq during that period as opposed to the 1990-1996 period. The reporting in those annual reports may be divided into five main sub headings. These are:

1. Humanitarian Supplies under resolution 986 (1995), (ii) Humanitarian Exemptions under resolution 661 (1990), (iii) Oil Industry Spare Parts, (iv) Operations of UN and Humanitarian Agencies, and (v) Other Matters.
2. Humanitarian Supplies: This sub-heading covers the reporting of humanitarian supplies under resolution 986 on Oil-for-Food. The main feature in all the seven annual reports between 1996 and 2003 was the number of requests put on 'hold' by the US/ UK. Although the size of the items put on hold is not necessarily very informative because putting a small item on hold may render a larger item useless, nevertheless, it is worth visiting this sub-heading in the annual reports. Here is a summary table of applications.

Table 8.1
Number of Humanitarian Applications approved, put on hold or blocked 1997-2003

Annual Reports	Humanitarian Applications		
	Approved	Hold	Blocked
2nd 1997[12]	662, value $1,139 million	88	20
3rd 1998[13]	1,375, value $2.87 billion	27	7
4th 2000[14]	1,835, value $3.4 billion	358, value $872.2 million	Not available
5th 2001[15]	2,519, value $5 billion	682, value $1.5 billion	Not available

6th 2002[16]	2,104, value $5.27 billion	721, value $2.8 billion	Not available
7th 2003[17]	800, value $2 billion	806, value $2.49 billion	Not available

It is apparent from the above summary that both the number and value of items put on 'hold' had suddenly and exponentially increased.

3. Humanitarian Exemptions under Resolution 661 (1990): The reporting under this sub-heading covered items that were supposedly exempt under Resolution 661 (1990) from scrutiny by the Committee. However, it can easily be seen that that was not in practice what happened and most of these items were subject to the same control and veto by single members of the Committee. Here is a table summarizing the mean reporting:

Table 8.2
Number of Humanitarian Exemption Applications approved,
put on hold or blocked 1997-2000

Annual Reports	Humanitarian Exemption Applications		
	Approved	Hold	Blocked
2nd 1997 [18]	5,203, value $8.5 billion	424	5,234
3rd 1998 [19]	3,849, value $6.5 billion	2,849, value $4.8 billion	3,090, value $5.2 billion
4th 2000 [20]	2,654, valu2 $4.4 billion	427, value $7.6 billion	2,823, value $24.9 billion
5th 2001 [21]	2,052, value $6.5 billion	288, value $681 million	2,733, value $13 billion
6h 2002 [22]	2,168, value $8 billion	682, value $2 billion	3,313, value $27.5 billion
7th 2003 [23]	3,847, value $13.85 billion	831, value $3 billion	4,218, value $24 billion

4. Oil Industry Spare Parts: After years of absence of maintenance resulting from the lack of spare parts, it became clear to the

world that Iraq was soon going to be unable to produce enough oil to cover the food bill. The UN Secretary General sent a team of experts to Iraq to study the needs of the oil industry. The subsequent report was submitted by the Secretary General to the Security Council. Consequently the Security Council decided in Resolution 1175 (1998) to allocate sums of money to meet any reasonable expenses for the purchase by Iraq of the necessary parts and equipment to enable it to increase the export of petroleum and petroleum products as provided under Resolution 1153 (1998). However, the procedure for approving applications to export oil spare parts to Iraq did not elicit any better treatment by the Committee than other applications. The following table tells part of the story:

Table 8.3
Number of Oil Spare Parts Applications approved,
put on hold or blocked 1997-2003

Annual Report	Oil Spare Parts Applications		
	Approved	Hold	Pending
3rd 1998[24]	3	1	30
4th 2000[25]	800, value $401 million	318, value $168 million	283, value $289 million
5th 2001[26]	1,507, value $825 million	764, value $510 million	5, value $ 1.9 million
6th 2002[27]	922, value $850 million	274, value $375 million	429, value $504 million
7th 2003[28]	143, value $107 million	309, value $306 million	145, value $508 million

(iv) Operations of UN and Humanitarian Agencies: Not even the UN or other humanitarian agencies received better treatment at the hands of the Committee. If some members of the Committee argued that certain items imported by Iraq could be used to boost Iraq's defenses, no such argument could be raised about the activities of UN agencies. We will cite five examples of the many occasions reported by the Committee in which it refused such applications without justification.

1. The Committee could not accede to two other UNDP requests, one concerning a project entitled "Provision of consultancies and training to essential humanitarian sectors" and the other

a project entitled "Rehabilitation of seed multiplication system through the strengthening of seed quality control in Iraq.[29]

2. The Committee was unable to approve a request from the World Food Programme (WFP) for a general sanctions waiver for all the equipment that has to be purchased by WFP for its operation under Resolution 986(1995).[30]

3. The Committee could not approve a request dated 24 September 1996 from Jordan for the Committee's authorization of one or more regular weekly flights between Amman and Baghdad by Royal Jordanian Airlines in order to carry United Nations personnel and for humanitarian reasons... [31]

4. The Committee considered a request from WHO for an overall arrangement for medical evacuation flights for Iraqi nationals but failed to approve it.[32]

5. The fifth example reveals not only how the Committee behaved but also the sinister role of the IAEA, the guardian of the nuclear industry. This is how the Committee reported the matter:

> During its 189th meeting, on 24 August 1999, the Committee considered a communication from IAEA in which the Committee was requested to advise whether the Agency could dispatch a fact-finding mission to Iraq, at the request of the latter, to gather data on possible radioactive residues resulting from depleted uranium ammunition. The Committee concluded that the matter did not fall within the purview of the Committee, unless IAEA wanted to import equipment submitted to the sanctions regime for the purpose of such a mission. A response to that effect was made to IAEA.[33]

It is clear that the IAEA pretended to act in accordance with its mandate and wrote to the Committee. The Committee responded that it was not within its purview despite the fact that the Committee generally made it clear that everything relating to Iraq was within its remit. However, as IAEA members could not fly with their equipment to Iraq, the request was shelved without anyone taking responsibility. The people of Iraq were left to suffer the hideous effects of radioactivity.[34]

6. Other Matters: The annual reports dealt with several other matters under this sub-heading. Among such matters reported were references to several reviews of the sanctions regime, none of which resulted in any modification. There are repeated

references to discussions by the Committee to ease the procedure to speed up the process of applications on 'hold' but none of these reports advised us as to who was discussing what, considering that the Committee was in fact the Security Council sitting as a Committee. There are also several refusals by the Committee to accede to requests by disadvantaged states who had applied in accordance with Article 50 of the UN Charter for exemption from the sanctions in order to import Iraqi oil.

We believe that the political message of the Sanctions Committee is best displayed in the following action:

An Iraqi request to donate €1 billion of oil revenue to the Palestinian people was on the agenda of the Committee in early 2001. The President of the Security Council requested recommendations on this matter, and the Committee met a number of times in early 2001 to consider the possibilities and implications. The Chairman informed the Committee of his contact with the Palestinian representative, who had welcomed the Iraqi gesture and hoped that this matter might be dealt with by the Committee independently of the sanctions regime against Iraq. Debates ensued, with diverse opinions expressed in the Committee. The Chairman concluded that there was no agreement on the issue, and he would so inform the President of the Security Council.[35]

The Report of One Security Council Meeting Tells the Whole Story

The Sanctions Committee met in private and if any records were made of its deliberations then they have not been made public. It remains a matter of conjecture to determine what had happened during the hundreds of meetings. There is some evidence to suggest that most of the Security Council members were not in accord with the decisions of the Committee which had to be unanimous, with one member able to veto the other fourteen. It is possible that members other than the US/UK discovered that they had made a mistake when they adopted the resolution imposing sanctions on Iraq, as it was formulated such that it needed no further resolution to renew but did need a new resolution to revoke. Such a sentiment and belief was revealed in one important session of the Security Council, which may be seen as reflecting the true dialogue inside the Committee.

The Security Council met on 24 March 2000, almost ten years after the imposition of total sanctions on Iraq, to discuss the report of the Secretary-General (S/2000/208). Three members, the US, UK and the Netherlands spoke in support of maintaining the sanctions and the other twelve members highlighted the plight of Iraqis, the destructive practice of putting applications on hold and called for the lifting of sanctions. We are not presenting our judgment of what they said but let them speak in their own words.

The Secretary General now had this to say on the morality of sanctions and their impact on children:

> Let me conclude by saying that the humanitarian situation in Iraq poses a serious moral dilemma for this Organization. The United Nations has always been on the side of the vulnerable and the weak and has always sought to relieve suffering. Yet here we are accused of causing suffering to an entire population. We are in danger of losing the argument, or the propaganda war—if we have not lost it already—about who is responsible for this situation in Iraq: President Saddam Hussein or the United Nations. ...
>
> I am particularly concerned about the situation of Iraqi children, whose suffering and, in all too many cases, untimely death, have been documented in the report prepared last year by UNICEF and the Iraqi Ministry of Health. That report, which has been echoed by many other observers, showed that, in the center and south of Iraq, infant mortality and morbidity have increased dramatically and reached unacceptable levels.[36]

On the spare parts for the oil industry and putting applications on hold, the Secretary General had this to say:

> However, Iraq's oil industry is seriously hampered by a lack of spare parts and equipment, and this threatens to undermine the program's income in the long term. That is why I have repeatedly recommended a significant increase in the allocation of resources under the program for the purchase of spare parts for the oil industry.
>
> I understand that the Council is now ready to consider these recommendations favorably, and I would

very much welcome that. But I should also mention that many of the holds on contract applications, imposed by members of the Committee established pursuant to resolution 661 (1990), do have a direct negative impact on the humanitarian program and on efforts to rehabilitate Iraq's infrastructure, most of which is in appalling disrepair. We need a mechanism to review these holds, in order to ensure the smooth functioning of the program.[37]

Mr. Ward, representative of Jamaica, summed up the sentiment of the other members of the Security Council on the deaths of Iraqi children in saying:

One does not need to be a mother or a father for one's heart to bleed at what the Iraqi children are going through; one needs only to be human. We cannot use political concerns to address humanitarian needs.[38]

Mr. Levitte, representative of France, said on the fate of Iraqi children:

According to the United Nations Children's Fund (UNICEF), the mortality rate for children under five rose from 56 per 1,000 in the period 1984-1989 to the current 131 per 1,000. The infant mortality rate is among the highest in the world. One dramatic statistic in a recent British parliamentary report deserves mention: If the progress in health observed during the 1980s had been maintained through the following decade, 500,000 children would have survived......This "embargo generation" is a lost generation.[39]

On the unacceptable procedure of holds he had this to say:

I would like to point out in particular the high rate in certain sectors essential to improving the humanitarian situation, such as electricity, water and agriculture. In these sectors, the rate of holds exceeds 50 per cent and has even reached 100 per cent in phase V of the telecommunications sector. With such high rates, the humanitarian program can no longer function in these sectors.[40]

On the matter of allowing Iraq to import spare parts for its oil industry he said:

> Spare parts with a total value of only $250 million have actually been delivered, whereas the Council has made available the equivalent of $1.2 billion in four phases. The decisions taken by the Council are therefore being largely ignored.[41]

It is fair to say that France was not in agreement with its US and UK allies on sanctions.

Mr. Wang Yingfan representative of China expressed Chinese dissatisfaction with the devastation caused by sanctions in saying:

> Many contracts in the petroleum, power-generating, water-treatment and other sectors are interrelated. Under such circumstances, as long as one contract is on hold, even if the others have been approved, it is as if none of the related contracts had been approved either. For instance, Iraq has been permitted to import power generators, but the import of electricity cables is denied. It is common sense that without those cables none of the generators, with a total value of hundreds of millions of dollars, can serve any useful purpose, even though the installation might have been completed and the generators might be running. ..As a matter of fact, the 10-year sanctions have brought incalculable suffering to innocent Iraqi civilians. This is an objective and incontrovertible fact. This is by no means the original intention and purpose of the Security Council in imposing the sanctions.[42]

On the double standards in the Security Council in which China was, no doubt, complicit he had this to say:

> We believe that the Security Council, in addressing humanitarian issues, should proceed in accordance with the same standards and apply the same criteria to all regions and countries, avoiding both politicization and any kind of double standard. The same attention and input should be given to every case, be it the humanitarian crisis in Iraq, Kosovo, East Timor, African countries or elsewhere.[43]

Mr. Lavrov the Russian Federation representative was more outspoken in his criticism. On the general effects of sanctions he said:

> The report of the Secretary-General, which is based on a broad range of facts, shows clearly that the scale of the humanitarian catastrophe in Iraq is inexorably leading to the disintegration of the very fabric of civil society there. The economic consequences of the many years of sanctions have been reflected in all aspects of the lives of the people of the country. The total impoverishment of the population—which obviously falls short of generally recognized health standards—serious employment problems, the impossibility of having a normally functioning educational system and other problems have led to a situation where an entire generation of Iraqis has been physically and morally crippled. They are in essence outcasts of the world community.
>
> The industrial infrastructure of Iraq has been damaged, including the water supply and the energy and communications sectors. The few remaining means of transportation cannot provide for the sustainable distribution of food and medicine. The epidemiological situation in the country poses a threat on a regional scale. Mortality rates among the most vulnerable groups of the population have reached threatening proportions, as stated in the reports of the United Nations Children's Fund (UNICEF).[44]

Mr. Lavrov exposed the very serious and hidden continuous war against Iraq, which was going on with little reporting when he said:

> Today we cannot fail to react to another problem that has been pointed out. The socio-economic and humanitarian situation in Iraq is worsening because civilian facilities in Iraq are constantly the targets of air strikes by the United States and Great Britain. This is happening in the so-called no-flight zones established unilaterally, without the United Nations taking any decision, and which encompass almost 65 per cent of Iraq's territory.
>
> Our data show that United States and United Kingdom aircraft invaded Iraqi airspace nearly 20,000

times between December 1998 and mid-March 2000. We are particularly concerned about reports of strikes against facilities that are being used in the United Nations humanitarian operation, in particular against food distribution warehouses and against metering stations along oil pipelines.

According to these analyses, 42 per cent of these air strikes have resulted in human casualties. Over the past year, 144 innocent civilians have died and 466 people have been wounded as a result of these air strikes. Our data show that 57 people have been killed and 133 wounded in southern Iraq, and that 87 people have been killed and 313 wounded in the north. Claims that these strikes were not directed against civilian targets do not hold water. Facts—including facts from international experts—attest to the contrary. Nor does the notion that these air strikes were in retaliation for actions by Iraqi anti-aircraft defenses hold water: our data show that facilities unrelated to anti-aircraft defense systems are being hit.[45]

Mr. Hasmy, representative of Malaysia expressed the Malaysian view on the legality and morality of sanctions when he said:

For almost a decade, the most comprehensive and punitive sanctions ever imposed on a people have destroyed Iraq as a modern State, decimated its people and ruined its agriculture, educational and health-care systems, as well as its infrastructure. The devastating effects of the sanctions testify to the failure of comprehensive sanctions as a policy tool. Such sanctions violate basic human rights—the right to live with dignity and, indeed, the right to life itself. The sanctions regime has brought about a humanitarian crisis of enormous proportions. This is beyond dispute. The tragedy is that, while much of the devastation can be prevented, it has been allowed to continue. The situation is so deplorable that, to their great credit, a group of concerned legislators in the United States Congress have felt compelled to pronounce themselves on the subject. They have characterized the sanctions regime as "infanticide masquerading as policy". Clearly, the sanctions do more than hurt; they kill, especially those who are most vulnerable. To add insult to injury, the entire program of deprivation being imposed on the Iraqi people and the mechanism instituted for that purpose are being paid for with proceeds from the sale of their own oil.[46]

On the hidden agenda of the US and UK in imposing sanctions, he said:

The original United Nations resolutions imposed sanctions to pressure Iraq to eliminate its programs of weapons of mass destruction. Policy statements emanating from some capitals, however, suggest that sanctions will remain in place until certain political objectives have been achieved. This policy clearly undermines the original objective of the sanctions, around which the international consensus against Iraq was originally based, and makes children and families in Iraq virtual hostages to the political deadlock between Governments. The continuing demonizing of Iraq must stop if we are serious in our professed concern for the plight of the Iraqi people.[47]

Needless to say, Mr. Hasmy's claim related to political objectives was later vindicated when the US/UK invaded Iraq in 2003. Mr. Hasmy went on to accuse the SC of breaching international law, saying:

By sustaining economic sanctions against Iraq in the full knowledge of their deplorable consequences, the Security Council will continue to undermine the Charter of the United Nations. It is time for us to view the matter not, for the most part, through the narrow prism of security—which is important, but which has substantially been addressed—but also and equally frequently through the broader prism of humanity.[48]

Executive Director of the Iraq Programme Addresses the Security Council on the Evils of Sanctions

No less damning views were also expressed by Benon V. Sevan, Executive Director of the Iraqi Programme when he addressed the Security Council on Thursday, 21 September 2000. He expressed the frustrations and dismay of several other UN officials who worked in Iraq, like Halliday and von Sponeck.[49] Here are a few excerpts from his address. They need little explanation or comment.[50]

I am sure some of you will now tell me: "Benon, come on, not again, you sound like a broken record!" Well, so be it. As the Executive Director of the Iraq Programme, I feel duty bound to draw the attention of the Council to the unacceptably high level of holds placed on applications. Just as playing a broken record hurts the ear, every hold placed on an application for an essential supply affects the implementation of the program, or to put it another way, it hurts the Iraqi people.

The increasing number of holds has become a major concern for the Secretary-General who has been following very closely the progress in our efforts to reduce the number and value of holds. As stated in paragraph 46 of the report before you, in many sectors, infrastructure remains heavily incapacitated despite the ordering by the Government of Iraq of essential inputs. Complementary items have frequently been kept on hold long after the central items with which they were intended to be used have been delivered. Thus many key supplies and equipment essential to all sectors remain either on hold by the Committee or in effect on hold in an Iraqi warehouse, waiting for the arrival of a complementary item.

Despite the commendable efforts made since the end of last April to bring about a reduction in the number of contracts on hold, I regret to say that the total value of holds, which had dropped to $1.6 billion, as at 31 May, has now reached yet again, $1.982 billion, or just under $2 billion, as at 18 September, involving 1,172 applications. Of these, 503 applications, worth $266 million, were for oil spare parts and equipment.

Increasingly, we have been facing a new situation whereby even when experts from UNMOVIC do not consider that items are on the 1051 list, some members insist that the items concerned are covered or should have been covered under resolution 1051 (1996).

It is neither the size nor the value of the items placed on hold that determine their relative value for the implementation of a project. What is the use, for example, if approval is given for the purchase of a very expensive truck and the application for the purchase of its ignition key is placed on hold?

The contracts signed by the Government of Iraq, however, contain no such provisions. In the present contracts there are no provisions for performance bonds, despite the size, technical complexity and the value of contracts. In brief, commercial protection for Iraq is seriously lacking. As a result, much is arriving in Iraq, defective or non-compliant with the terms of contracts. At present, there is no penalty against a supplier who does not meet the terms of a contract. He is paid once it is certified that the supplies have crossed the border into Iraq.

These are all legitimate concerns and I should like to make an urgent appeal through the Council to the Committee members to reconsider this very important matter. The Office of the Iraq Programme is ready to assist the Committee in that regard.

Electricity in particular is a major concern— not only is the supply of electricity insufficient, it is precarious, as seen with the recent fire in the transmission lines at the Mussaiyab Power Station, which resulted in the loss of 600 MW. This increased power outages in Baghdad to eight hours a day and up to 20 hours in other affected governorates. The entire electricity grid is in a precarious state and is in imminent danger of collapsing altogether should another incident of this type occur.[51]

We believe that with the limited information available on the Sanctions Committee, we have managed to expose the 'genocide tool' which was cleverly created by the US/UK at a moment of negligence or indifference by other members of the SC some of whom regretted having approved its creation. We believe that some members of the Security Council committed genocide willfully while others by omission having created such a possibility.

SANCTIONS AS GENOCIDE

When a country is put under total blockade for some thirteen years during which nothing was allowed in or out and even essential medicine and medical equipment was subject to restrictions, then any of the results in Article 2 of the *Genocide Convention* were either intended by the perpetrators, or the perpetrators had no doubt that their actions would lead to these results, or they knew that these results would occur in the ordinary sense of events—each of which amounts to specific intent under English Law.

It is accepted that the Government of Iraq between 1990 and 2003 was considered, under the dictates of the foreign policy of the US, a pariah. Iraq was not even given its natural right to address the Security Council. Perhaps officials in Iraq thought that it would have been an exercise in futility and a waste of resources for the Iraqi Government to seek the opinion of any judicial authority on the total blockade.

It is equally accepted that the governments of Iraq since 2003 have neither the interest nor the political will to indict their masters with whom they have signed so-called security agreements, which are no less than acquiescence in occupation.

However, it is inconceivable that such an anomalous state of affairs will last forever. Sooner or later a national government will emerge in Iraq and will be forced by popular will to seek redress for the genocide committed during the blockade years. We would venture even further and claim that once the effect of the use of uranium weapons becomes more pronounced, the pressure will be even stronger to seek such redress.[1] Once such a government exists it can bring a case against the UK before the ICJ; or attempt to gain an indictment before the ICC, though clearly there are a range of issues concerning ratification and jurisdiction that will come into play in the latter case. In view of the new direction which the ICJ seems to be following, Iraq may get a fairer hearing there. However, even before the ICC, it will still be able to argue 'intent' under the broader definition of the Statute, based on foreseeability and knowledge. Notwithstanding this, we suggest that an objective Court ruling on the questions of law and fact are likely to find along the lines set out below.

The Court will find, if it examines all evidence thoroughly and without bias, that genocide was committed in Iraq even when applying the restrictive definition of intent in *dolus specialis*. If we were to forget about the millions who died unnecessarily, as could be proven from the multitude of reports by UN agencies and NGOs, and accept the single incidence of the half a million children which the Secretary of State of the USA, Albright acknowledged had died,[2] while articulating that according to her their deaths were worth it, then the Court could find that genocide was committed by the admission of its perpetrators, acting in their official capacity i.e. raising questions about state responsibility.

Intent in genocide will have to be accepted by any court to mean that the criminal perpetrators intended the consequences of their actions if they knew to a degree of certainty that the consequences of imposing total blockade of Iraq would lead to its destruction regardless of whether or not they deliberately sought to realize those consequences. Every international report from that of UN Special Envoy Mr. Ahtisaari to UNICEF's 2003 report proved that the destruction of Iraq was taking place.[3] There cannot be the slightest doubt that all members of the Security Council knew that genocide was taking place. The numbers alone are sufficient to demonstrate that—dwarfing all numbers in any other accepted cases of genocide.

Clearly the conditions whose imposition could be said to bring about the physical destruction in whole or part as required in Article II, sub-paragraph (c) have been fulfilled. We believe that Robinson's suggestions are almost identical to the events as they transpired in Iraq, strengthening the argument that these activities fall within the remit of genocide. As Robinson put it:

> Instances of Genocide that could come under subparagraph(c) are such as placing a group of people on subsistence diet, reducing required medical services below a minimum, withholding sufficient living accommodation, etc., provided that these restrictions are imposed with intent to destroy the group on whole or in part.[4]

The above conditions and more, such as withholding basic material and chemicals for water purification, were imposed on Iraq during the thirteen years of total blockade with an intent that could be argued as falling within that defined by the *Rome Statue*, and that should therefore be considered acts of genocide against the nationals of Iraq. It is clear that there was intent to cause harm as the US/UK refused to pay attention to any of the studies and reports, including those of UN organizations, which showed the adverse effects of sanctions. Thus in the context of the *Genocide Convention*, when it was highlighted to the two governments that the conditions they were imposing on Iraq were leading to the destruction of the nationals of Iraq, they persisted nonetheless. Clearly, even if strict intent was not visible at first, the disregarding of compelling evidence in the course of the action has to equate to having knowledge about the impact of the actions. The circumstances of the actions demonstrate intent beyond mere foresight or foreknowledge of impact, to actual knowledge. And if knowledge is present during a continuing act that is ongoing into the future, then intent may be amplified to be regarded as a crime that was not only intended at the time that it occurred but also as planned into the future. What is particularly heinous is that despite such knowledge there was no desisting from the actions.

Complicity in Genocide

Article III of the *Genocide Convention* reads:

The following acts shall be punishable:
Genocide;
Conspiracy to commit Genocide;
Direct and public incitement to commit Genocide;
Attempt to commit Genocide;
Complicity in Genocide.

It is clear that the intention of the drafters all along was to punish those who are accessories to the destruction of a group, thus the Convention lists the actions above. It should be emphasized here that the terms: conspiracy, incitement, attempt and complicity may have different meaning under different legal systems in the world which means that different interpretation of the Article are bound to be made. Out of all the above subparagraphs we would like to concentrate on sub-section (e). From the work that we have undertaken, and the attempts of one of the authors to engage the legal system in the UK, we would like to highlight that parties other than the US and the UK were complicit in committing Genocide in Iraq.

On the question of complicity in genocide the ICJ held:

> The question arises whether complicity presupposes that the accomplice shares the specific intent (*dolus specialis*) of the principal perpetrator. But whatever the reply to this question, there is no doubt that the conduct of an organ or a person furnishing aid or assistance to a perpetrator of the crime of genocide cannot be treated as complicity in genocide unless at the least that organ or person acted knowingly, that is to say, in particular, was aware of the specific intent (*dolus specialis*) of the principal perpetrator. If that condition is not fulfilled, that is sufficient to exclude categorization as complicity.[5]

There is one entity that we strongly believe was complicit in the act of genocide committed in Iraq, namely the Security Council, whether acting under its name or as the Sanctions Committee. It is admittedly rare for literature in public international law to lay accusations at the door of the Security Council, due to its exalted status in the United Nations Charter. However, we need to make it clear here, that as a practicing lawyer and commentator and researcher, we believe that nobody—including no entity—ought to be above the law. It should not be possible for states or combinations of states to commit major jus cogens crimes and be relieved of culpability under the pretext that they operated collectively in whatever guise—that of institutions or of treaties, or of intergovernmental entities, whatever the covering entity might be, any more than for individuals to do so, as officials of states. This necessarily means that the United Nations Security Council could be in breach of International Law and therefore ought to be liable to questioning about its decisions.

Naturally it is clear that the structures and nature of public international law means that a case will not be filed against the Security Council insofar as there is no mechanism which presently holds a mandate to address such a case—to say nothing of whether such an international will to do so might be summoned. But it nonetheless remains important in the context of documenting human rights abuses and the right to redress for criminal acts that action be considered against member states that took part in imposing and maintaining the total blockade on Iraq. Further questions that need addressing but which were not tackled in our work, are those concerning the extent to which norms of collective responsibility bind members of the United Nations Security Council, and the extent to which collective litigation can be pursued against a group of states.

To return to the specific context of Iraq, it needs to be reiterated that the original purpose of imposing sanctions on Iraq was to remove the Iraqi army from Kuwait. We may go along with that decision for the sake of argument, despite our belief that total blockade as articulated above constitutes genocide, which is itself a peremptory norm, and should not be used as a means of coercing any state into any action. The Security Council members that accepted the demand of the US and UK to impose a total blockade on Iraq may have an argument, albeit weak, based on the 1990 Resolutions. However, notwithstanding these arguments, it is clear *that once the Iraqi army had been forced to withdraw from Kuwait, the continuation of sanctions had no foundation in law*. Imposing a total blockade on a state in order to disarm it is a punitive measure of collective punishment contrary to a fundamental principle of international law, that states have a right to self defense, and in exercise of that right, to arm themselves. The failure to respect this norm is to violate Iraqi state sovereignty well beyond any punitive measures addressed in the UN Charter, and to bring into question one of the founding principles of multilateral organizations: whether they can violate international law, and do so with impunity.

We submit that every state that acquiesced in the continuation of sanctions on Iraq, when all international bodies were reporting the genocidal effects of sanctions, ought to be considered guilty of complicity in genocide. To fail to do this signals a weakening of public international legal norms, and subjects the discipline to the politics of power - indeed, in matters where it matters most, throws it out the window.

Members of the Sanctions Committee gave themselves the right, which was never sanctioned by any due process of law, to withhold the import into Iraq of material vital to the sustenance and continuation of the lives of ordinary people. We contend that any member of the Sanctions Committee who took part in any decision at any stage during the thirteen years of sanctions to block vital imports to Iraq (including essential medical supplies) ought to be liable to being charged with having been complicit in imposing conditions leading to genocide in Iraq.

This assertion is supported by Article IV of the Convention which reads:

> Persons committing Genocide or any of the acts enumerated in Article III shall be punished, whether they are constitutionally responsible rulers, public officials or private individuals.

The purpose of this Article was to temper the immunity given to heads of state, to contest the plea concerning 'acts of state' versus that of individual action, and to question pleas concerning the chain of command, and 'superior orders' when it comes to evading culpability for the crime of genocide.

It is worth pointing out here that the representative of the USSR suggested an amendment to the Genocide Convention that would have added that "command of law or superior orders shall not justify Genocide".[6] However, such an amendment was rejected by states, irrespective of the supposedly landmark Nuremberg Principles, fearing it would have made it difficult to ratify as it might have conflicted with some domestic legislation. The Article as it was adopted requires intent on behalf of soldiers, for example, carrying out superior orders. However, the plea of superior orders is no defense in the case of members of the Sanctions Committee, because they were not simple tools implementing the Security Council resolutions, but themselves as Council members, had the freedom of action and interpretation and would thus be liable to being found complicit in imposing genocide on Iraq and vetoing purchase of basic commodities. Their argument of being under the constraint of pressure by other states should have no more validity than that of individual officials in relation to government policy as decided by Nuremberg.

A Significant Challenge to the Legality of Security Council Resolutions: The Ruling of the European Court of Justice (ECJ)

For too long decisions of the Security Council were considered almost sacred: neither challenged nor even discussed. It was accepted that article 103 of the Charter effectively meant that whatever the Security Council decides goes. Even the International Court of Justice (ICJ) has denied itself jurisdiction even if the case is before it, once the Security Council is seized of the matter.[7] It took a more independent legal body than then ICJ to attempt to change this unacceptable state of affairs. This came in the ECJ ruling in the *Kadi* case,[8] which did not concern Iraq but did at least concern sanctions.

Mr. Kadi and others brought legal action against a Council of EU Regulation, which froze their assets in implementing a Security Council resolution intended to freeze assets of supporters of Bin Laden and the Taliban. The Court of First Instance (CFI) rejected the applications by the claimants but found that it was, none the less, empowered to check, indirectly, the lawfulness of the resolutions of the Security Council in question with regard to *jus cogens*.[9]

The claimants appealed and the UK cross-appealed on the matter of the right to challenge the Security Council resolution with regard to *jus cogens*. The ECJ annulled the judgment of the CFI and made its own judgment on the applications. However, the ECJ made no decision on the ruling of the CFI or the cross-appeal by the UK on the question with regard to *jus cogens*. We submit that that matter is still active and the ruling of the CFI is a serious challenge to the prevailing view that Security Council resolutions are above the 'rule of law'.

Equally important outcomes of the hearing of the *Kadi* case before the ECJ has been its ruling on the right of the Community to refuse to implement a UN resolution if it conflicts with basic fundamental rights upheld by the Community and also its ruling on the functioning of the Sanctions Committee.

Thus on the possible conflict between a Security Council resolution and basic rights, the ECJ held:

> The Community judicature must, therefore, in accordance with the powers conferred on it by the EC Treaty, ensure the review, in principle the full review, of the lawfulness of all Community acts in the light of the fundamental rights forming an integral part of the general principles of Community law, including review of Community measures which, like the regulation at issue, are designed to give effect to the resolutions adopted by the Security Council under Chapter VII of the Charter of the United Nations.[10]

The ECJ applied the above principle to functioning of the Sanctions Committee and observed that matters such as (i) the inability of a person on Committee's list to assert his rights;[11] (ii) the veto of any one member of the Committee,[12] (iii) the inability of person on the list to assert his right in person or be represented during a procedure by the Committee to consider his application to be removed from list,[13] and (iv) that the Committee need neither communicate reason or evidence for a name to be on the list nor give reasons for rejecting an application to remove a name from list,[14] were all causes for review by virtue of the above principle of upholding basic fundamental rights as enshrined in the Treaty.

The Sanctions Committee in the *Kadi* case is almost identical to the Sanctions Committee for Iraq and their guidelines are also identical. We suggest that the ruling of the ECJ in *Kadi* case enables any Iraqi who was subjected for years to such denial of basic rights to sue the guilty European state, for example the UK, for damages on the grounds that the measures breached his/her fundamental rights as upheld by the Treaty.

CONCLUSION

THE NEED FOR AN APPROPRIATE JUDICIAL INQUIRY

Imposing sanctions on Iraq was one of the most heinous of crimes committed in the 20th century. Yet it has received little attention in the Anglo-American world. Despite the calamitous destruction resulting from the sanctions, no serious attempts by legal professionals, academics or philosophers have been undertaken to address the full scope of the immorality and illegality of such a criminal and unprecedented mass punishment.

Modern political Iraq was created by the Sykes-Picot Agreement following the end of WWI and the disappearance of the Ottoman Empire, out of parts of the old political Mesopotamia. All governments of Iraq between the 1920s and 2003 continuously rejected the carving out of the current state of Kuwait. Such a persistent objector is entitled under customary international law to reject the borders created and imposed by the colonialist powers even if they were later upheld by the UN. The Western imperialists' plans for the Arab world have been the same over the last 200 years as asserted by the British Foreign Secretary in 1949.[1] It started with the encroachment by the British on the edges of the Ottoman Empire during the 19th century, which resulted in the full occupation of Iraq during WWI. The control of Iraq by the British took several forms of military presence and treaties until the overthrow of the monarchy in 1958. Although the British control over Iraq and the rest of the Gulf waned post WWII, there was no vacuum as the USA moved in. The imperialist plan for the Arab world has been based on two limbs. Firstly, Iraq should be prevented from becoming a developed polity, as it would challenge the artificially created statelets on the Gulf, having always been a persistent objector. Secondly, any Arab unity should be prevented at any cost. Both objectives were pursued with vigour by the UK in the first half of the 20th century and by the UK and USA in its second half.

The creation of the State of Israel was precisely to serve the purpose of having a geographical barrier between the Middle East Arabs and North African Arabs in addition to solving the Jewish problem for the civilized Europeans.

We believe that we have established that different governments in Iraq, irrespective of their political affiliation to the West as in between 1920 and 1958 or their relative independence post 1958, had worked within available means to build a proper prosperous, functioning modern state. The Ba'ath, after assuming power in 1968, had three factors that made it easier for it to advance development beyond what its predecessors had achieved. Firstly, the Ba'ath had a long-term strategy. Secondly, it had continuity of political control over Iraq. Thirdly, it had more revenue from the sharp rise of oil prices post 1973 and its nationalization. All these factors enabled the Ba'ath to transform Iraq between 1970 and 1980 into a semi-industrialized state as Ahtisaari labeled it in 1991.[2]

It was a phenomenal achievement, as we have shown, for the Ba'ath state to have been able to develop Iraq on every level in such a short time. The comparison between the ten years of the Ba'ath development of Iraq and the almost ten years of the so-called democratic Iraq since the invasion of 2003 is unavoidable. Despite the normal flow of oil, US technology and support, and the facilities available to it from Europe, not one single development took place in Iraq post 2003. For almost ten years, democratic Iraq has not been able to solve its electricity problems. Iraqis still rely on local generators to provide them with basic electricity for lighting and refrigeration. Air conditioning, so much needed in temperatures of over 50 degrees Celsius, is a luxury the Iraqis can only dream about. We need to remind ourselves that in the 1980s, during the Ba'ath rule, Iraq not only provided cheap electricity to everyone, but exported the surplus to Turkey!

Between 1990 and 2003, the USA/UK and their allies not only destroyed what the Ba'ath had built, but in fact all that had been built in modern Iraq since the 1920s. All aspects of life were devastated through the massive attack of 1991 and the following almost 13 years of total siege. When Ahtisaari visited Iraq in April 1991, he commented that semi-industrialized Iraq had been bombed into the Stone Age.[3] We wonder what Ahtisaari would have said, had he visited Iraq on the eve of the invasion in 2003.

The cause of the unprecedented destruction and killing that has befallen Iraq as outlined in the book has yet to be explained. We know of nobody, be that a politician, a jurist, an academic, a media commentator or anyone else who has come up with a rational reason for such massive genocidal acts against the people of Iraq. If it is alleged that it was because Iraq invaded Kuwait, then we should remember that both Israel and the USA had invaded so many countries in the 20th century. Egypt invaded and annexed the Hala'ib triangle from the Sudan, an area which is larger than Kuwait, without a word of objection from the so-called world community. If it was about alleged WMD which everybody with high school knowledge of science knew Iraq did not have in the 1990s and certainly never used, then we should remember that both the USA and Israel, individually, have had massive arsenals and have used them. [We refer to the nuclear weapons used by the US and DU, cluster bombs, phosphorous, Napalm etc used by both, which are all classified as WMD.] If it was about respecting human rights, then we should remember that the UK/USA and their European allies support the most oppressive regimes in Arabia, the Gulf and elsewhere in the world. It should also be obvious to everyone that Iraq never threatened, let alone attacked, the USA, the UK or any European state that was so ready to send their troops to attack Iraq or ensure the maintenance of their total siege.

We can only conclude that it was absolute evil which was a fundamental element of the imperialist plan for the Middle East Arab World—the same evil that was written about in the Bible, the Qur'an, and by Hegel to name only a few.

How was it possible for such genocide to be allowed following the post WWII conventions and awareness of the scourge of wars which the new UN was created to prevent, a student of international law or politics would legitimately ask. The reason, we believe, lies in the basic flaw of the UN Charter which simply imposed the will of WWII victors on the rest of the world by setting up the Security Council which usurped the will of the international community, gave itself absolute powers to decide and veto, and ended up being a court of law in which it was prosecution, judge and jury with no appeal. In imposing sanctions on Iraq and maintaining them for nearly 13 years, the SC was precisely that and got away with more than murder—with genocide!

We have called for a major reform of the UN creating a balanced and just system in which no single state, however mighty it may, would be able to hold the world to ransom, and where disputes are settled by an international court that is independent of the UN and whose judgments are enforceable.

We have catalogued breaches and crimes committed during the years of total sanctions. One purpose is to highlight the scale of death and destruction so that such measures are never again taken against any other country in the future. The second and no less important purpose is to ensure that legal action could be taken against the perpetrators of these crimes and breaches.

In addition to breaching the basic human rights of the people of Iraq as has been accepted by all states of the world, aggression, crimes against humanity, war crimes and genocide were committed as have been detailed in the previous chapters. These crimes have always been defined under customary international law before they were incorporated in the Geneva Conventions and the Statute of the International Criminal Court.

Who are the perpetrators?

We have shown that there are three categories of perpetrators of crimes against Iraq. These are: States, Governments Officials and members of international bodies. The first category includes every state that voted in resolution 687 (1991) to impose total genocidal sanctions on Iraq following its withdrawal from Kuwait and the end of hostilities. The second category includes every member of the USA and UK governments who took part in perpetrating these crimes. For the USA the list should include every member of the Bush senior, Clinton and Bush junior administrations. It should also include military commanders who supervised the imposition of sanctions and military attacks on Iraqi civilian installations between 1991 and 2003. Last but not least it should include every representative of the USA who sat on the Sanctions Committee and decided to deprive Iraqis of their basic life needs.

For the UK the list should include every member of John Major and Tony Blair cabinets. Similar to the case of the USA, the list should also include all military commanders and UK representatives on the Sanctions Committee.

The third category should include any member of a UN body that either existed or was created for Iraq, who took part in a planned campaign of deception and misinformation which managed to deceive people at large into believing that Iraq was not carrying out its duty as demanded by the unjust SC resolutions. Among members of this category are Dr. Mohamed ElBaradei and members of his board at the IAEA; Rolf Ekéus, First Chairman of UNSCOM and his successor Richard Butler; and Dr. Hans Blix who, in his capacity as head of UNMOVIC, knowingly kept on telling the world up to the eve of the invasion that he was not sure that Iraq was clean of WMD when he, a renowned scientist, knew full well that with the available technology, any traces of nuclear radiation and chemical residues were capable of being sniffed out in Iraq, especially so since they had inspected every corner of it, even the President's bedroom!

How to Initiate Legal Action

There are several venues for initiating legal action against each of the above categories of perpetrators. We are aware that the Iraqi governments following the 2003 invasion, similar to the Iraqi governments of the 1920s, have been nothing more than agents and tools of the USA. There is nothing spectacular about this reality. In fact the opposite would have been surprising. It is inconceivable that an occupying power would take all the effort and cost to invade and occupy a country only to let it choose a government opposed to the invader's interests. However, like in any occupation, a time will come when the people of Iraq will take control of their own affairs and sweep away all the invasion agents. It is then that we believe the nationalist Iraqi government will bring action before two international courts—the ICJ and the European Court—against each state which voted for the total sanctions against Iraq following its withdrawal from Kuwait. Such action should be based on the fact that imposing total sanctions was genocidal and that the SC had no authority to breach a peremptory norm of customary international law. It is highly likely that the ICJ will find it more difficult to take on the SC as it has historically shied away from even looking into the legality of its resolutions.

However, in the case of the European Court, albeit its jurisdiction applies only to European states, the opportunity of success is much higher considering that the Court has created a precedent in the case of *Kadi* [4] and that its duty is to see that SC resolution comply with the rule of law within the community. Any state found guilty would be forced to pay war reparations. Such a judgment would have a deterrent effect on any state contemplating imposing genocidal total sanctions on any other state in future.

Although individuals have no access to the ICJ, they have, nevertheless, access to domestic courts in Europe. Any Iraqi who had suffered through the imposition of sanctions has a case to bring against European states which enforced the sanctions against him, relying on the European Court judgment in the case of *Kadi*. Thousands of Iraqis should be able to find redress to their suffering following such just judgment by the European Court which put an end to the bizarre state of affairs that prevailed in Europe in which acts of states were outside the rule of law, however illegal these states acts were.

In the case of individual members of the USA/UK administrations and members of international bodies referred to above, there are a couple of routes to initiate legal action. The ICC has no jurisdiction in crimes committed before it came into force. This means that crimes committed in Iraq during the siege are outside its jurisdiction. We are not overtly sorry for that. We believe that the ICC was created to try people with whom the superpowers were dissatisfied. Article 16 of the Statute of the ICC made it subject to the intervention of the SC which could stop any action in the court indefinitely without giving reason. No justice could be expected of such a court which would be unable to indict any of the permanent members of the SC. When the President of the ICC was asked following a lecture he gave in the Middle Temple in 2007 in London about the possibility of indicting Mr. Bush and Mr. Blair, he responded with a laugh!

However, each and every one of the war crimes, crimes against humanity and genocide which were committed against Iraq is indictable before domestic courts in all 'civilized' states either under legislation promulgated following the adoption of the Geneva Conventions and the Genocide Convention or by virtue of accepting that crimes against customary international law are automatically indictable under domestic courts. Individual Iraqis who had suffered under the sanctions regime are able to choose which route to follow depending on in which state they are initiating legal action. In the USA, both the Geneva Conventions and the Genocide Convention were ratified prior to 1991. The ratification of a convention in the USA gives domestic court jurisdiction to try any crime under that Convention. It should be open to any Iraqi to initiate legal action for breach of these Conventions. If the courts find that the implementing legislation would not allow such action to be brought then complaints based on customary international rules should be available to complainants.

In the case of the UK the matter is slightly more complicated. Although the UK passes domestic legislation immediately after acceding to any treaty that requires changes to UK law to give it domestic jurisdiction, it nevertheless always adds a condition to that legislation in the form of the need of the consent of the Attorney General to initiate criminal proceeding. We know of no single case in which the AG has ever granted consent to indict a British official under such legislation. We believe that such a route may be futile to follow so long as the AG in the UK is unanswerable to anyone. There is, however, another route open to Iraqis who had suffered from sanctions imposed and maintained by British officials, that being invoking customary international law. War crimes and crimes against humanity have always been crimes under customary international law. Genocide has always been a peremptory norm of international law from which no derogation is admitted. All that the Geneva Conventions, the Genocide Convention and the Statute of the ICC did was to incorporate them into treaties. This incorporation has not meant that customary law is not valid anymore. Customary international law exists in parallel with treaties and conventions. Most jurists and judges have come to accept that customary international law is enforceable in British courts. We have our doubts following the judgment of Lord Bingham in the case of *Jones and others* [5] in which he stated that although aggression is a crime under customary international law, it required Parliament to legislate that it was so before it could become indictable before a British court. A criminal action initiated against Tony Blair or any member of his cabinet by an Iraqi could test the ruling of Lord Bingham. However, a failure before the Supreme Court in the UK could still be challenged before the European Court.

After having argued the different routes available to a free Iraqi government and to Iraqi individuals we still would like to consider the possibility of another route to punish the perpetrators of crimes against Iraq and exact reparations. We call for the setting up of a special tribunal like that of Nuremberg and an application of the same principles which were applied in Nuremberg and upheld by the USA/UK and their allies as high moral and legal principles and precedents. Such a tribunal could be set up from an international panel of judges and prosecutors which will apply identical procedure and principles to that of Nuremberg. It seems to us that it would be almost impossible for the people who argue the high moral and legal values of Nuremberg to refuse having these [6]principles applied to them.

The Nuremberg tribunal was staffed with judges and prosecutors from the victors of WWII: the USA, UK, USSR and France. The accused were indicted for four main crimes: Crimes against Peace, Wars of Aggression, War Crimes and Crimes against Humanity. We argue that all these crimes in addition to genocide should form the bases of indictment.

It is a sad state of affairs that after so many unnecessary deaths, so much destruction, one war, twelve years of siege, invasion and occupation we ended with the primary perpetrators of genocide in Iraq either being awarded top diplomatic positions as in the case of Tony Blair, or enjoying life with glory in highly paid positions as in the case of John Major. If no redress is even attempted then the world will slump into such moral decay that similar genocides will be repeated on an even increasing scale.

As there is no statute of limitations with regard to bringing action in any of the crimes committed against Iraq, it is hoped that this book will serve not only as an indictment of and barrier to future global imposition of sanctions, but also as a tool in bringing the actual perpetrators of this crime to a Nuremberg-style day of judgment.

ENDNOTES

Introduction

1 Gordon, Joy, 'When intent makes all the difference in the world: economic sanctions on Iraq and the accusation of genocide', *Yale Human Rights and Development Law Journal, Vol. 5*, 2002, p. 58, n.1.

2 Memo from White House Counsel Alberto Gonzales to Pres. George W. Bush <http://news.lp.findlaw.com/hdocs/docs/torture/gnzls12502mem2gwb.html>

3 Obama can complain about Israeli politicians in private but is in full compliance in public. See: Guernigo, Yann Leu, 'Sarkozy tells Obama Netanyahu is a "liar" ', Reuters, 8 November, 2011 <http://www.reuters.com/article/2011/11/08/us-mideast-netanyahu-sarkozy-idUSTRE7A720120111108>

4 Many religious fatwas related to women's rights have been issues. See for example: Al-Fawzan, Saleh, on women's voice: <http://ar.islamway.com/fatwa/7640> (in Arabic).

5 See for example: Kibble, Mlabo 'Creative Chaos" and the War in Libya', *The Current Analyst*, 22 August 2011. <http://www.currentanalyst.com/index.php/external-actors/163-creative-chaos-and-the-war-in-libya>

6 Human Rights Watch, 'Libya: Lagging Effort to Build Justice System', 22 January 2012 <http://www.hrw.org/news/2012/01/22/libya-lagging-effort-build-justice-system>

7 Nagy, Thomas J., 'Safeguarding Our American Children by Saving Their Iraqi Children', in Ismael, Tareq Y. and Haddad, William W., *Iraq The Human Cost Of History*, Pluto Press, 2004, pp. 150-151.

8 Al Khafaji, Isam, 'Not Quite an Arab Russia: Revisiting Some Myths on Iraqi Exceptionalism', in: Ismael, Tareq Y. and Haddad, William W., *Iraq The Human Cost Of History*, Pluto Press, 2004.

9 **On the Building of Iraq.** eg: Kiryakos, Saad, 'The 17-30 July Revolution, (in Arabic)'/ Alnasrawi, Abbas, *The Economy Of Iraq/ Oil, Wars, Destruction of Development and Prospects, 1950-2010*, Greenwood Press Westport, Connecticut , 1994/ Alrubaie, Falah, 'An Evaluation to Industrial Development in Iraq During 1975-1990'-Omar Almukhtar University, Libya,January 2004 (in

Arabic)/ Mukhtar, K.E., '*The Genesis of Iraqi Oil Industry and The Role of the IPC Ltd*'/ Sanford, Jonathan E., *Report for Congress: Iraq's Economy: Past, Present, Future,* June 2003/ Jaradat, A. A., 'Agriculture in Iraq: Resources, Potentials, Constraints, and Research Needs and Priorities', Submitted to: Department of State—Middle East Working Group on Agriculture October 5-6, 2002/ Situation Analysis of Education in Iraq 2003, UNESCO, April, 2003/ Abbas, Kadhim & Abdullah, Iyad, 'The Flourishing of Education under the Ba'ath Rule', (in Arabic), 2009/ Abbas, Kadhim & Abdullah, Iyad, 'The Flourishing of Health under the Ba'ath Rule', (in Arabic) 2009.

On the destruction of Iraq eg.: Acherio, Albert , 'Effect of the Gulf War on Infant and Child Mortality in Iraq', *New England Journal of Medicine*/ 'Unsanctioned Suffering: A Human Rights Assessment of UN Sanctions on Iraq', *Center for Economic and Social Rights*, May 1996/ Report to the Secretary General on Humanitarian Needs in Kuwait and Iraq in the immediate Post –Crisis Environment by a Mission Led by Martti Ahtisaari, the Under-Secretary-General for Administration and Management 10-17 March 1991, UN SCOR, Annex, UN Doc. S/22366"/ *The Human Rights Implications of Economic Sanctions on Iraq: Background Paper Prepared by the Office of the High Commissioner for Human Rights for the Meeting of the Executive Committee on Humanitarian Affairs* (New York, 5 September 2000)/Clark, Ramsey, *The Fire This Time*, Thunder's Mouth Press, 1994/ Herring, Eric, 'Between Iraq and a Hard Place: A Critique of the British Government's Case for Sanctions', *Review of International Studies, Vol. 28, No.* 1 (April 2002),/ Mueller, John and Karl, 'The Methodology of Mass Destruction: Assessing Threats in the New World Order', in Herring, Eric (ed.). *Preventing the Use of Weapons of Mass Destruction* (London: Frank Cass, 2000), p. 177 (see also pp. 164, 180). Reprinted from the *Journal of Strategic Studies,* Vol. 23, No. 1 (2000)/ Mueller, John, 'Public Opinion as a Constraint on US Foreign Policy: Assessing the Perceived Value of American and Foreign Lives', National Convention of the International Studies Association, Los Angeles, CA, 14-18 March 2000/ Robinson , Piers. *The CNN Effect: The Myth of News, Foreign Policy and Intervention* (London: Routledge, 2002)/ UNESCO. "The Education Sector: Pre-sanctions to 1995/96," in UN Office of the Humanitarian Coordinator for Iraq. *Special Topics on social conditions in Iraq: An overview submitted by the UN system to the Security Council Panel on Humanitarian Issues (*Baghdad, 24 March 1999)/ Boone, Peter, Gazdar,Haris & Hussain, Althar, '*Sanctions against Iraq: Costs of Failure*' (New York: CESR, November 1997/ UNICEF. "Results of the 1999 Iraq Child and Maternal Mortality Surveys," UNICEF, 2000. As found at: www.unicef.org/reseval/iraqr.htm>; Ali, Mohamed M. and Shah, Iqbal H.. 'Sanctions and childhood mortality in Iraq', *The Lancet*, Vol. 355 (27 May 2000)/ Garfield, Richard, 'Morbidity and Mortality among Iraqi Children from 1990 through 1998: Assessing the Impact of the Gulf War and Economic Sanctions' (1999)/ UNICEF. 1999, Iraq Child and Maternal Mortality Surveys (12 August 1999)/ Ismael, Tareq Y. and Haddad, William W., *Iraq The Human Cost Of History*, Pluto Press, 2004.

10   Gordon, Joy, 'When Intent Makes All the Difference in the World: Economic Sanctions on Iraq and the Accusation of Genocide', *Yale Human Rights & Development Law Journal, Vo. 5* (2002), pp. 1-27.

Chapter One

1   Battle of Bagdad, Hulagu Khan, <http://en.wikipedia.org/wiki/Hulagu_Khan>
2   Salih, Zaki, *Britain and Iraq: A Study in British Foreign Affairs*, London, Books & Books 1995, pp. ix-x.
3   *Ibid*, p. xi.

4   Lauterpacht, E., Greenwood, C. J. , Weller, Marc, *The Kuwait Crisis: Basic Documents*, Grotus Publication Limited, United Kingdom, 1991, pp. 17-18.

5   Dekker, Ige F., Post , H. H. G., *The Gulf War of 1980-1988: the Iran-Iraq War in international legal perspective*, T.M.C. Asser Instituut, The Hague, 1992, p. 8.

6   Al-Ani, Abdul-Haq, *The Trial of Saddam Hussein,* Atlanta, Clarity Press, p. 62.

7   See Memorandum by the Marquess of Lansdowne, 21 March 1902, in: Lauterpacht, E., Greenwood, C. J., Weller, Marc, *The Kuwait Crisis: Basic Documents*, Grotus Publication Limited, United Kingdom, 1991, p. 17-18.

8   *The Kuwait Crisis: Basic Documents*, Op.Cit, p.27.

9   Simons, Geoff, *Iraq, From Sumer to Saddam*, Macmillan Press Ltd., 2nd Edition, London, 1996, pp. 213-214.

10   <http://www.smithsonianmag.com/people-places/unruly.html?c=y&page=7> "Six years after becoming king, Ghazi crashed his sports car into a utility pole in Baghdad after an evening of drinking. His two British physicians summoned an Iraqi colleague to the scene of the mortally wounded king. "I was fearful lest, if no Iraqi doctor was in attendance, Anglophobic mischief-makers might originate canards to the effect that [we] were responsible for the king's demise," Dr. Henry C. Sinderson, the monarch's chief physician, wrote in his memoirs. Even so, violent street demonstrations erupted in Baghdad the next day. In Mosul, a mob killed the British consul. For years, many Iraqis insisted that Ghazi was killed by the British and their allies. He was succeeded by his son Faisal II."

11   Simons, Geoff, *op.cit.* pp. 257-259.

12   As quoted in Saleh, Zaki, Op.Cit, p. xl.

13   Numerous books and articles have documented the destruction of Iraq in 1991 and afterwards. Though we will discuss this destruction in detail in a later Chapter, the reader could see the following:Clark, Ramsay, *The Fire This Time*, Thunder's Mouth Press, March 1994;Center for Economic and Social Rights, *The Human Cost of War in Iraq*, New York; Ismael, Tareq Y. and Haddad, William W., *Iraq The Human Cost Of History*, Pluto Press, 2004

14   The End of History, Francis Fukuyama, <http://www.wesjones.com/eoh.htm>

15   See Al-Ani, Abdul-Haq, *The Trial of Saddam Hussein,* Atlanta, Clarity Press, p.36.

16   Hazran, Yusri, 'The Rise of Politicized Shi'ite Religiosity and the Territorial State in Iraq and Lebanon', *The Middle East Journal*, 10/01/10. See also: <http://www.mareeb.net/vb/showthread.php?t=6324> (Arabic).

Chapter Two

1   Beirut's catastrophes, past and present (in Arabic)<http://www.yabeyrouth.com/pages/index368.htm>

2   Hussein- McMahon Communications <http://www.mideastweb.org/mcmahon.htm>

3   Balfour Declaration<http://en.wikipedia.org/wiki/Balfour_Declaration_of_1917>

4   Hussein bin Ali, Sharif of Mecca<http://en.wikipedia.org/wiki/Hussein_bin_Ali,_Sharif_of_Mecca.

5   Al-Ani, Abdul-Haq, *The Trial of Saddam Hussein*, Clarity Press Inc. Georgia, 2008, p.62.

6   Fisk, Robert, *Iraq, 1917,* <http://www.globalpolicy.org/component/content/article/169/36413.html>

7   Nuri As-Saeed<http://en.wikipedia.org/wiki/Nuri_al-Said>

8   Nuri left his house by boat as soon he heard of the disturbance and before any unit could get to him. He arrived at the Isterabadi family house in Kadimyiah and stayed the whole day hoping that the parties to the Baghdad Pact would come to his rescue. The next day he decided to seek a way out of Iraq and thought of going to Iran through the Governorate of Imara in southeast Iraq. He went,

accompanied by a woman and wearing an Abayia, to the house of Muhammad Al-Uraibi in the district of Battaween on the east bank of the Tigris. Muhammad Al-Uraibi was the sheikh of the Ilbo-Mhimmed, a very large Meidaan tribe in Imara and a member of the Chamber of Deputies. We used to live on the same road opposite Al-Uraibi's house. However, when he rang the bell he was told that the sheikh was not home. Whether or not they recognized him and refused him hospitality will never be known. He went eastward to the end of the road; turned left and then turned right again into another road some fifty meters away passed the local primary school. It was at the end of the road that somebody noticed his pyjama sticking out from under the Abayia and recognized him. An Iraqi army sergeant passing by gunned him down. Later, on the 15th of July, 1958, his body was pulled through the streets of Baghdad.

9   Naji Shawkat<http://en.wikipedia.org/wiki/Naji_Shawkat>

10   Hikmat Sulayman <http://en.wikipedia.org/wiki/Hikmat_Sulayman>

11   Ahmad Mukhtar Baban   <http://mobdii.org/pdfs/15/58111230289650pdffile.pdf>

12   General Omar Ali, the Kurdish officer who led the Iraqi regiment in Palestine in 1948 insisted until his death that the British conspired to oust Nuri. The following is a narration of his explanation as told to me by his son. Nuri wanted new and serious arms for the Iraqi army but the British were reluctant. He hinted that he might seek them from other sources but the British did not take his threat seriously. Sometime in the spring of 1958, he had a heated argument with the British Ambassador to Baghdad in the latter's office. Nuri was furious with the British refusal, banged the Ambassador's desk and stormed out of the room swearing that he was going somewhere else for arms, clearly hinting at the USA. However close the UK was to the USA, it was not going to relinquish Iraq to it. This, Omar Ali insisted all his life, was the reason why the British instructed the officers in the Iraqi army to stage the July 1958 coup and this explained why, according to Omar Ali, the Baghdad Pact members' request to intervene was turned down by Britain.

13   Muhammad Fadhel al-Jamali<http://en.wikipedia.org/wiki/Muhammad_Fadhel_al-Jamali>

14   Simon, Reeva S., *Iraq between The Two World Wars*, Columbia University Press, New York 1986, p. 67.

15   Nuri al-Saʾid had been in London in July 1956 when Nasser announced the nationalization of the canal; Nuri immediately counseled Prime Minister Eden that "you have only one course of action open and that is to hit, hit now, and hit hard." A month later Nuri again called for strong British action, defining the Suez issue as "a matter of life or death for the West as well as for Nasser." Other Iraqi leaders echoed Nuriʾs bellicose views, one urging the British to give Nasser "a bloody nose, " another stating that "the crux was whether Her Majestyʾs Government were determined and able to bring Nasser down within a comparatively short time." Quoted in James P. Jankowski, *Nasser's Egypt, Arab nationalism, and the United Arab Republic,* Lynne Rienner Publishers, London, 2001, p. 84.

16   Seale, Patrick, *The Struggle for Syria: A Study of Post-war Arab Politics, 1945-1958*, 2nd edn., London, 1987, pp. 199-201.

17   Yesilbursa, Behcet Kemal, The *Baghdad Pact: Anglo-American Defence Policies in the Middle East, 1950-1959.*, Frank Cass, London, 2005, p. 90.

18   Simon, Reeva S., *op.cit.*, p. 63.

19   <http://en.wikipedia.org/wiki/Arab_Federation>

20   Abdel Karim Qasim, <http://en.wikipedia.org/wiki/Abdul_Karim_Qassim>

21   Abdul Salam Arif, <http://en.wikipedia.org/wiki/Abdul_Salam_Aref>

22   The sequence of events following the coup has been argued by Al-Ani, Abdul-Haq, *The Trial of Saddam Hussein* Al-Ani, pp.37-39.

23   <http://en.wikipedia.org/wiki/Golden_Square_%28Iraq%29>

24   Younis As-Saba'awi, Colonel Fahmi Said, and Colonel Mahmud Salman were executed on 5 May 1942. Colonel Kamal Shabib was executed on 17 August 1944 and Colonel Salah al-Din al-Sabbagh was executed on 16 October 1945.

25   Almutair, J., 'Qasim tactics Against Himself, 3,' (Arabic Text), *AlHiwar AlMutamadin*, 2350, 22 July 2008. <http://www.ahewar.org/debat/show.art. asp?aid=141599>

26   Al-Ani, *op cit*, p.40.

27   See Al-Saadi, Sabri Zire, 'Liberalization Strategy For Iraq›s Oil-Hostage Economy: Alternative To Oil Power Dominance and Neo-Liberal Subordinate Economic Policy (Part 1/2)', Note 7, *Middle East Economic Survey, VOL. XLIX*, No 42, 16-Oct-2006. <http://www.mees.com/postedarticles/oped/v49n42-5OD01.htm>

28   See: Barzani Revolts 1960–1975 and their aftermath.<http://en.wikipedia.org/wiki/Iraqi_Kurdistan>

29   Al-Ani, *op cit*, p. 39-40.

30   Al-Ani, *op cit*, p. 40-41.

31   Al-Ani, *op cit*, p. 41-43.

32   Arif Abdul-Razzaq first attempted coup was on 14 September 1965.

33   Believers in «Rational Socialism» thought socialism was inevitable not because of a historical process, but because people would eventually come to share their view that socialism was a better and fairer system. They felt that rational people would simply realize that socialism could deliver the greatest personal freedom and satisfaction. <http://www.ashbytechnicalwriting.com/battle/battle6.html>

34   Remember for example that at the time of writing this chapter, the direct cost to the USA of the Iraq war had exceeded $500 billion!

35   These happenings have been dealt with in Al-Ani, *op cit*, pp. 44-45.

36   Batatu, Hanna, *The Old Social Classes and the Revolutionary Movements of Iraq*, Princeton University Press, New Jersey, 1988, p. 1074.

37   "The recent conflict has wrought near-apocalyptic results upon the economic infrastructure of what had been, until January 1991, a rather highly urbanized and mechanized society. Now, most means of modern life support have been destroyed or rendered tenuous. Iraq has, for some time to come, been relegated to a pre-industrial age, but with all the disabilities of post-industrial dependency on an intensive use of energy and technology."Report on humanitarian needs in Iraq in the immediate post-crisis environment by a mission to the area led by the Under-Secretary- General for Administration and Management, 10- 17 March 1991, S/22366, 20 March 1991.<http://www.casi.org.uk/info/undocs/s22366.html>Retrieved on June 27, 2009.

38   Al-Ani, *op cit*, Chapter 1.

39   An anecdote circulating among Ba'athists is that prior to 1968 when members of the party were complaining about the low level of popular support, Saddam Hussein used to say: Give me political authority and I will give you a Party.

40   Mukhtar. K. E., *op cit*. 2006, p. 5.

41   Alnasraw, Abbas, *op cit*, Chapter 1, p.11.

42   See for example: <http://www.kurdefrin.com/vb/t6444.html> (in Arabic).

43   Ibrahim, Nabil, 'History of Barazani and Talabani Gangs' (In Arabic), Part 3. <http://www.albasrah.net/ar_articles_2009/0509/nabil3_140509.htm>

44   "A Charter for National Action, prepared by the Ba'ath Party, was published in the press for public discussion and became the basis for cooperation with the ICP and other parties. In March 1972 Ba'thist and ICP leaders met to discuss the content of the charter and express their views about basic principles such as socialism, democracy, and economic development. A statute was drawn up expressing the principles agreed on as the basis for cooperation among the parties of the NPF. It also provided for a 16-member central executive com-

mittee, called the High Committee, and a secretariat. The NPF officially came into existence in 1973."<http://www.britannica.com/EBchecked/topic/293631/Iraq/22908/The-revolution-of-1968>

45   <http://countrystudies.us/iraq/82.htm>

46   <http://abutamam.blogspot.com/2005/12/corrosive-israeli-mossad-in-iraqi.html>See also: <http://israelkurdistannetwork.blogspot.com/2007/09/kurdish-israeli-political-relations.html>

47   One such story was told by Salah Omar Ali, one of Saddam Hussein closest lieutenants to one of the authors. He claimed that during the 6th Non-Aligned Conference in September 1979 in Cuba, Saddam Hussein confided in him that Iran was so weak that all it needed was one push for it to collapse from within.

48   <http://www.albaghdadia.com/programs/history/4723-2009-05-25-15-00-59.html> (in Arabic).

49   <http://www.albaghdadia.com/programs/history/4730-2009-05-25-17-55-39.html> (in Arabic).

50   Statement by former NSC official Howard Teicher to the U.S. District Court, Southern District of Florida <http://www.webcitation.org/5flvP0UgC>
      see also: <http://en.wikipedia.org/wiki/French_support_for_Iraq_during_the_Iran_Iraq_war> and <http://en.wikipedia.org/wiki/British_support_for_Iraq_during_the_Iran-Iraq_war>

51   Alnasraw, Abbas, *op cit*, p. 86.

52   *Ibid*.

53   Alnasrawi, Abbas, *op cit*, p. 100.

54   *Ibid*

55   "But we have no opinion on the Arab-Arab conflicts, like your border disagreement with Kuwait. I was in the American Embassy in Kuwait during the late '60s. The instruction we had during this period was that we should express no opinion on this issue and that the issue is not associated with America. James Baker has directed our official spokesmen to emphasize this instruction...."<http://en.wikipedia.org/wiki/April_Glaspie>

56   <http://www.cvni.net/radio/e2k/e2k007/e2k07article.html>.

57   The Balfour Declaration <http://www.mideastweb.org/mebalfour.htm>

58   Since the 1970s, influential groups of Washington foreign-policy hawkish strategists have believed that in order to ensure its global dominance, the United States must seize control of the Middle East and its oil. This is argued in: Dreyfuss, Robert, 'The Thirty-Year Itch', *Mother Jones*, March-April 2003 <http://motherjones.com/politics/2003/03/thirty-year-itch>

59   For writings of Michel Aflaq, see:<http://albaath.online.fr/English/index-English.htm>

Chapter Three

1   Khadouri, Majid, *Socialist Iraq*, The Middle East Institute, Washington, D.C. 1978, p. 111-112

2   *Ibid*

3   *Ibid*, p. 111

4   Alnasrawi, Abbas, *The Economy of Iraq/ Oil, Wars, Destruction of Development and Prospects, 1950-2010*, Greenwood Press Westport, Connecticut, 1994, page 61

5   Khadouri, op cit, p. 116

6   *Ibid,* p. 112

7   *Ibid,* p. 112-113

8   *Ibid,* p. 114

9   The National Development Plan 1970-1974, April 1970, Government Pres- Baghdad 1971

10	Alnasrawi, op cit, p. 62
11	*Ibid,* p. 64
12	The National Development Plan, op.cit, p. 134
13	*Ibid,* p. 136
14	*Ibid,* p. 136-137
15	*Ibid,* p. 139
16	*Ibid,* p. 141
17	*Ibid,* p. 142
18	*Ibid* p.147
19	*Ibid*
20	*Ibid* p.149
21	*Ibid* p.157
22	*Ibid,* p.73
23	Khadouri, op cit, p. 133-134
24	Alrubaie, Falah, *An Evaluation to Industrial Development in Iraq "During 1975-1990"*-Omar Almukhtar University, Libya, January 2004 (in Arabic), p. 5-8 <http://mpra.ub.uni-muenchen.de/8331/>
25	Alnasrawi, op cit, p. 66
26	Mukhtar, K.E., *The Genesis of Iraqi Oil Industry and The Role of the IPC Ltd.,* p. 3 <http://www.aiforum.org.au/docs/Presentation_to_AIF_symposium_IP11.pdf
27	*Ibid,* p. 6>
28	Alnasrawi, *The Economy Of Iraq,* Op.cit. p. 12
29	Chapin Metz, Helen, *A Country Study: Iraq,* P. 131-132 <http://lcweb2.loc.gov/frd/cs/iqtoc.html>
30	*Ibid,* p. 132
31	Alnasrawi, Abbas, *Iraq: economic embargo and predatory rule,* 2000, p. 3-4 <http://www.casi.org.uk/info/alnasrawi9905.html>
32	Alnasrawi, *The Economy Of Iraq,* Op.cit. p. 9
33	*Ibid*
34	Kiryakos, Saad, *The 17-30 July Revolution,* (in Arabic), Part II <http://www.almansore.com/drasat/DR-SaadDawoodPart228-09-07.htm>
35	Khadouri, op cit, p. 125
36	Kiryakos, op.cit, Part II
37	Chapin Metz, op.cit, p. 133
38	The Iraqi Government tried after WWII to open up the country to competition, and the company which received the new concession was bought out by IPC and, under the name of the Mosul Petroleum Company and became part of the IPC 'family' of associated companies.
39	*Ibid,* p.134
40	*Ibid,* p.135-136
41	Kiryakos, op.cit, Part III http://www.almansore.com/drasat/DR-SaadDawood-Part306-10-07.htm
42	Khadouri, op cit, p. 129
43	*Ibid,* p.130
44	*Ibid,* p.132
45	Chapin Metz, op.cit, p. 138
46	Kiryakos, op.cit, Part III
47	Al-Ani, Abdul-Haq, *The Trial of Saddam Hussein,* Atlanta, Clarity Press, p. 261
48	Kiryakos, op.cit, Part III
49	Chapin Metz, *op.Cit,* p. 152
50	Chapin Metz, *op.cit,* p. 149
51	*Ibid,* p. 149-150
52	Sanford, Jonathan E., *Report for Congress: Iraq's Economy: Past, Present, Future,* June 2003, p. 34

53   Sanford, Jonathan E., *Op.Cit.* p. 35
54   Chapin Metz, op.cit, p. 142
55   <http://iraqilegislations.org/LoadLawBook.aspx?SP=FREE&SC=120120017863
        483&Year=1970&PageNum=1>
56   <http://iraqilegislations.org/LoadLawBook.aspx?SP=FREE&SC=301220051440
        056&Year=1975&PageNum=1>
57   Khadouri, op cit, p. 122
58   Ibid
59   Kiryakos, op.cit, Part IV <http://www.almansore.com/drasat/DR-SaadDawoo-
        dPart406-11-07.htm>
60   Chapin Metz, op.cit, p.147
61   Ibid, p.147-148
62   Ibid, p.148
63   Jaradat, A. A., *Agriculture in Iraq: Resources, Potentials, Constraints, and Research
        Needs and Priorities*, Submitted to: Department of State – Middle East Working
        Group on Agriculture October 5-6, 2002, p. 27
64   *Ibid*, p. 28-29
65   *Ibid*, p. 135
66   Chapin Metz, op.cit, p.143
67   Jaradat, A. A, op.cit, p.144
68   Jaradat, A. A, op.cit., p. 29-30
69   Chapin Metz, op.cit, p. 118
70   Iraq Sanctions: Humanitarian Implications and Options for the Future, Chapter
        4 <http://www.globalpolicy.org/component/content/article/170/41947.html>
71   Alnasrawi, *The Economy Of Iraq*, op.cit. p. 81
72   Alnasrawi, *Iraq: economic embargo and predatory rule*, op.cit, p.4-5
73   *Ibid*, p. 6
74   Chapin Metz, op.cit, p. 119
75   Alnasrawi, *Iraq: economic embargo and predatory rule*, op.cit, p. 5-6
76   Alnasrawi, *The Economy Of Iraq*, op.cit. p. 100
77   Alnasrawi, *Iraq: economic embargo and predatory rule*, op.cit, p. 6
78   Chapin Metz, op.cit, p. 120
79   *Ibid*, p. 121
80   amir Al-Khalil. *Republic of Fear: Saddam's Iraq*, London: Hutchinson Radius,
        London, 1990, pp. 93-94

Chapter Four

1   Khadouri, op cit, p. 137
2   See: *Gül refuses to recognize Kurdish language*, Al Jazeera Channel, 31 December
        2010 (Arabic) <http://www.aljazeera.net/NR/exeres/0922EC49-6D3B-4696-
        91CE-1A2B8BC10EF.htm?GoogleStatID=1> and/ *Gül: Turkish will remain sole
        official language*, Kurdish News Agency, 31 December 2010, <http://www.
        aknews.com/en/aknews/4/206890/>
3   Katzman, Kenneth, *The Kurds in Post-Saddam Iraq*, Congressional Research
        Service, October 2010, P. 1 <http://www.fas.org/sgp/crs/mideast/RS22079.pdf>
4   Iraq - The Politics of Alliance: The Progressive National Front <http://www.
        country-data.com/cgi-bin/query/r-6634.html>
5   *Ibid*
6   *Ibid*
7   *Ibid*, p. 138
8   Al-Azzawi, Souad, Deterioration of Iraqi Women's Rights and Living Conditions
        Under Occupation, Global Research, January 13, 2008   (http://www.global-
        research.ca/index.php?context=va&aid=7785)

9   Neshat, Saeid N., *A Look into the Women's Movement in Iraq*, p. 56 in Far-zaneh Journal, 6:11 (2003) <http://www.iiav.nl/ezines/web/Farzaneh/1993/Vol1Nr1/.../arti4n11.pdf>

10   Law 110 for Official Holidays dated 9 November 1972, granted Christians, Jews, Mandaeans and Yezidis the right to enjoy their religious holidays in addition to the Muslim holidays. <http://www.legislations.gov.iq/LoadLawBook.aspx?SP=REF&SC=061220058853418&Year=1972&PageNum=1>

11   *The Plight of Iraq's Religious Minorities*, The Pew Forum on Religion and Public Life,15 May 2008 <http://pewforum.org/The-Plight-of-Iraqs-Religious-Minori-ties.aspx>

12   *Christians In Iraq*, The New American, 10 November 2008 <http://www.the-newamerican.com/world-mainmenu-26/asia-mainmenu-33/504>

13   *Swiss voters back ban on minarets*, BBC News, 29 November 2009 <http://news.bbc.co.uk/2/hi/8385069.stm>

14   *Iraqi Christians Fear Eradication*, Assyrian International News Agency, 12 May 2010 <http://www.aina.org/news/20101205134445.htm>

15   *Ibid*

16   For a list of attacks on Christians in Iraq since 2003, see <http://www.bbc.co.uk/news/world-middle-east-11463544>

17   Shi'a-Sunni Relations, Global Security <http://www.globalsecurity.org/military/world/iraq/religion-shia-sunni.htm>

18   The Political Report of the Sixth Congress of the Regional Command (In Arabic), Baghdad, 1970

19   Khadouri, op cit, p. 139

20   <http://iraqilegislations.org/LoadLawBook.aspx?SP=FREE&SC=021220052939259&Year=1970&PageNum=1>

21   Khadouri, op cit, p. 140

22   <http://iraqilegislations.org/LoadLawBook.aspx?SC=060320061760921>

23   Situation Analysis of Education in Iraq 2003, UNESCO, April, 2003, p.48 <http://unesdoc.unesco.org/images/0013/001308/130838e.pdf>

24   Humanitarian Assistance Capacity in Iraq: Part I, *CARE International and Johns Hopkins University*, January 2003, p. 4, <http://www.who.int/disasters/repo/9353.pdf

25   Ibid, page 13

26   Ibid, page 5

27   Abbas & Abdullah , op.cit Part I 2009 <http://www.alrafdean.org/node/109440>

28   Abbas & Abdullah , op.cit Part II 2009 <http://www.alrafdean.org/node/109543>

29   Chapin Metz, op.cit, p. 114

30   Abbas & Abdullah , op.cit Part II 2009

31   <http://iraqilegislations.org/LoadLawBook.aspx?SP=FREE&SC=021220052939259&Year=1970&PageNum=1>

32   The National Development Plan 1970-1974, April 1970, Government Press-Baghdad 1971, p. 143.

33   Abbas, Kadhim & Abdullah, Iyad, *The Flourishing of Health under the Ba'ath Rule*, (in Arabic) 2009 <http://www.wata.cc/forums/showthread.php?t=54240

34   Health Systems Profile- Iraq, Regional Health Systems Observatory- EMRO, p. 43 <http://gis.emro.who.int/HealthSystemObservatory/PDF/Iraq/Health%20service%20delivery.pdf>

35   Humanitarian Assistance Capacity in Iraq, *Op.cit.*, p.11

36   *Ibid*

37   Selected Health Information on Iraq, *United Nations Humanitarian Coordination For Iraq, Health Coordination Group (HCG)*, March 2003, p.3<http://www.who.int/disasters/repo/10062.pdf>

38   Humanitarian Assistance Capacity in Iraq, op.cit, p. 18

39   Selected Health Information on Iraq, op.cit., p. 3

40   Humanitarian Assistance Capacity in Iraq, op.cit, p. 7

41   *Ibid*, p. 14

42   Abbas, Kadhim & Abdullah, Iyad, op.cit.

43   *Ibid*

44   *Ibid*

45   The Health Conditions of the Population in Iraq Since the Gulf Crisis, *World Health Organization*, March 1996 <http://www.who.int/disasters/repo/5249 html

Chapter Five

1   The contents of the meeting have been documented in: Salinger, Pierre & Laurent, Eric, *Secret Dossier; The Hidden Agenda Behind the Gulf War,* Penguin Books, London, 1991, pp. 48-62.

2   Blum, William, *Killing Hope- US military & CIA interventions since World War II*, Zed Books, London, 2004, p. 322.

3   *Ibid.*

4   *Ibid.*

5   See: Salinger, *op. cit.*, p. 239.

6   'Economic Sanctions against Iraq' in: Hull, Richard E. *Imposing International Sanctions: Legal Aspects and Enforcement by the Military.* Washington, DC: National Defense University Press, 1997. <http://permanent.access.gpo.gov/lps51586/Imposing%20International%20 Sanctions%20-%20March%2097/chapter1.html>

7   R.W. Apple Jr., 'The Iraqi Invasion; Invading Iraqis Seize Kuwait And Its Oil; U.S. Condemns Attack, Urges United Action', *New York Times,* 3 August 1990.

8   Cordesman, Anthony H. and Wagner, Abraham R. *The Gulf War,* Westview Press, Boulder, CO., 1996, p. 53.

9   Economic Sanctions against Iraq, *op.cit.*

10   Hoskins, Eric, 'The Humanitarian Impacts of Economic Sanctions and War in Iraq', in Weiss, Cortright, Lopez & Minear (eds) *Political Gain and Civilian Pain: Humanitarian Impacts of Economic Sanctions,* Lanham/Oxford: Rowman & Littlefield, 1997, p.100-101.

11   Gordon, Joy, 'When intent makes all the difference in the world: economic sanctions on Iraq and the accusation of genocide', *Yale Human Rights and Development Law Journal*, Vol. 5, 2002, p. 58.

12   Council Regulation (EEC) No. 2340/90 of 8 August 1990, in Lauterpacht, E., Greenwood, C. J., and Weller, Marc, *The Kuwait Crisis: Basic Documents,* Cambridge University Press, 1991, p. 13-14.

13   Center for Economic and Social Rights, UN sanctioned suffering: A Human Rights Assessment of United Nations Sanctions on Iraq, New York, CESR, May 1996, p. 35.

14   Falk, Richard, 'Iraq, the United States, and International Law: Beyond the Sanctions', in Ismael, Tareq Y. and Haddad, William W., (eds), *Iraq: The Human Cost of History*, Pluto Press, London, Virginia, 2004, p. 23.

15   Economic Sanctions against Iraq, *op.cit.,* p.23-24.

16   Craddock, Percy, *In Pursuit of British Interests: reflections on Foreign Policy under Margaret Thatcher and John Major,* John Murray, London, 1997, p. 177.

17   Friedman, Thomas, 'The Iraqi Invasion; U.S. Is Seeking to Forestall Any Arab Deal for Kuwait', *The New York Times,* 5 August 1990.

18   Riding, Alan, 'Confrontation in the Gulf; NATO, Bereft of a Military Role, Redefines Itself as the West's Political Galvanizer', *The New York Times,* 9 August 1990.

19   'Why America is in the Gulf', address by Secretary Baker on the Persian Gulf crisis, US Department of State Dispatch, 5 Nov.1990.

20   Economic Sanctions against Iraq, *op.cit.*

21   Apple Jr., R.W., 'Ships Turn Away From Ports As Iraq Embargo Tightens; U.S. Military Force Pours In; Americans Escape', *The New York Times*, 14 August 1990.

22   UN Security Council, Letter dated 16 August 1990, from the Charge D'Affaires A.I. of the United States Mission to the United Nations Addressed to the President of the Security Council (S/21537), 16 August 1990.

23   Rosenthal, Andrew, 'Confrontation In The Gulf; US Says Gulf Moves' Cost Will Far Exceed $25 Billion', *The New York Times*,1 September 1990.

24   Hoffman, David, 'Bush, Gorbachev Toughen Stand Against Iraq', *The Washington Post*, 10 September 1990.

25   The Persian Gulf Crisis (August 2, 1990-February 28, 1991) <http://www.presidentialtimeline.org/html/exhibits.php?id=20>

26   Eronen, Mikko, 'Finland accepts the use of force in the Persian Gulf' (in Finnish), *Helsingin Sanomat*, 20 November 1990.

27   Elsner, Alan, 'Flashback to 1990: Jim Baker's Quick Trip to Yemen', *Huffington Post*, 3 January 2010.<http://www.huffingtonpost.com/alan-elsner/flashback-to-1990jim-bake_b_409725.html>

28   John Pilger reveals how the Bushes bribe the world<http://www.newstatesman.com/pdf/johnpilger.htm>

29   See : 'Gulf War: Jim Baker note for President Bush (meeting Mitterrand & Dumas'), Margaret Thatcher Foundation, <http://www.margaretthatcher.org/document/110741 and: 'Gulf War: Jim Baker note for President Bush (meeting MT & Hurd)', Margaret Thatcher Foundation, <http://www.margaretthatcher.org/document/110720>

30   John Pilger , *op.cit.*

31   *Ibid.*

32   Dowd, Maureen, 'War In The Gulf: White House Memo; Bush Moves to Control War's Endgame',*The New York Times*, February 23, 1991.

33   Lewis, Paul, 'Confrontation in the Gulf: The U.N.; France and 3 Arab States Issue an Appeal to Hussein', *The New York Times*, January 15, 1991.

34   Clark, Ramsey, *The Fire This Time: U.S. Crimes in the Gulf*, Thunder's Mouth Press, March 1994, p. 36.

35   Chapter 2, *Needless Deaths In The Gulf War*, Civilian Casualties During the Air Campaign and Violations of the Laws of War, New York: Human Rights Watch, (c)1991. <http://www.hrw.org/legacy/reports/1991/gulfwar/CHAP2.htm>

36   Marcy, Sam, 'The general blows it; Fired for leaking Pentagon plan to terror-bomb Iraq civilians', Sept. 27, 1990.<http://www.workers.org/marcy/cd/sam90/1990html/s900927b.htm>

37   Gellman, Barton, 'Allied Air War Struck Broadly in Iraq; Officials Acknowledge Strategy Went Beyond Military Targets', *The Washington Post,* 23 June 1991, www.envirosagainstwar.org/know/1991USHitCivilianTargets.pdf>

38   *Ibid.*

39   *Ibid.*

40   Clark, *op.cit.* p. 160.

41   *Ibid*, p. 156.

42   Chapter 2, *Needless Deaths In The Gulf War, op.cit.*

43   Morgan, Stephen John, 'US used Neutron Bomb to Take Baghdad', 24 April 2007.<http://searchwarp.com/swa150515.htm. The effects of the use of Depleted Uranium have been extensively researched and discussed in: Al-Ani, Abdul-Haq & Baker, Joanne, *Uranium in Iraq: the Poisonous Legacy of the Iraq Wars,* Vandeplas publishing, 2009

44   Clark, *op.cit,* p. 45

45   *Ibid*

46   Michaels, Henry, 'What are cluster weapons?', *World Socialist Web Site*, 5 April

2003.<http://www.wsws.org/articles/2003/apr2003/side-a05.shtml>

47   Arkin, W, Durrant, D & Cherni, M, *op.cit*, p. 107-111.

48   Thomas, William, 'Report: U.S. Dropped Nuclear Bombs on Afghanistan, Iraq; Conventional bunker-busters could mask the detonation of tactical nuclear bombs', <http://www.twf.org/News/Y2007/1221-Nuclear.html>

49   Chapter 4, *Needless Deaths in the Gulf War*, Civilian Casualties During the Air Campaign and Violations of the Laws of War, New York: Human Rights Watch, (c)1991.<http://www.hrw.org/legacy/reports/1991/gulfwar/CHAP4.htm>

50   Clark, *op.cit*, p. 65.

51   *Ibid,* p. 64.

52   *Ibid,* p. 65.

53   *Ibid.*

54   *Ibid.*

55   *Ibid.*

56   *Ibid,* p. 67.

57   *Ibid,* p. 65.

58   *Ibid.*

59   *Ibid.*

60   *Ibid.*

61   *Ibid.*

62   "Fineman, Mark, 'Refugees From Iraq Describe Hellish Scenes', *Los Angeles Times*, 5 February 1991, <http://articles.latimes.com/1991-02-05/news/mn-564_1_asian-refugees>

63   Quoted in Clark, *op.cit*, p. 74

64   Walker, Paul, 'U.S. Bombing: The Myth of Surgical Bombing in the Gulf War', Citizens For Government Accountability, <http://www.citizensforgovernmentac-countability.org/?p=1357>

65   Clark, op.cit, p. 75

66   Al-Husaini, Hashim, 'Al-Amiriya Shelter, The Silence of the Lambs', *The Arab Review*, Summer 1995, Vol. 4, No. 3.

67   Navy Secretary John Lehman stated in a speech, "Smart Weapons", given at the exclusive Bohemian Grove in California in July 1991 that the Pentagon estimates that 200,000 Iraqis were killed by the US and its allies during the Gulf War. See: 'Inside the Bohemian Grove: The Story People Magazine Won't Let You Read EXTRA!' (Nov./Dec. '91) <http://www.theforbiddenknowledge.com/hardtruth/bohemian_grove2.htm>

68   UNITED STATES CENTRAL COMMAND/ OPERATION DESERT SHIELD/DESERT STORM Executive Summary , 11 July 1991.

69   Healy, Melissa & Broder, John M. 'Number of Iraqis Killed in War May Never Be Known/ Casualties: One historian puts deaths at 30,000 to 40,000, The Pentagon has no plan to produce a formal estimate', *Los Angeles Times* ,8 March 1991.

70   Arkin, W, Durrant, D & Cherni, M, 'On Impact: Modern Warfare and the Environment—A case study of the Gulf War', A Greenpeace study prepared for a "Fifth Geneva" Convention on the Protection of the Environment in Time of Armed Conflict (3 June 1991, London, UK) p. 10.

71   *Ibid.*

72   Clark, *op.cit*, p. 43.

73   *Ibid.*

74   Rockwell, Paul, 'Never to Forget: The War Crimes of George W. Bush & Donald Rumsfeld', *Newtopia Magazine*, 1 February 2005, <http://www.newtopiamaga-zine.org/issue20/features/nevertoforget.php>

75   Report of the WHO/UNICEF Special Mission To Iraq, S/22328, 4 March 1991.

76   *Ibid,* p. 7-8.

77   *Ibid.*

78	*Ibid.*
79	I*bid,* p. 11.
80	*Ibid,* p. 13.
81	*Ibid.*
82	*Ibid.*
83	*Ibid.*
84	*Ibid,* p. 17.
85	Al-Azzawi, Souad Nagi, 'The Great Recosntruction Campaign 1991-1993' (in Arabic).<http://www.albasrah.net/pages/mod.php?mod=art&lapage=../ar_articles_2008/1108/i3mar1_131108.htm>
86	Report to the Secretary-General on humanitarian needs in Kuwait and Iraq in the immediate post-crisis environment by a mission to the area led by Mr. Martti Ahtisaari. Under-Secretary-General for Administration and Management, dated 20 March 1991, UN document S/22326>
87	Report to the Secretary-General on humanitarian needs in Iraq prepared by a mission led by Sadruddin Aga Khan, Executive Delegate of the Secretary-General, dated 15 July 1991, UN Document S/22799, p. 12.
88	*Ibid.*
89	*Ibid,* p. 12-13.
90	*Ibid,* p. 13.
91	*Ibid.*
92	*Ibid,* p. 40.
93	Quoted by Clark, *op.cit*, p. 83.
94	Economic Sanctions against Iraq, *op.cit.*
95	*Ibid.*
96	UN Security Council Resolution 687 (1991).<http://www.fas.org/news/un/iraq/sres/sres0687.htm>
97	Cockburn, Andrew, 'Why Clinton is Culpable, Iraq's WMD Myth', *Counter Punch*, 29-30 September 2007, <http://www.counterpunch.org/andrew09292007.html>
98	*Ibid.*
99	Economic Sanctions against Iraq, *op.cit.*
100	Memorandum of understanding between the Secretariat of the United Nations and the Government of Iraq on the implementation of Security Council Resolution 986 (1995), S/1996/356, 20 May 1996.
101	Crossette, Barbara, 'U.S. Blocks a Plan to Allow Iraq to Sell $2 Billion in Oil', *The New York Times*, 1 August 1996.<http://www.nytimes.com/1996/08/01/world/us-blocks-a-plan-to-allow-iraq-to-sell-2-billion-in-oil.html>
102	Economic Sanctions against Iraq, *op.cit.*
103	Gordon, Joy, 'Cool War: Economic Sanctions as a weapon of Mass Destruction', *Harper's Magazine,* November 2002.
104	*Ibid.*
105	*Ibid.*
106	*Ibid.*
107	*Ibid.*
108	*Ibid.*
109	Gordon, Joy, *Cool War, op. cit.*
110	Humanitarian Assistance Capacity in Iraq: Part I/ A Situation Analysis and Literature Review, CARE International and Johns Hopkins University/ Center for International Emergency, Disaster and Refugee Studies, January 2003.
111	*Ibid.*
112	*Ibid.*
113	*Ibid.*
114	Daponte, Beth Osborne and Garfield, Richard, 'The Effect of Economic Sanctions

on the Mortality of Iraqi Children Prior to the 1991 Persian Gulf War', *American Journal of Public Health, Vol. 90, No. 4*, April 2000.

115   *Ibid.*

116   *Ibid.*

117   Fawzi, Mary C. Smith, Ziadi, Sarah, 'Sanctions, Saddam and Silence: Child Malnutrition and Mortality in Iraq', *The Washington Report on Middle East Affairs*, January 1996. <http://www.washington-report.org/component/content/article/167-1996-january/1776-sanctions-saddam-and-silence.html>

118   Crossette, Barbara, 'Iraq Sanctions Kill Children, U.N. Reports', *The New York Times*, 1 December 1995.

119   Nearly one million children malnourished in Iraq, says UNICEF.<http://www.unicef.org/newsline/97pr60.htm>

120   Garfield, Richard, 'Morbidity and Mortality Among Iraqi Children from 1990 Through 1998: Assessing the Impact of the Gulf War and Economic Sanctions', <http://www.casi.org.uk/info/garfield/dr-garfield.html>

121   *Ibid.*

122   UNESCO, *Situation Analysis Of Education In Iraq*, 2003, p. 5.

123   Iraq Education Sector Scoping Study/ Geopolicity, 2009.

124   UNESCO, *Situation Analysis Of Education In Iraq*, 2003, p. 15.

125   *Ibid*, p. 57.

126   UNESCO, *Situation Analysis Of Education In Iraq*, op.cit., p. 59.

127   *Ibid*, p. 59.

128   *Ibid*, p. 38.

129   *Ibid*, p. 60.

130   Humanitarian Assistance Capacity in Iraq, *op. cit.*

131   *Ibid*

132   *Ibid*

133   Alnasrawi, Abbas, 'Iraq: economic embargo and predatory rule', 2000, p. 3-4.<http://www.casi.org.uk/info/alnasrawi9905.html>

134   UNSG letter to SC, S/1998/330, 2.

135   UNSG Report to SC. S/2000/1132, para 32.

136   Jaradat, A. A., 'Agriculture in Iraq: Resources, Potentials, Constraints, and Research Needs and Priorities', 2003, p. 5-6 <http://afrsweb.usda.gov/research/publications/publications.htm?SEQ_NO_115=150003>

137   *Ibid* p.31.

138   *Ibid* p.32

139   Global Watch, 'FAO/WEP Mission to Iraq Finds that Malnutrition is still Widespread', 16 October 1997 <http://www.fao.org/english/newsroom/global/GW9718-e.htm>

140   *Ibid.*

Chapter Six

1   1982 Lebanon War, Wikipedia <http://en.wikipedia.org/wiki/1982_Lebanon_War>Retrieved 24 July 2009.

2   'Osama Bin Laden Warns America', CBS news<http://www.cbsnews.com/stories/2004/10/30/terror/main652425.shtml>Retrieved 24 July 2009.

3   Security Council Resolutions, 1982,<http://www.un.org/documents/sc/res/1982/scres82.html>

4   Security Council Resolutions 1982,<http://daccessdds.un.org/doc/RESOLUTION/GEN/NR0/435/39/IMG/NR043539.pdf?OpenElement>

5   a. The draft resolution (661) was originally faxed from the United States Mission to all members of the SC in an almost identical version at 5.48 p.m. on Friday, 3 August 1990. On August 6, an attempt was made to justify this on the ground that Iraq had failed to carry out the withdrawal of its forces from

Kuwaiti territory or by interpreting various statements made at Baghdad on Sunday or what the Permanent Representative of Iraq had said. But that was not the truth. The plan to impose sanctions on Iraq actually existed before the SC members entered this new phase of Security Council deliberations, at a time when no one even knew about the statement made by the Iraqi Government, also on 3 August, to the effect that it was going to commence the withdrawal of its troops from Kuwait. (See: *Speech by the Cuban representative in the SC on August 6, 1990*, in Provisional verbatim record of the two thousand nine hundred and eighty-third meeting of the Security Council).<http://daccess-ods. un.org/TMP/2625531.55422211.html>

b. When the Sanctions were first imposed on Iraq, the United States insisted on making the importation of food conditional: Iraq could not import food except in "humanitarian circumstances". The Congressional Research Service reported within weeks that Iraq's food availability was in crisis, and CIA Director William Webster reiterated this in December 1990. Despite this, the US was intransigent in interpreting "humanitarian circumstances" in the most extreme way possible—that Iraq could not import food until there was irrefutable evidence of advanced stages of famine. On that basis, the United States, invoking the consensus decision-making rule, prevented Iraq from importing any food, including powdered milk for infants, for eight months. (Gordon, Joy, Invisible War, Harvard University Pres 2010, pp. 212-213).

c. Even though UN Security Council Resolution 661 had exempted food and medicines from the sanctions, the US administration declared that exports of food to Iraq would be fully subject to the sanctions. The only objective of such move was causing suffering to the Iraqi population. Here is how *The New York Times* explained the issue: "The extent of the blockade, which the Administration calls an "interdiction," remained unclear. In a briefing for reporters at Kennebunkport, Marlin Fitzwater, the White House spokesman, said that even food and medicines were covered by the quarantine, at least until the Administration was convinced that an exception for materials in those categories was justified on humanitarian grounds." (*The New York Times*, 14 August 1990).

6   The Finnish Daily *Helsingin Sanomat* - Ulkomaat – 14 November1990 (in Finnish).

7   See for example *Helsingin Sanomat* - Kotimaa – 16 November 1990 and *Helsingin Sanomat* - Kotimaa – 29 November 1990 (in Finnish)

8   See Johansson, Patrik, "*UN Security Council Chapter VII resolutions, 1946-2002- An Inventory*." Uppsala: Department of Peace and Conflict Research, 2005.<http://www.pcr.uu.se/publications/UCDP_pub/Chapter%20VII%20 Resolutions_050921.pdf>

9   The Bossuyt Report, The Adverse Consequences of Economic Sanctions on the Enjoyment of Human Rights, Commission on Human Rights, Su-Committed on the Promotion and Protection of Human Rights, E/CN.4?sub.2/2000/33, June 21, 2000.

10   On sanctions against South Africa: A/RES/35/206C of 16 December 1981; A/ RES/37/69C of 9 December 1982; A/RES/38/39 [D] of 5 December 1983; A/ RES/39/72 [A] of 13 December 1984; A/RES/40/64 [A] of 10 December 1985; A/RES/41/35 [B] of 10 November 1986; A/RES/42/23 [C] of 20 November 1987; A/RES/43/50C of 5 December 1988; A/RES/44/27C of 22 November 1989; On the trade embargo against Nicaragua: A/RES/40/188 of 17 December 1985; A/RES/41/164 of 5 December 1986; A/RES/42/176 of 11 December 1987; A/ RES/43/185 of 20 December 1988; A/RES/44/217 of 22 December 1989; A/ RES/52/10 of 5 November 1997; A/RES/53/4 of 14 October 1998; A/RES/54/21 of 9 November 1999; A/RES/55/20 of 9 November 2000; A/RES/56/9 of 27 November 2001; A/RES/57/11 of 12 November 2002; A/RES/58/7 of 4 November

2003; A/RES/59/11 of 28 October 2004; A/RES/60/12 of 8 November 2005; A/RES/61/11 of 8 November 2006; A/RES/62/3 of 30 October 2007; A/RES/63/7 of 29 October 2008; A/RES/64/6 of 28 October 2009; and A/RES/65/6 of 26 October 2010. On the US embargo against Cuba: A/RES/47/19 of 24 November 1992; A/RES/48/16 of 3 November 1993; A/RES/49/9 of 26 October 1994; A/RES/50/10 of 2 November 1995; A/RES/51/17 of 12 November 1996.

11   See Principles and responses in International Humanitarian Assistance and Protection (1995).

12   Convention (IV) respecting the Laws and Customs of War on Land and its annex: Regulations concerning the Laws and Customs of War on Land. The Hague, 18 October 1907.

13   Convention (IV) relative to the Protection of Civilian Persons in Time of War. Geneva, 12 August 1949.

14   Protocol Additional to the Geneva Conventions of 12 August 1949, and relating to the Protection of Victims of International Armed Conflicts (Protocol I), 8 June 1977.

15   *See for example: 'US soldiers 'killed Afghan civilians for sport and collected fingers as trophies', The Guardian, 9 September 2010; 'Killings of Civilians in Afghanistan: US Special Forces Covered Up Massacre', Global Research, 8 April 2010; 'US 'killed 47 Afghan civilians', BBC News, 11 July 2008; 'US Killed 700 Civilians in Pakistan Drone Strikes in 2009', Antiwar.com, 2 January 2010.*

16   <http://www.usaid.gov/iraq/updates/may03/iraq_fs34_051503.pdf>

17   *Nagy, Thomas J., 'Safeguarding "Our" American Children by Saving "Their" Iraqi Children: Gandhian Transformation of the DIA's Genocide Planning, Assessment, and Cover-up Documents', in Ismael, Tareq Y. and Haddad, William W., Iraq- The Human Cost of History, Pluto Press, 2004, p. 148.*

18   Universal Declaration of Human Rights, <http://www.un.org/en/documents/udhr>

19   *International Covenant on Civil and Political Rights,<www2.Ohchr.org/english/law/ccpr.htm>*

20   *International Covenant of Economic, Social and Cultural Rights,<www2.Ohchr.org/english/law/cescr.htm>*

21   *International Covenant on Civil and Political Rights,<www2.Ohchr.org/english/law/ccpr.htm>*

22   International Human Rights, Office of the High Commissioner for Human Rights,<http://www.ohchr.org/en/professionalinterest/pages/internationallaw.aspx>

23   *Ibid.*

24   Fact Sheet No.2 (Rev.1), The International Bill of Human Rights,*www.ohchr.org/Documents/Publications/FactSheet2Rev.1en.pdf>*

25   Universal Declaration of Human Rights, <http://www.un.org/en/documents/udhr>

26   See: Khadduri, Imad, 'The fig leaf of moral impotence', March 10, 2003 <http://www.iraqsnuclearmirage.com/YellowTimes/The_Fig_Feaf_of_Moral_Impotence.htm>

27   *Convention on the Rights of the Child, www.unicef.org/crc/>*

28   *Albright was asked by Lesley Stahl on CBS's 60 Minutes on May 12th 1996: "We have heard that half a million children have died [as a result of sanctions]. I mean, that's more children than died in Hiroshima. And, you know, is the price worth it?" Albright replied: "I think this is a very hard choice, but the price—we think the price is worth it." <http://www.youtube.com/watch?v=FbIX1CP9qr4>*

29   *Paul, J. A., 'Sixteen Policy Recommendations on Sanctions', Global Policy Forum, March 1998, www.globalpolicy.org/security/sanction/jpreccs.htm>*

Chapter Seven

1   Drumond, Paula, 'Genocide Convention Analysis and the Dialogue Between IR and International Law', 49th International Association Annual Convention, March 2008.
2   Lippman, Matthew, 'A Road Map to the 1948 Convention on the Prevention and Punishment of the Crime Genocide', *Journal of Genocide Research*, vol. 4, n. 2, 2002, p.179.
3   Drumond, Paula, op cit.
4   Robinson, N., *The Genocide Convention, A Commentary*, Institute of Jewish Affairs, World Jewish Congress, New York, 1960, p. 17
5   Statement after the adoption of the Convention by the General Assembly of the UN. For the full text see ST/DPI/SER. A/68 and the United Nations Bulletin, December 15, 1948.
6   Mistral Gabriela, *an Appeal to World Conscience, the Genocide Convention*, UN Review, June, 1956.
7   Perlman, Philip, B., 'The Genocide Convention', *Nebraska Law review, Vol. XXX*, No. 1, pp. 1-10, Nov. 1950.
8   Cited in Woolsey, L. H., The New Policy Regarding US Treaties, 47 AJIL, 449.
9   Genocide Convention Implementation Act of 1987 - Ronald Reagan address – transcript<http://findarticles.com/p/articles/mi_m1079/is_n2142_v89/ai_7018358/?tag=content;col1>
10   Woolsey, op cit.
11   Memo from White House Counsel Alberto Gonzales to Pres. George W. Bush <http://news.findlaw.com/usatoday/docs/torture/gnzls12502mem2gwb.html>
12   Robinson, N., op cit, p. 50.
13   Ibid, p. 49
14   Drumond op. cit
15   Robinson, N., op cit. p. 46.
16   The Genocide Convention', *The Listener*, London. 10 March 1949.
17   Robinson, N., op cit, p. 46
18   See <http://en.wikipedia.org/wiki/Universal_jurisdiction>
19   Schabas, William, 'United States Hostility to the International Criminal Court: It's all about the Security Council', *European Journal of International Law, vol. 15, n. 4,* September 2004, p. 706.
20   Articles 5 and 6 of the Rome statute of the international criminal court.
21   Al-Ani, Abdul-Haq, *The Trial of Saddam Hussein*, Atlanta, Clarity Press, 2008, p. 99-100
22   Iraqi Council of Ministers Order No. 20 of 2005 <http://www.kululiraq.com/modules.php?name=News&file=article&sid=7222 (in Arabic)
23   Lippman, Matthew, op cit., p. 190
24   Judgment of the ICJ in the case of Corfu.., Preliminary Objections... Robinson, p. 56.
25   Robinson, op cit. p. 58
26   Drumond, op cit. p.2
27   See for example: Gordon, Joy, *Invisible War- The United States and the Iraqi Sanctions*, Harvard University Press, 2010, pp. 221-230
28   Jorgic v. Germany 74613/01, ECHR, 2007-IX
29   Robinson, op cit. p.58
30   ICJ, (Bosnia and Herzegovina v. Serbia and Montenegro), Judgment of 26 February 2007 Judgment of 26 February 2007.
31   Deborah W. Denno, 'Selected Model Penal, Code Provisions' , *Fordham University School of Law,* 2009 <http://law.fordham.edu/assets/Faculty/model_penal_code_selected_sections%281%29.pdf> accessed 1 October 2011
32   (a) 'Basic offense. Whoever, whether in time of peace or in time of war and with

the specific intent to destroy, in whole or in substantial part, a national, ethnic, racial, or religious group as such'. 18 U.S.C. § 1091

33 Law Commission Of England and Wales, Report on the meaning of intention (Murder, Manslaughter and Infanticide (Report No. 304 HC 30) at para 3.27) <http://www.justice.gov.uk/lawcommission/docs/lc304_Murder_Manslaughter_and_Infanticide_Report.pdf>

34 The term 'specific intent' was first used by Lord Birkenhead in *DPP v Beard* [1920] AC 479

35 *R v Majewski* [1977] AC 443, 478-479

36 Schabas, William A, *Genocide in International Law – The Crime of Crimes* (2nd ed, CUP, 2009) (Schabas 2009); Joy Gordon, 'When Intent Makes All the Difference in the World: Economic Sanctions on Iraq and the Accusation of Genocide' (2002) *vol 5 Yale Human Rights & Development Law Journal 57*

37 Greenawalt, Alexander K A ,'Rethinking Genocidal Intent: The Case for a Knowledge-Based Interpretation' (1999) *Pace Law Faculty Publications 2259*

38 Schabas 2009, 257

39 Bergsmo, Morten, 'Intent' in D. Shelton et al (eds) *The Encyclopedia of Genocide,* New York: Macmillan Reference 2005, 524, 529

40 Case Concerning the Application of the Convention on the Prevention and Punishment of the Crime of Genocide (Bosnia and Herzegovina v. Serbia and Montenegro) 26 February 2007 para 297

41 William A. Schabas, 'The Jelisic Case and the Mens Rea of the Crime of Genocide' (2001) 14 *Leiden Journal of International Law 129*

42 Schabas 2009, 260

43 Marin, Pilar Martinez and Rae, James DeShaw, 'Without Intent? Mens Rea in the Crime of Genocide', Paper Presented at International Studies Association (ISA) Conference San Francisco, California March 26, 2008 <http://www.allacademic. com//meta/p_mla_apa_research_citation/2/5/1/5/5/pages251552/p251552-1. php>

44 Under English Law we can understand the meaning of 'intent' because we can look it up in authorities. However, we are not sure that it is just as clear when it comes to the definition of these different 'dolus'. Where do they exist? Are they recognized legal terms under international law or specific domestic jurisdictions and if so what authorities exist to back up these definitions? The fact they have been used by the ICJ and other ad hoc tribunals and asserted by some academic does not clarify their legal value.

45 Johan D van der Vyver 'Prosecution and Punishment of the Crime of Genocide' (1999) 23 *Fordham International Law Journal*, 306-08, 308

46 Bergsmo 527

47 Bergsmo 526

48 *Prosecutor v. Akayesu* (Case No. ICTR-96-4-T) Judgment, 2 September 1998 (*Akayesu* case)

49 Schabas 2009, 260, n 84

50 Greenawalt 2265

51 ibid 2265-66

52 ibid 2291

53 ibid 2294

54 Nagy, Thomas J., 'Safeguarding Our American Children by Saving Their Iraqi Children' in, Ismael , Tareq Y and Haddad, William W, *Iraq The Human Cost Of History,* Pluto Press, 2004, 150-151

55 Greenawalt 2291

56 Lippman, Matthew, 'The Convention on the Prevention and Punishment of Genocide: Fifty Years Later', 15 *Arizona Journal of International and Comparative Law*, 415, (1998) at 507.

57	Greenawalt 2269
58	Bergsmo 529. It is not clear how Bergsmo reached this conclusion which seems to agree with the views of Van der Vyver..
59	Schabas 2009, 254
60	Schabas 2009, 265
61	On the need for a subjective test of intent Professor Thomas Nagy has this to say: Some scholars contend that the word "intent" in the treaty's definition calls for a smoking gun. As if this smoking gun must be produced by the leadership of the country through a declaration stating something to the effect of: "We are engaged in mass killing of this particular national or racial or religious group for the specific purpose of exterminating them" Few perpetrators are so blatant or so single-minded in their motivations. Nagy, Thomas J., Safeguarding Our American Children by Saving Their Iraqi Children, Ismael , Tareq Y and Haddad, William W, *Iraq The Human Cost Of History,* Pluto Press, 2004, 150
62	Schabas 2009, 266
63	Bergsmo 527
64	Jackson, Helen H, *A Century of Dishonor* (NY: Dover Publication, 2003)
65	Greenawalt 2261
66	ibid
67	Gordon, Joy, 'When Intent Makes All the Difference in the World: Economic Sanctions on Iraq and the Accusation of Genocide' (2002) vol 5 *Yale Human Rights & Development Law Journal* 66
68	Ibid.
69	Ibid.
70	Clark, Ramsey, Report to UN Security Council re: Iraq, 26 January 2000 <http://www.mail-archive.com/kominform@lists.eunet.fi/msg00124.html>
71	Bisharat, George, 'Sanctions Against Iraq are Genocide' (*Seattle pi,* 2 May 2002) <http://www.seattlepi.com/default/article/Sanctions-against-Iraq-are-genocide-1086527.php#ixzz1Of44ALAp>
72	Boyle, Francis, On Behalf of Iraq's 4.5 Million Children, A Petition for Relief from Genocide, 23 November 2002 <http://www.counterpunch.org/boyle1123.html>

Chapter Eight

1	Gordon, Joy, 'When intent makes all the difference in the world: economic sanctions on Iraq and the accusation of genocide', *Yale Human Rights and Development Law Journal, Vol. 5,* 2002, p. 58, n.1
2	Paragarpah 6(f) of the Guidelines, S/22660, 2 June 1991.
3	Cockburn, Andrew, 'Why Clinton is Culpable, Iraq's WMD Myth', *Counter Punch,* 29-30 September 2007, <http://www.counterpunch.org/andrew09292007.html>
4	Security Council, 4120th Meeting, 24 March 2000, S/PV.4120 (Resumption 1), 10.
5	Sanctions Committee report to SC, S/1995/992, 28 November 1995.
6	Sanctions Committee report to SC, S/2002/84, 18 January 2002, para. 3.
7	Sanctions Committee report to SC , S/2002/476, 23 April 2002, para. 3.
8	Sanctions Committee report to SC . S/2002/802, 22 July 2002, para. 3.
9	Sanctions Committee report to SC , S/2002/1167, 18 October 2002, para. 3.
10	Sanctions Committee report to SC , S/2003/61, 17 January 2003, para. 3.
11	Sanctions Committee report to SC, S/2003/507, 29 April 2003, para. 3. It looks rather comical that the Committee should meet even after the invasion of Baghdad on 9 April when it was clear to the invaders that no such systems existed in Iraq and decide nonetheless to keep the matter on its agenda.
12	Second Annual Report, S/1997/672, 28 August 1997, para. 19.
13	Third Annual Report, S/1998/1239, 31 December 1998, para. 34.

14   Fourth Annual Report, S/2000/133, 18 February 2000, para. 2.6

15   Fifth Annual report, S/2001/738, 27 July 2001, para. 19.

16   Sixth Annual Report, S/2002/647, 10 June 2002, para. 22.

17   Seventh Annual Report, S/2003/300, 12 March 2003, paras. 15-16.

18   Second Annual Report, S/1997/672, 28 August 1997, para. 25.

19   Third Annual Report, 31 December 1998, 31 December 1998, para. 42.

20   Fourth Annual Report, S/2000/133, 18 February 2000, para. 34.

21   Fifth Annual Report, S/2001/738, 27 July 2001, para. 28.

22   Sixth Annual Report, S/2002/647, 10 June 2002, para. 31.

23   Seventh Annual Report, S/2003/300, 12 March 2003, para. 36.

24   Third Annual Report, S/1998/1239, 31 December 1998, para. 41.

25   Fourth Annual Report, S/2000/133, 18 February 2000, para. 32.

26   Fifth Annual Report, S/2001/738, 27 July 2001, para. 26.

27   Sixth Annual Report, S/2002/647, 10 June 2002, para. 28.

28   Seventh Annual Report, S/2003/300, 12 March 2003, para. 20.

29   Second Annual Report, S/1997/672, 28 August 1997, para. 27.

30   *Ibid*, para. 28

31   *Ibid*, para. 32

32   *Ibid*, para. 33

33   Fourth Annual Report, S/2000/133, 18 February 2000, para. 57.

34   *See:* Al-Ani ,Abdul-Haq & Baker, Joanne, *Uranium in Iraq: The Legacy of the Iraq Wars*, (Vandeplas Publishing, 2009).

35   Sixth Annual Report, S/2002/647, 10 June 2002, para. 33.

36   Security Council, 4120th Meeting, 24 March 2000, S/PV.4120, 2-3.

37   *ibid* 2

38   Security Council, 4120th Meeting, 24 March 2000, S/PV.4120 (Resumption 1) 6

39   Security Council, 4120th Meeting, 24 March 2000, S/PV.4120, 15

40   *Ibid.* 16.

41   *Ibid.* 16.

42   *Ibid.* 18.

43   *Ibid.* 19.

44   *Ibid.* 5.

45   *Ibid.* 6.

46   Security Council, 4120th Meeting, 24 March 2000, S/PV.4120 (Resumption 1) 7-8.

47   *Ibid.* 10.

48   *Ibid.* 10.

49   Former U.N. Humanitarian Coordinator for Iraq Denis Halliday opposes U.N.'s sanctions, CNN Interactive Chat Transcript, 16 January 2001. <http://www.cnn.com/COMMUNITY/transcripts/2001/01/16/halliday/>

50   Introductory statement by Benon V. Sevan, Executive Director of the Iraq Programme at the informal consultations of the Security Council, Thursday, 21 September 2000 <http://www.un.org/Depts/oip/background/latest/bvs000921.html>

51   *Ibid.*

Chapter Nine

1   DUB

2   Rahul Mahajan, 'We think the Price is Worth it', (*FAIR*, Nov/Dec 2001) <http://www.fair.org/index.php?page=1084>

3   The best available tool to a researcher on sanctions on Iraq is the work done by the Campaign against Sanctions on Iraq (CASI) which had compiled numerous reports of UN organs and agencies, Governments and intergovernmental institutions and NGOs and religious bodies. All these are available at <http://

www.casi.org.uk/info/index.html>; Report to the Secretary-General; on humanitarian needs in Kuwait and Iraq in the immediate post-crisis environment by a mission to the area led by Mr. Martti Ahtisaari Under-Secretary-General for Administration and Management, dated 20 March 1991, UN document S/22366, <http://daccess-dds-ny.un.org/doc/UNDOC/GEN/N91/089/88/IMG/N9108988.pdf?OpenElement>; Report to the Secretary-General dated 15 July 1991 on humanitarian needs in Iraq prepared by a mission led by Sadruddin Aga Khan, Executive Delegate of the Secretary-General UN Document S/22799, <http://daccess-dds-ny.un.org/doc/UNDOC/GEN/N91/228/18/IMG/N9122818.pdf?OpenElement>; Acherio, Albert and others, 'Effect of the Gulf War on Infant and Child Mortality in Iraq' (1992) 327 *New England Journal of Medicine 931* <http://www.ncbi.nlm.nih.gov/pubmed/1513350>; Crossette, Barbara, 'Iraq Sanctions Kill Children, U.N. Report's, *The New York Times*, 1 December 1995,<http://www.nytimes.com/1995/12/01/world/iraq-sanctions-kill-children-un-reports.html>;

Fawzi, Mary C. Smith, Ziadi, Sarah, 'Sanctions, Saddam and Silence: Child Malnutrition and Mortality in Iraq', *The Washington Report on Middle East Affairs*, January 1996 <http://www.washington-report.org/component/content/article/167-1996-january/1776-sanctions-saddam-and-silence.html>; *'Unsanctioned Suffering: A Human Rights Assessment of United Nations Sanctions on Iraq,* Center for Economic and Social Rights', May 1996, <http://www.cesr.org/downloads/Unsanctioned%20Suffering%201996.pdf>; Report of the second panel established pursuant to the note by the president of the Security Council of 30 January 1999 (S/l999/100), concerning the current humanitarian situation in Iraq, Annex II of S/l999/356, 30 March 1999, <http://www.casi.org.uk/info/panelrep.html>; The Education Sector: Pre-sanctions to 1995/96 ' in UN Office of the Humanitarian Coordinator for Iraq. *Special Topics on social conditions in Iraq: An overview submitted by the UN system to the Security Council Panel on Humanitarian Issues* (Baghdad, 24 March 1999) <http://www.casi.org.uk/info/undocs/spec-top.html>#11>; *The Human Rights Implications of Economic Sanctions on Iraq: Background Paper Prepared by the Office of the High Commissioner for Human Rights for the Meeting of the Executive Committee on Humanitarian Affairs (New York,* 5 September 2000), <http://www.cam.ac.uk/societies/casi/info/undocs/sanct31.pdf.>; Iraq: a decade of sanctions, by the International and Development Affairs Committee of the Church of England's Board for Social Responsibility, which is available on the Campaign Against Sanctions on Iraq <http://www.casi.org.uk/info/churcheng/cofejuly2000.pdf>; UNICEF, 1999 Iraq Child and Maternal Mortality Surveys <http://www.fas.org/news/iraq/1999/08/990812-unicef.htm>; UNICEF press release, Iraq surveys show 'humanitarian emergency', 12 August 1999, (CF/DOC/PR/1999/29) <http://www.unicef.org/newsline/99pr29.htm>; UNICEF press release. Child malnutrition prevalent in central/south Iraq, 29May 1997 (CF/DOC/PR/1997/17) <http://www.unicef.org/newsline/prgva11.htm>; UNICEF press release. Nearly one million children malnourished in Iraq, says UNICEF, 26 November 1997 (CF/DOC/PR/1997/60) <http://www.unicef.org/newsline/97pr60.htm>; UN Food and Agriculture Organization. *Assessment of the Food and Nutrition Situation-Iraq (Rome,* September 2000 <http://www.fao.org/docrep/005/x8147e/x8147e00.htm> Report of the Secretary-General pursuant to Paragraph 5 of Resolution 1302 (2000) S/2000/1132 (29 November 2000) <http://daccess-dds-ny.un.org/doc/UNDOC/GEN/N00/760/04/PDF/N0076004.pdf?OpenElement>; Report of the Secretary-General pursuant to Paragraph 5 of Resolution 1360 (2001) S/2001/919 (28 September 2001) <http://daccess-dds-ny.un.org/doc/

UNDOC/GEN/N01/549/26/PDF/N0154926.pdf?OpenElement>; Report of the Secretary-General pursuant to paragraph 5 of resolution 1302 (2000) (8 September 2000) S/2000/85 <http://daccess-dds-ny.un.org/doc/UN-DOC/GEN/N00/280/49/PDF/N0028049.pdf?OpenElement>; Report of the Secretary-General pursuant to paragraph 5 of Security Council resolution 1281(1999)(1June 2000)S/2000/520 <http://daccess-dds-ny.un.org/doc/UNDOC/GEN/N00/453/72/PDF/N0045372.pdf?OpenElement>; Introductory statement by Benon V. Sevan Executive Director of the Iraq Program at the informal consultation of the Security Council Thursday, 21 September 2000 <http://www.un.org/Depts/oip/background/latest/bvs000921.html>; Report of the Secretary-General pursuant to paragraph 5 of resolution 1360 (2001) (19 November 2001), S/2001/1089 <http://daccess-dds-ny.un.org/doc/UNDOC/GEN/N01/637/99/PDF/N0163799.pdf?OpenElement>; Humanitarian Assistance Capacity in Iraq: Part I/ A Situation Analysis and Literature Review, CARE International and Johns Hopkins University/ Center for International Emergency, Disaster and Refugee Studies, January 2003, <http://www.who.int/disasters/repo/9353.pdf>; Daponte, Beth Osborne and Garfield, Richard, 'The Effect of Economic Sanctions on the Mortality of Iraqi Children Prior to the 1991 Persian Gulf War' (2000) 90(4) *American Journal of Public Health 546-552* <http://www.ncbi.nlm.nih.gov/pmc/articles/PMC1446193/>; Gordon, Joy, 'Cool War: Economic Sanctions as a weapon of Mass Destruction' (*Harper's Magazine*, November 2002) <http://www.harpers.org/archive/2002/11/0079384>; For General works see: Graham-Brown, Sarah, *Sanctioning Saddam: The Politics of Intervention in Iraq* (London: I.B. Tauris, 1999); Arnove, Anthony (ed.). *Iraq Under Siege: The Deadly Impact of Sanctions and War* (London: Pluto Press, 2000); Conlon, Paul, *United Nations Sanctions Managements Case Study of the Sanctions Committee, 1990-1994* (Ardsley, New York: Transnational Publishers, 2000); Cockburn, Andrew and Cockburn, Patrick, *Out of the Ashes: The Resurrection of Saddam Hussein* (London: HarperCollins, 1999); Cordesman, Anthony H., and Hashim, Ahmed S., *Iraq: Sanctions and Beyond* (Boulder, CO: Westview Press, 1997); Simons, Geoff, *The Scourging of Iraq: Sanctions, Law and Natural Justice* (Basingstoke: Macmillan, 1998, 2nd edn); Hoskins, Eric, 'The Humanitarian Impacts of Economic Sanctions and War in Iraq' in Weiss, Thomas G., Cortright, David, Lopez, George A., and Minear, Larry, (eds) *Political Gain and Civilian Pain: Humanitarian Impacts of Economic Sanctions* (Lanham/Oxford: Rowman & Littlefield, 1997); Boone, Peter, Gazdar, Haris, Hussain, Althar, *Sanctions against Iraq: Costs of Failure* (New York: CESR, November 1997) and Ismael, Tareq Y., and Haddad, William W., (eds) *Iraq The Human Cost of History* (London: Pluto Press, 2004)

4   Robinson 63-64. Of course the clear backdrop that Robinson had in mind here were the conditions concerning the concentration camps of WWII and the so-called Death March, where Ottoman soldiers marched Armenians into the Syrian Desert to their certain deaths. See. Castellino, Joshua, 'Death March' Shelton, D. et al (eds) *The Encyclopedia of Genocide* (New York: Macmillan Reference 2005) 226-229

5   Case Concerning the Application of the Convention on the Prevention and Punishment of the Crime of Genocide (Bosnia and Herzegovina v. Serbia and Montenegro), February 26, 2007, para 421

6   Robinson 72. On the question of 'command of law' the matter is easier to comprehend. Domestic law is, as a matter of principle, subservient to international commitments. Thus if a state chose to abide by an international obligation as is indicated by the fact that it ratified it, it cannot invoke domestic law as a defense for non-fulfillment of that obligation. It follows that all people whether citizens of the US, the UK or any other State, who committed the crime of genocide in

any act whether as members of the Sanctions Committee or during the military campaign could not and should not be able to use this defense. This incidentally is precisely what the Supreme Court of the US held in the *Abrams v United States*, 250 U.S. 616 (1919) where the Court interpreted specific 'intent' to mean that the defendants were responsible for the natural consequences of their intended actions even if those actions were motivated by unrelated concerns. Such was the ruling of the British House of Lords in the case of *DPP v Smith* [1961], in which the House applied a purely objective test to intent in murder asserting the standard of the reasonable man, who would have understood the harmful consequences of his actions.

7   The ICJ held in the Lockerbie case that it could not proceed with a disputed case before it on the application of an international convention once the SC adopted a resolution in the matter. Questions of Interpretation and Application of the 1971 Montreal Convention arising from the Aerial Incident at Lockerbie (*Libyan Arab Jamahiriya v. United Kingdom*), Preliminary Objections, Judgment, I. C.J. Reports 1998, 9 (Lockerbie Case) paras 39-40.

8   Joined Cases C-402/05 P and C-415/05 P, Yassin Abdullah *Kadi* and Al Barakaat International Foundation v Council of the European Union and Commission of the European Communities, Judgment of 3 September 2008.

9   *Kadi* case, para. 87.

10   *Kadi* case, para. 5.

11   *Kadi* case, para. 323.

12   *Ibid.*

13   *Kadi* case, para. 324.

14   *Kadi* case, para. 325.

Conclusion

1   As quoted in Saleh, Zaki, *Britain and Iraq: A Study in British Foreign Affairs*, London, Books & Books 1995, p. xl

2   "The recent conflict has wrought near-apocalyptic results upon the economic infrastructure of what had been, until January 1991, a rather highly urbanized and mechanized society. Now, most means of modern life support have been destroyed or rendered tenuous. Iraq has, for some time to come, been relegated to a pre-industrial age, but with all the disabilities of post-industrial dependency on an intensive use of energy and technology." Report on humanitarian needs in Iraq in the immediate post-crisis environment by a mission to the area led by the Under-Secretary- General for Administration and Management, 10- 17 March 1991, S/22366, 20 March 1991 <http://www.casi.org.uk/info/undocs/s22366.html>

3   *Ibid.*

4   Joined Cases C-402/05 P and C-415/05 P, Yassin Abdullah *Kadi* and Al Barakaat International Foundation v Council of the European Union and Commission of the European Communities, Judgment of 3 September 2008.

5   *R v Jones; Ayliffe v DPP; Swain v DPP* [2006] UKHL 16, [2007] 1 AC 136.

INDEX OF TABLES

INDEX